"*Big Life* is doing what Paul did. The reason we remember Paul is not just because of his great words in the Epistles. We remember Paul because of all the churches he planted. That is what the Big Life Ministry does; it spreads the Word of God and the salvation of Jesus Christ to people who are then empowered to set up new churches. Their new faith is constantly reinforced and nourished."

—Lieutenant Colonel Oliver L. North

"In the book of Acts, mission work was relatively uncomplicated. The message spread like wildfire because hearers became witnesses. Witnesses became disciples, and disciples became leaders. The resulting growth was a result of multiplication, not mere addition.

Big Life Ministries takes us back to these first principles and is seeing the power of God at work in the lives of people across many nations.

People are coming to faith with amazing testimonies of God's power and grace. And as they take their first steps they are commissioned to witness to others. Straight away. No messing about. Go and tell others about this Jesus who has turned your world upside down.

I welcome this book. The story of Big Life needs to be told."

—David Kerrigan
General Director,
Baptist Missionary Society (United Kingdom)

A BIG
LIFE

Peter Hone

A BIG
LIFE

Ordinary People Led by an Extraordinary God

Foreword by Charles Colson and
Afterword by Mike Huckabee

TATE PUBLISHING
AND ENTERPRISES, LLC

Published by Tate Publishing & Enterprises, LLC
127 E. Trade Center Terrace | Mustang, Oklahoma 73064 USA
1.888.361.9473 | www.tatepublishing.com

Tate Publishing is committed to excellence in the publishing industry. The company reflects the philosophy established by the founders, based on Psalm 68:11,
"The Lord gave the word and great was the company of those who published it."

Book design copyright © 2011 by Tate Publishing, LLC. All rights reserved.
Cover design by Stephanie Woloszyn
Interior design by Kate Stearman

Published in the United States of America

ISBN: 978-1-61346-647-6
1. Religion / Christian Church / Growth
2. Religion / Christian Ministry / Missions
11.10.18

To Elize

You are my heart, my love, my North Star.

Acknowledgements

This book is in no way meant to glorify John, Kathy or Benjamin, nor any of the hundreds of God's people serving sacrificially across the world in the Big Life Ministry. None of them would allow it anyway. But I am grateful for the hours given up by all of those I interviewed, the patience shown in answering my endless questions, and for their courage in opening their hearts completely. The time and the tears were worth it, at least for me.

Thanks to Benjamin and his team for the time in India and Nepal. Crossing the Nepal border as a 'tourist' on a rickshaw with two dozen DVD players piled on my lap was a little unusual, as was interviewing my friend while marching through the jungle to get to the next village. May your fire never die, Ben.

To my unofficial editors, Jeff Gibson, Jeanette Pala, and Jeff Pylant, thank you for your contribution.

To the Big Life U.S. team, for your prayer, love and support. Sincere thanks to Jim Nichols for all the technical help.

To Kerry Rard, Nadine Mace (Gal 1:10), Jim Tindall, Brian Pala, my son Toby Hone and so many others who went out of their way to love and encourage me when it was tough.

To Gil and Dot Janneke, mom and dad, for starting this journey.

To my wife, Elize and my son, Danny who shared my frustrations and my joy as they accepted an often absent husband and father, and encouraged me unfailingly to finish what I had started.

My sincere thanks to all at Tate Publishing, especially Donna Chumley, who listened when the Lord spoke, and Ryan Womack, who edited with patience and skill.

Author's Note

The original Greek word, Ekklesia, was used in the Bible to describe the gatherings in the early church. Ekklesia is defined in the New Testament Greek Lexicon as:

1. An assembly of Christians gathered for worship in a religious meeting.

2. Those who anywhere, in a city, village, constitute such a company and are united into one body.

In order to put a practical definition to the functioning of the Ekklesia, I have used the following definition of a church, or fellowship, which is embraced by the Ministry of Big Life-

> "A group of baptized believers who identify themselves as a church and who regularly perform the five functions outlined in Acts 2:42-47 and given to us in the Great Commission and Great Commandment: Teaching, Fellowship, Worship, Ministry, and Evangelism."

"But before all this, they will seize you and persecute you. They will hand you over to synagogues and put you in prison, and you will be brought before kings and governors, all on account of my name. And so you will bear testimony to me. But make up your mind not to worry beforehand how you will defend yourselves. For I will give you words and wisdom that none of your adversaries will be able to resist or contradict. You will be betrayed even by parents, brothers and sisters, relatives and friends, and they will put some of you to death. Everyone will hate you because of me. But not a hair of your head will perish. Stand firm, and you will win life."

—Jesus of Nazareth. Luke 21:12-19

Foreword
By Charles Colson

Former Special Counsel to President Richard Nixon
Founder of Prison Fellowship Ministries

Over thirty-five years of ministry, I've heard thousands of Christians say, "I'm just an ordinary Christian; I can't do much. I can't make a difference."

Maybe you've thought that at times. It's a natural reaction in this world which exalts celebrities and powerful institutions. But I cringe every time I hear someone say that. I'm not quite sure if it's an excuse for not doing anything, or if people really believe that they are powerless and impotent. But God shows us through the centuries that he empowers ordinary men and women for his purposes. He raises them up often from the most unlikely places. Look at my life—I rose to the top, the office right next to the President of the Unites States. Then I crashed and went to prison. I thought my life was over. I was powerless and broken. But in fact my most important mission was just beginning. God did something much greater than I had ever been able to do on my own.

I was the unlikeliest person to be called, yet I've been given the greatest privilege of my life to serve him in prisons around the world. God delights in using the weak things of the world to shame the wise and mighty.

So you are never a nobody. You can do anything if you follow God's call and rely on him.

One of the best examples of this is the subject of this book. John Heerema had a successful landscaping business and was a faithful worshiper at First Baptist Church of Naples, Florida; a wonderful, goodhearted guy who loved the Lord. He and his wife, Kathy, had a beautiful family, a nice home, an established business, and a good income. He could ride out the rest of his days living in a comfortable, secure environment, attending church regularly, listening to great sermons and doing his Bible studies.

But John Heerema decided he wasn't going to be one of those people who just sits in the pew and feels helpless. He recognized that with God all things are possible. And he had a vision, a real sense of calling, a heart to spread the gospel to people who have never heard it.

That was the beginning of a very exciting journey, the kind which really warms my heart. John Heerema gave it all up; one man stepping out in faith, beginning a ministry to the people in the 10/40 window, the most strategic mission field in the world.

The story of how God took John Heerema, one of your 'ordinary Christians', and turned him into a missionary, is incredible. As you will read in these pages, the ministry of Big Life is having an extraordinary impact in empowering others in those strategic areas to do ministry, seeing churches built, disciples made, communities changed.

It is a story of what God can do with one man fully consecrated to him.

What makes this story so thrilling for me is that it represents the new wave of missions in the world. The old model, of American missionaries moving abroad, taking their families, relocating, learning the language, getting settled in. This worked a couple of generations ago. People could stay faithfully in the mission field all their lives and make a real impact. But it is high cost, and it doesn't result in multiplication.

The most successful missions today are not transporting Americans abroad at high costs, living in a culture they are unfamiliar with, but rather spending our resources to train and equip indigenous leadership. This is the new model that Heerema is demonstrating.

I discovered the effectiveness of the new model in the early days of Prison Fellowship. Friends from Britain asked us to help establish a ministry in England. That was pretty simple, because they were skilled, mature Christians. Soon thereafter we were invited into Northern Ireland, and then Scotland. But very soon we began to get inquiries from Third World countries. Would we be willing to come to those countries and set up ministry?

That was in the fledgling days of Prison Fellowship, when we were devoting all of our resources to try to meet a huge growing domestic need for prison ministry. We basically made the decision on economic grounds that we couldn't send people to those countries. But we would train local leadership in those countries to do prison ministry.

With a small international staff, we were able to meet with the Christian leaders in those countries, to begin to train volunteers, to provide resources and materials. We worked on an arrangement whereby they could call themselves Prison Fellowship Ecuador, for example, or Prison Fellowship Sri Lanka, so long as they signed our statement of faith, applied for re-certification every two years, gave us reports on their work, and of course fulfilled the statement of purpose.

Over the past thirty-five years that model has produced for the most part very effective ministries in 113 countries around the world. There are now thousands of trained PF volunteers working in countries around the world. Our overhead costs have been kept to a bare minimum; our direct costs have involved only our people visiting those countries to conduct training conferences when necessary.

This is the future of missions: to hold it with a light touch and empower people locally. This, after all, is the Ephesians 4 model of the church.

John Heerema and the people of Big Life are on the front lines. They are doing it right. Instead of multiplying staff, they are multiplying resources, and collaborating with others. Perhaps their story will inspire you or your church to begin to think in terms of equipping and empowering rather than trying to control the ministry of God around the world.

And remember, God loves to confound the wisdom of the world, doing his greatest work through 'ordinary' men and women.

—Charles Colson
March 2011

Prologue
Pakistan

He raised the small plastic cup to his lips and sipped gingerly, holding it delicately between thumb and forefinger because the tea was scalding hot, steam rising and swirling even on this blistering hot day. It probably wasn't good tea, but it tasted good to Faizal. When you have just returned to the city after months in the mountain wastes of Afghanistan training to be a Taliban freedom fighter, any tea tastes good.

They had first approached him outside the mosque where many young Muslims were recruited. The clerics told of the fatwa announcing the call to arms. He was excited and surprised to find he was no stranger to them. They knew all about his family's standing in the community, his strong religious education at the Madrassa, the Koranic school, and his strict upbringing as a devout Muslim. They said they wanted him, and they were calling him in the name of jihad. He was to be a warrior for Allah, given the honor of fighting to expel the infidels from Afghanistan.

His father, a prominent Pashtun leader, was so proud. To have a son called to jihad in this manner was a privilege. When the war had begun a few years ago and the Taliban fighters were driven back from Kabul, many had been conscripted to fight; but they were poor fighters, poorly trained, and they were defeated. But now the Taliban had regrouped, they were organized, and they chose their soldiers more carefully, selecting men who were strong in mind as well as body—men who understood the holy vision of the Koran, obedient men with passion who would never accept defeat.

Faizal became skilled in modern weaponry and in the art of guerilla warfare that has always been so successful in the maze of mountain strongholds that is

Afghanistan. He learned to kill efficiently and to hate the arrogant, invading infidel and everything for which he stood.

He was comfortable handling both light and heavy weapons and many kinds of explosives, most of which he could improvise himself. He could blow up a bridge or a railway track in minutes. He was taught hand-to-hand combat, survival techniques, communications, and how to set up spy networks. He learned to assess the weak points in different kinds of enemy aircraft and armored vehicles and to master the weapons that were effective in destroying them. And he learned how to conceal a device on his body if he was ever given the honor of being called to be a suicide bomber. He had no fear of death, knowing that his reward in paradise was assured. He was a Muhajid, a warrior called to jihad.

Now he was back home. He would work in his father's business until he was called again—this time not for training, but for war. He would pray that this would be soon because his purpose and his destiny were rapidly approaching. Faizal knew this because he could feel it in his heart. Something was about to happen.

As he sipped his tea, he looked around this busy, open tea stall. No one paid him any attention. He smiled, wondering how they would regard him if they knew he was a Taliban soldier. His mind drifted back to his training. It had been difficult sleeping five hours a night on the hard ground in a thin tent, a loaded weapon constantly at his side. Some nights he froze, not sleeping at all, and the food had been pitiful.

But Faizal's heart stirred as he remembered the commander's address the day he left to return home. He recalled the set of the man's jaw and the steel in his eyes as much as he recalled the passion in his words: "The infidels are ruling this world, and they are bent on the demonization of Islam. They are terrorists, and it is the duty and the holy purpose of all Muslims to take up arms and crush those who would oppress and murder Muslims throughout the world. They must be killed, slaughtered, and annihilated wherever we find them."

Faizal had wept as he cheered. He was ready to fight, ready to kill, and ready to sacrifice.

A welcome breeze lifted the fringe of his hair, and he lifted his face and closed his eyes to enjoy the momentary relief from the heat. As he opened them again, he saw a dust devil a little way off, red sand rising and twirling as it danced in circles a foot above the ground, slowly moving toward him. In among the red was a flash of white, and he watched until it died, and a scrap of paper landed at his feet. He reached down and picked it up. It was a part of a torn page of a book, but a very thin and fragile page. The words were printed, very small, but clear. He read it.

"Blessed are the poor in spirit, for theirs is the kingdom of heaven."

Faizal looked away for a second, and then he read it once more. He had no idea what it was, but he knew it was not the Koran so he crumpled it in his fist, intending to throw it away. But even as he raised his arm to toss it, he knew he could not. He had to finish reading it. Opening his hand, he smoothed out the paper and read on.

"Blessed are the merciful, for they will be shown mercy."

Something inside him stirred. Mercy? There could be no mercy for his enemies. Mercy had no part in his recent training. And surely the kingdom of heaven is for the strong, not the poor in spirit. He could not accept this. But as he read the words over and over, he felt their power, and he knew with his whole heart and his whole mind that this was truth. From where did this teaching come?

Some weeks later, he received the call to jihad. He packed up his things, bid his proud father farewell, then left his home. But he did not report to the Taliban because he could not. Instead, he stayed at the home of a close friend, hiding out from his family, the Taliban, and the world. Faizal was in an agony of doubt. It was not fear that had changed him because Faizal was no coward. No, it wasn't fear; it was something else, something that he did not yet understand.

He carried the scrap of torn page everywhere, and he kept looking at it, reading it, and wondering why it was so powerfully affecting him. What else could prevent him from responding to the call for jihad when it had been his life's ambition a month ago? He finally showed it to his friend who thought he recognized "the kingdom of heaven" as Christian.

A week later, Faizal met with a Christian, a former Muslim, on the outskirts of the city. The Christian was stunned to be contacted by this man who revealed after some questioning that he was a Taliban fighter, and he agreed to meet but insisted that it be in the back room of a café in the Christian part of town.

"You can't meet him there. He is a Christian. It is dangerous to trust him—suicidal," said Faizal's friend. But by now, he was focused on only one thing: a small scrap of paper. Faizal found the Christian friendly but unsure of him. Their small talk was awkward, so Faizal took out the scrap of paper and just handed it to him.

"What is this? Is it Christian?" he asked bluntly.

The man read it then nodded.

"Yes, it's Jesus," he replied.

"It's about Jesus, Jesus the prophet?" Faizal asked, frowning.

"No, this has been torn from a Bible. This is not *about* Jesus. These are the words *of* Jesus." The Christian stared into Faizal's face defiantly. "And Jesus is not just a prophet. He is God, and the Savior of the world."

But Faizal was not listening to this. He was thinking of what the Christian had said before. The words of Jesus? *The words of Jesus?*

Everything seemed to stop. Suddenly, there was nothing in Faizal's existence except the realization that Jesus Christ had spoken to him. He recognized instantly that he had been called in pure love, and then he fell to his knees and cried out in utter despair at the brutal awareness of his own sin. The Christian also fell to his knees, putting his arms around Faizal, comforting him. After some minutes, he led him in a prayer of repentance, forgiveness, and acceptance—a prayer of salvation.

When Faizal was praying later that night, he could think only of the finality of his life that would accompany his new faith. But this was only the beginning of everything, and soon Jesus was leading him to new life and directing him to the work he had for him to do. Soon, Faizal was talking not of death, but of mercy, and directing Muslims to the kingdom of heaven.

Soon, he was serving his God through a ministry named Big Life.

India

As the sky grows darker, there is a growing anticipation in the balmy evening air. The cacophony of incessant insect noise is interrupted by the rude bass calls of the frogs from the nearby river. Maybe a hundred and fifty villagers are slowly gathering in groups, having made their way to the north of the village, where the children play and the adults meet and talk. The women's saris reflect bright colors as they move, even in the dim yellow glow from the bare light bulbs that hang in the trees. The men stand toward the back of the semicircle of onlookers, aloof and watchful.

Children of all ages, being children, sit at the very front, cross-legged, squeezing shoulder to shoulder into any available space. They jabber to each other, their smiles shy and nervous, but they intend to miss none of the excitement. Wide eyes shine as they stare up at the large white canvas sheet, secured by ropes between the branches of two tall trees. It ripples gently in the warm breeze. The low hum of a generator is replaced by the whine of the projector as it comes to life, and then there's the harsh *clack*, *clack*, *clack* of the movie reel until it catches onto the empty spindle. The children wave, shout, and point, unable to contain their joy as the canvas sheet becomes a movie screen and the ancient box speaker, somewhere in the branches above, explodes with loud and uncertain orchestral music.

Everyone reacts at once, chattering and shouting to his or her neighbor. What is this? But as the movie begins and the characters speak in Bengali, they settle down to listen and to watch.

Soon, as the story progresses, these Hindu villagers will learn the true story of a man who died terribly on a cross so that they could know the living God. Even as they watch, the Indian men of the Big Life ministry who brought this movie to them are earnestly praying in the darkness that the Holy Spirit will move among these people.

They know that it is a matter of life and death.

PART ONE
1959–2010

JOHN

"…he went to him and begged him to come and heal his son…"

John 4:47

Homewood

ack Heerema was in turmoil as he drove home from the hospital. His newborn, his second son, was deformed. Jack and his wife, Jean, had decided some months ago to name him John, after the disciple that Jesus loved. As he drove, Jack struggled to think coherently, to understand how this could be. In his mind, he repeated the doctor's words over and over, as if somehow they would change, and this terrible news could be just a mistake.

"It's *talipes equinovarus*, clubfeet. It's severe and will probably require surgery." Then, in a gentler voice, he went on to answer Jack's first question before he could ask it. "There is a high probability he will not be able to walk. I'm so sorry, Jack."

Jack broke down at the sight of his son's feet. How could this happen? How could they even think of operating on such a tiny, helpless thing? His emotions swung from grief to anger. This is 1959, not the dark ages. How could they tell him his son would not walk? They must be able to do something. But as anger gave way to acceptance, he knew the doctors were telling him only what they knew to be true.

Jack knew otherwise; his God was faithful. He would console and restore. Still, he felt desperate for Jean. She was a gentle, loving wife and mother, and she would take this hard. He needed to support and love her right now. That was at least one good thing he could do. They prayed together, seeking comfort for their pain, and before Jack left the hospital, he went to the small chapel and fell to his knees to pray again for little John.

Now, staring through the windshield on the lonely journey home on this mild May morning, he continued to pray, asking for understanding and strength for the ordeal to come. This was not going to be easy, but with God's help, he would fight. He would pray. And God would heal his son.

At two weeks, the doctors decided to delay surgery, and they put casts on both John's legs. It was a pitiful sight, but it made Jack and Jean firmer in their absolute belief that God would heal John and that the healing had already begun.

Homewood was a small town south of Chicago with a fairly large tight-knit Dutch immigrant community of which the Heeremas were a well-respected family. Jack ran a modest but successful plumbing business with his brothers and attended the Homewood Reformed Church where he served as the chairman of deacons. He was a man of God and a man of action, and soon, not only his church, but friends in every local reformed church in the area were praying for his son's restoration.

As John grew, his frustration with the casts was obvious as he constantly tried to kick them off. Sometimes he succeeded, and Jack and Jean would have to return to the doctor to have them refitted. Their own frustration came from the doctor's regular monthly insistence that there was little improvement in John's condition and that the prognosis remained poor. The Heeremas would have none of it, believing by faith that the Lord would heal John in His time and in His way. They continued to pray and exhort their church and relatives to keep supporting them in prayer.

After two years, the casts were exchanged for braces. John was active now, and the braces provided ease of movement. Jack and Jean took him for regular checkups, and after one of these the doctor invited them into his office.

"He seems to be doing better," said Jean, more hopeful than certain.

The doctor looked away for a second, seeming to search for words. He spoke slowly, carefully. "Jean, to be honest, there is little improvement so far. Little change. I know you are positive, loving parents, but the prognosis is not good. It may be necessary to think about how the family can live and cope with this situation. You may soon need to think about the need for a wheelchair…"

"No," said Jack. He said it with such finality that the doctor and Jean were silenced. They just looked at him. His frown and his jaw were set in concrete. "There will be no wheelchair. My son will be healed, I know it."

"Well," said the doctor, "I would hate to dash your hopes. Let's review it again next time." The meeting was over.

It seemed inevitable that the Heeremas would have to face reality, but late into his second year, John showed a great determination to stand. He was uncomfortable, in pain, but resolute. With agonizing slowness, after many months of trying, he at last stood unaided on his crooked feet, and very soon after, at three years old, he walked. The more he walked, the straighter his stance became. Talk of wheelchairs and an uncertain future was forgotten as the Heerema family gave praise and thanks to the Lord for his deliverance. But John's ordeal was not yet over; he would wear his braces for another eight years.

The expected surgeries did eventually come. His left foot was troublesome, responding slowly to the corrective brace, and just after John's seventh birthday, the doctors operated. The Heeremas were told it was successful, but two years later, it was necessary to repeat the operation on the same foot.

The braces were an increasing burden as John went through his elementary and middle school years. He wore a leather belt around his waist under his pants. From this a reinforced steel cable, hinged behind each knee, went down into the heel of his shoes to force his feet to turn outward. There were extended periods when John's feet would want to curl inward, and the pressure caused him constant, sometimes excruciating pain. He was often laid up at home, missing school.

But the real pain, the real test, was to his spirit. John had a love for sports, and his handicap prevented him from competing as he wanted, no matter how hard he tried to be normal. He was not allowed to do PE or sports at school, and outside of school, other kids would point out his braces and laugh at the strange way he ran.

John learned to accept the mocking. He didn't care, just so long as he could play. One time, John's braces were being repaired, and the guys were all outside playing baseball. John begged his brother, Jim, to take him there and let him play.

"John, you can't play without your braces. You know that."

"Jim, I can stand with my crutches. Please, Jim."

"John, how can you play with crutches?"

"I can do it, let me show you!"

Jim couldn't say no, it would just break his brother's heart. It almost broke Jim's heart, watching John throw down his crutches as he came up to bat, trying to swing the bat while balanced on his crooked feet. Jim took to bringing John along to play baseball and basketball with the bigger kids, Jim's friends. He told John it was to toughen him up, but it was really just so Jim could keep an eye on his little brother and protect him, because he was going to play, no matter what. John would play every day if he could. But never, ever on a Sunday.

Jack Heerema would not allow either of his boys to play sports on Sundays. When they complained that they wouldn't make the team, he told them to try harder—end of discussion. Sunday was the Lord's day, and the Heeremas went to church and worshiped as a family. On Wednesday nights, they all went to Bible study. Jack was a Sunday school teacher, a youth leader, and a member of the church board. A quiet, fastidious man, he saw his duty as providing for and raising a godly family dedicated to the service of the Lord.

His family treated him as a normal boy, so John learned to accept his situation and to make the best of it. But he knew that his braces made him different, and although he never complained about them, he hated them. In the summer of his ninth year, with the church camp a week off, he approached his mom and nervously asked if he could wear sneakers for that week and leave the braces at home. She looked at him, a little taken aback. He had never asked for this before.

"Why, John? You know you're supposed to wear them."

"My feet feel real good, Mom, and I'd like to try the sneakers." His mouth worked nervously as he tried to find the right words. "It's only a week…"

She immediately saw how desperately he wanted this. She knew he had come to her because if his dad said no, it would be no. Some seconds passed, and he spoke up again, afraid that her silence might mean she would refuse him.

"There'll be swimming and stuff, and I'd like to just be able to do that…" His voice trailed off once more.

Jean's heart filled with compassion for her son. Eight years, two surgeries, and no complaints. He could take a week off. She smiled. "I'm sure it will be fine, John. I'll talk to your father." He didn't answer her; he didn't thank her. He couldn't; he was too choked up. He just hugged her hard and ran off.

It was quite a camp. John wore his sneakers proudly, and for the first time ever, he felt just like everyone else. He swam, he played baseball, and he had fun. He felt alive and free. And on the fourth night, he felt the unmistakable touch of the Holy Spirit. It was early evening, his group was all together in their cabin, talking before dinner, and John was sitting on his bed, listening. The counselor, Adam, was speaking about God, salvation, grace, and all those things that he heard from the pastor at church, and from his dad. But then Adam said something that resonated with John. Leaning forward, speaking softly, he held his hands apart as if he were holding an invisible soccer ball.

"You see guys, each of us has this space inside of us, like a vacuum. We all have a desire to be loved, and to feel peace with ourselves, and the world. It's only when we allow God to fill that vacuum that we find that love and peace."

John, nine years old, instantly understood that this was true. He didn't know how, but he knew it. He had struggled so much in his young life, he had known pain and frustration, and he felt that vacuum; now he knew he wanted to give it to God to fill. Later that night, they made a great bonfire, and as John stared into the dancing orange and blue flames, he heard the camp director ask if anyone wanted to share their experience of the week.

John stood up in his sneakers, without knowing he was going to do it or even realizing he was standing, and with tears streaming down his face, scared to death in front of all the people, he looked around. Everyone was silent, looking at him.

"I…I…" He was trying to find the words, trying to talk through his tears.

"It's okay, John, it's okay," said Adam, somewhere to his right.

"I want to say that…that I felt Jesus today, and I've asked him to live inside me, and fill my vacuum." He was sure it didn't make sense, but they understood. Suddenly he was surrounded by the love of many friends, and of Jesus, his new and greatest friend.

Soon after, the Heeremas moved the short distance from Homewood to South Holland, and Jack immediately had the family attending Thorn Creek Reformed Church. John became very involved with the youth group at church and even joined the choir. In 1971, at age twelve, the doctors at last had good news for John: his feet had improved significantly. There was still weakness and other troublesome concerns, but after ten years, the braces were finally removed. It was a great moment for the entire family. After twelve years, the Lord had answered their prayers.

John became best friends with John Van Proyen, who was a year younger and also raised in a Reformed Christian home. They rode their bikes, camped out, and went to youth group at church together. They quickly cemented a friendship that was to last right through high school, college, and into their adult lives.

John was an average student and had to work harder than his older brother and sisters to get where his father expected him to be. But through his trials, John had developed a quiet determination and self-sufficiency that enabled him to cope. He was resilient and tough. As he reached his mid-teens, he would find that he would need to call upon all that resilience.

Storms

He came through the front door, staggered to his room, and collapsed on the bed. The pain was so bad that he felt as if he'd been stabbed in the stomach with a hot knife. It had been like this for over a week, and it wasn't getting better. He heard footsteps and painfully pulled himself up so that as his mother came in he was sitting on the side of the bed.

"Are you okay, John?" Her face was etched with concern.

"Sure, Mom. Just a stomach ache. No big deal."

She cupped his face in her hands and frowned down at him.

"This is the second day you've come home in pain. I'm making a doctor's appointment right now."

As she walked out, he took a deep breath. It wasn't the second day. It was the last two weeks. He hadn't told her because he didn't want to worry her, but now he was worried himself. It was his fifteenth birthday in a couple of weeks, and he felt like he might not make it until then. He gingerly got up to find the aspirin.

Jean made an appointment for Monday of the following week while John swallowed aspirin to keep the pain at bay. On Friday, the last day of school before spring break, John had a burger for lunch. Thirty minutes later, he was on his knees, vomiting in the bathroom. He thought it was the food, until he saw with alarm that he was coughing up blood.

John was rushed to the hospital. By the time they reached the emergency room, he was barely conscious. He had an open stomach ulcer, and the bleeding was massive. The doctors stabilized him and attempted a blood transfusion; but it failed because they could not control the hemorrhaging. They couldn't operate because the bleeding was so severe. They feared they would lose him.

Jack and Jean Heerema were soon at the hospital, desperately praying for the Lord to intervene. Many of John's friends from his youth group arrived to support them and stayed the entire night. But the news was dire; the doctors did not expect John to make it through the night. If by some miracle he did, there would certainly be brain damage due to the massive loss of blood.

Once again, Jack was praying for his son. But this time, it wasn't to overcome a handicap. This time, he was pleading for his son's life.

Jean was soon surrounded by other concerned mothers. They were on the telephone most of the night and soon formed a remarkable prayer chain with members of their congregation forming two-hour continuous prayer groups to offer up prayer for John. The next day, after a long, tense night, John was critical but alive, and Jack, Jean and the pastorate of Thorn Creek had thousands of people praying for one more miracle. Jack enlisted his relatives, his friends, and his considerable business contacts all over south Chicago, while the church contacted every Reformed church in the community.

They got their miracle. Three weeks later, John walked out of the hospital after a remarkable and steady recovery. The doctors said it was extraordinary. There was not even a hint of brain damage. The entire community had witnessed the power of prayer, and the Church of Thorn Creek, and the Heerema family in particular, offered prayer once again to thank the Lord for his mercy and unfailing grace. It was a life-changing moment for John, and he was deeply convicted that although he had committed his life to the Lord at camp five years earlier, he had never gone forward to publicly proclaim it.

He tearfully and joyfully did this a week later along with four friends, all of whom had come to the Lord through John's experience. He had been praying that these friends would come to know Jesus Christ, and he was humbled and overwhelmed that it had happened this way. He knew that God had saved his life, and now he had a new understanding of the power of prayer. He was living proof of it. He promised himself that prayer would always be an important part of his life.

The doctors informed the Heeremas that the ulcer had developed as a direct result of the situation with John's clubfeet. No one really knew what he had been through, but all the years of worry, pain, and frustration had caused intense stress. He had dealt with it by effectively burying it, and it had come back at him with a vengeance.

High school was a great experience. John worked hard and achieved good grades. Even though he still struggled with his feet, he was able to play sports more competitively. Most of John's friends were Christians from his own or some other church, and as a result, he was able to avoid the poor choices so easily available to teenagers.

John was well-liked for his dry humor, and he loved to tell stories and be the center of attention. He was mocked a little for his tendency to exaggerate, but his friends saw this as just the way John was—not brash but enthusiastic about life. He had a vibrant personality, so he always seemed to have a girlfriend and a very active social life. He attended church regularly, either with friends or with his family. In the holidays, he worked at a wholesale florist and developed a love for horticulture, which eventually led to his choice of career.

But in his senior year, his feet once again became a major issue. This time, it was the right foot, and the surgeon decided to operate once again to straighten it. John thought it would be okay; the earlier operations on his left foot had been bearable. But he was older now, his bones had formed and matured, and the pain from the corrective surgery was excruciating. And before the year was out, the whole episode was repeated. It was another difficult time, but John remained close to the Lord, and the outcome was positive.

It was ironic, after all this, that when he was away at college, John began to drift away from the faith. He loved his father deeply, but Jack's expectations of his son were always demanding and John had grown up constantly trying to please him and never feeling that he was succeeding. His dad was strict about values and morals and the Christian life. Perhaps it was being apart from his dad for the first time, or maybe it was peer pressure and the temptations of the college party scene. But John succumbed. Although he didn't take drugs or sleep around, he drank, went to parties, and pursued his own desires.

College turned John into an ambitious young man, determined to be successful, to make money and live well, just like all his college friends. This became his focus. But he knew in his heart that his new lifestyle was not honoring to the Lord and not respectful to his parents. They had brought him up as a Christian, sacrificed to get him into college, and now he only went to church when they came to visit him. His prayer life became almost non-existent; a prayer each night for his family—that was it. He heard rumors that some people in his church back home were not impressed with him, but he ignored them and naïvely convinced himself that these rumors would not reach his father's ears, just a few pews away.

He eventually achieved his degree in plant and soil science in 1981. But he left college knowing deep inside that he'd lost more than he'd gained. He was plagued with constant feelings of guilt—guilt for pushing the Lord into the background, and guilt for deceiving his parents. In his reflective times he told himself that he would make it right with the Lord, while all the time drifting further away from Him. He secured the job he wanted as a golf course superintendent at an upscale country club northwest of Chicago, and after a few months, he thought he would be happy there. But the winter of 1981/82 was bitter, and the pristine golf course of the summer seemed a world away.

One day in January, John drove the two-hour journey from his apartment in Woodstock to South Holland to visit his parents. On the way back north, late in the evening, it started to snow. Before long, it became a snowstorm. The car radio gave steady reports of the storm worsening with a wind chill factor of ninety-one degrees below zero. The authorities began to close roads, until eventually all roads were closed and an emergency was declared. As he drove, visibility decreased, and John began to grow anxious. He had to get back to his apartment; he had nowhere else to go, so he decided to try to just get through it. His lights could just make out the vehicle in front, and he concentrated hard on following it. But as the driving snow continued to fall, he lost control and slid into a snowbank. He wasn't hurt, and he was pretty sure there was little damage to the car; but he was stuck, alone, and very scared.

He had no idea where he was, and he couldn't get out of the vehicle in this treacherous wind, even though the snowfall had begun to die down. If he did, if he lost sight of his car, he would risk freezing to death. He would have to sit it out, try to stay warm, and hope someone finds him.

It was maybe an hour later that John saw lights, and then a snowmobile pulled up noisily alongside. He was relieved; he was beginning to feel the cold.

John's car door was jerked open, and a big state trooper, bending over, barked into John's face. He could barely make out the words over the howl of the wind.

"Leave your vehicle and get in!"

As he got out of the car, the cold wind took his breath away. He had on a winter jacket, but no gloves or hat, and the cold just seemed to creep right under his clothes and grip his flesh. They took him to an old, derelict farmhouse a few miles away and dropped him there.

"Stay inside and try to stay warm. Don't leave this place, okay?"

Then they were gone, looking for others stranded like him. John looked around. It wasn't a very inviting place. The wind whined through the broken windowpanes, and the snow outside cast an eerie glow onto the few abandoned pieces of furniture John could make out in the gloom. He settled down in a corner out of the freezing wind and tried to stay warm. He was hungry, tired, and his hands, nose and ears were cold; but he knew that this could have been a lot worse—much worse. He was lucky, he supposed.

Lucky—do Christians say "lucky"? Do they believe in luck? He suddenly realized that throughout this entire episode, he had not thought of God at all. Even in the car, alone and stuck in the snowbank trying to work out what to do, God had not entered his mind. He had been close to panic but still had not cried out to him for help. Suddenly, with absolute clarity, he recalled for the first time in six years his promise to himself to stay close to God in prayer. He remembered how thousands of earnest and sincere prayers had saved his life back then, and now he'd left the Lord behind somehow.

What had happened to him? How far had he fallen since then? He bowed his head and tried to pray. He prayed that he would make it through the night, find his car tomorrow, that it would start, and that he could get home. Then he prayed, "Lord, if you will do this for me, I will move to Florida, and you will never have to worry about me freezing to death again."

That was it. The best he could do. He was making a deal with God. It was a graphic illustration of how shallow and pathetic his prayer life and his faith had become. Swamped by guilt, he told himself that when he got home, he would make it right. He would get back with God.

His eyes were adjusting to the gloom now, and he made out an old sofa in the middle of the room. The cushions were icy and smelled old, and who knows what was living in them. But they were soft and would warm up with his body heat, so he pushed the sofa against the wall, away from the windows, and lay down. He got as comfortable as he could, his freezing hands under his armpits, and settled down to try to sleep.

Then he heard a noise, and he sat bolt upright in a second, his heart beating like crazy. He was fully alert, eyes searching. And then he saw a shape as it passed a window and came closer. It was a dog, a big dog, standing ten feet away, bowing and waving its head in submission. John gave a sigh, suddenly feeling self-conscious and stupid at his overreaction.

"Are you cold, boy? Come," John said, and he came, tail wagging, and jumped up on the sofa. John was pleased. It was going to be a long, cold night, and they would need each other. A thought crossed John's mind that maybe the dog was a gift from God to help him through the night. But if it was a gift, he didn't feel he deserved it.

John was snowed in at his apartment on Super Bowl Sunday. The roads were closed again. He looked at all the whiteness out of his window, sighed, and put on his jacket, hat, and gloves. Then he stepped out into the minus eighty-four-degree wind chill and walked a mile to his old college buddy's apartment. He wasn't watching the Super Bowl alone.

As he watched TV, he smiled at the irony; the game was in Miami, in sweltering, eighty-degree heat. That's a difference of 164 degrees. At a break in the game, the commercials started, and John turned to his friend.

"I'm moving to Florida," he said.

His friend smiled and nodded, taking a swig of his beer.

"Me too."

But John was serious. He applied for golf superintendent positions in Florida that January, and in March, he was interviewed down in Naples. He was hired and agreed to start work at Hole in the Wall Golf and Country Club that summer. So on July 5th, 1982, John packed everything he owned into his car and drove down to Naples, Florida, to start his new life.

KATHY

"Come to me, all you who are weary and burdened, and I will give you rest. Take my yoke upon you and learn from me…"

Matthew 11:28–29

Snakes, Beasts,
and Crawling Things

Naples was a beautiful, growing city, situated on the southwest coast of Florida. The weather was hot and humid in the summer but warm and perfect in the winter. Dolphins swimming in the warm and gentle waters of the Gulf of Mexico were easy to spot. The beaches were white and tranquil. Naples was becoming a winter haven for the affluent from the northern states, and thousands of them, the "snow birds," were retiring to stunning homes around the waterways, in high-rise condominiums or around the upscale country clubs that were springing up to meet the demand.

Most people thought that Naples was a great place to be in 1982, with the easy lifestyle and all this development going on, but for eighteen-year-old Kathy Lacke, from Fort Atkinson, Wisconsin, it was anything but a great place. Her father, an X-ray technician, had accepted a job in Naples four years earlier, and moved his family to Florida to start a new life.

Kathy entered high school as a freshman as soon as she arrived and immediately fell in with the wrong crowd. In middle school, she had been an achiever, a straight-A student. She was a quiet, moody girl, but she had structure and routine and had grown up with the same group of friends in her small town. As she moved away from all of this and moved up to the demands of high school at the same time, her fragile self-esteem cracked, and her moodiness slowly turned to depression.

Under pressure, she suddenly saw herself as an underachiever and an outcast, and she gravitated to other troubled kids like herself, desperate to fit in. Her parents were concerned, and in an effort to make her happy and settled, they relaxed Kathy's boundaries. This gave her too much freedom, which she exploited fully. She sought happiness everywhere, trying every new thing her new friends tried, but she couldn't find happiness or any kind of lasting satisfaction. She found only emptiness and frustration.

Driven by feelings of negativity and hopelessness, she was constantly disappointing her parents. This led to further self-esteem issues, and she was unable to halt the downward spiral. Her brother Tony started as a junior in the same school and just blossomed, eventually gaining acceptance to an Ivy League college. Kathy saw her failure in stark contrast to Tony's success. She felt that she constantly let her whole family down, but try as she may, there was nothing she could do about it. She was plagued by guilt because in her mind, there was no one to blame but herself.

Kathy began to have dark dreams and extended bouts of insomnia. She tried to deal with this by sitting up at night writing poetry and prose, but these became dark too—dark and angry. She ranted about the ugliness of motherhood, and the writings that came from her mind and her pen often scared her. One long, rambling verse climaxed with Satan spawning an illegitimate child. One night when she couldn't sleep, she sat up and wrote for hours, her frantic ramblings describing the snakes, beasts, and crawling things that kept her awake each night. She drew pictures of these things and then recoiled in fear at what she had drawn. She scribbled her fear of sleep, that if she slept, she was certain she would suffocate and never wake up. These writings and drawings were a cry for help, a desperate attempt to cling to rationality and hope.

Years later, looking back, Kathy realized that if someone—anyone—had asked her to go to church, she would have gone, even if out of desperation, because she was dead inside. Although her parents were from a Catholic background, Kathy had rejected religion completely by the time she reached high school. She had never owned or even read a Bible.

Now she was directionless and felt worthless and hopeless. Her schoolwork grew progressively worse, and much of the time when the depression hit hard, she just didn't care. Her parents expressed their own frustration with her, and there was tension. But somehow, with their support, pressure, and encouragement, she managed to graduate. They were hugely relieved that they had all scraped through it, and Kathy was acutely aware of this too. She felt no sense of achievement.

Finishing school in June 1983, she found a job as a receptionist for a large accounting firm. Following the work ethic that she had seen in her mother, she dedicated herself to her job. She was able to put aside her self-esteem issues, as the company was quick with recognition and monetary rewards; after two years, she became personal assistant to the president. She loved her job, she was good at it, and she saw it as a way to put some purpose into her life at last.

Finishing school and starting work was a release for Kathy in other ways too. She saw the destructive path she was on at school and was able to steer away from it by cutting ties with her former school friends. There was only one girl, Jenny, that she stayed close to, and as their friendship grew, they began to see a lot of each other. In October 1983, Jenny told Kathy that a guy she'd been seeing had invited her for a day out on his boat. His roommate was going to be there too, so she needed a friend to go with her. Kathy agreed to go.

It was Saturday. They arrived at the dock, and Kathy's friend frowned as she searched, then waved at two guys perched upon a pretty small boat. As the girls approached, the guys jumped on to the dock to say hi. The first one, who turned out to be the roommate, was friendly and quite good-looking; but the other one was far more interesting. He smiled a little shyly and politely shook Kathy's hand. She was more than surprised.

"Hi," he said quietly. "My name's John Heerema."

It was a great day. They went out on the Gulf, had a few drinks and a lot of laughs. They agreed to do it again and met the following Sunday. It became a regular thing, and as Kathy and John spent time together over the next few months, they began dating. Kathy loved John's sense of humor and was able to laugh at him and at life for the first time since she arrived in Naples. He was unlike anyone she had met before. There was something decent and wholesome about him, and she felt safe and comfortable around him. Most importantly, she felt wanted, because he always treated her with respect.

Kathy intrigued John. They connected well and talked and laughed for hours, but there was always a sadness about her, something deep down that he wanted to explore and understand. She was often in her own world, thinking her private thoughts. When he asked her about her life, or her past, and tried to draw her out, she would respond to a point, but then she would withdraw, not seeming to know what to say or unwilling to answer his questions.

She struggled with this, thinking that her reluctance to open up would frustrate him and drive him away, but he would just give that shy smile and back off. She wondered where his patience and perseverance came from, and she worried constantly that he would lose interest, stop seeing her, and leave her alone once more. She was beginning to need him.

But it still didn't stop her lashing out at him when his probing questions touched a nerve. John had mentioned his faith often, but she knew that as their relationship progressed it was inevitable that John would want to talk more deeply about it, maybe even try to get her interested. She was dreading that day, not knowing how she would react. One evening he told her about his family and his upbringing in the church and that although he wasn't walking with the Lord right then, he still regarded himself as a Christian. He turned to her.

"What about you, Kathy? You ever think about God? About your spiritual life?"

"What?" She turned to face him directly. She was suddenly very angry. "My spiritual life? Let me tell you what I think, John. I think Christians are judgmental, intolerant hypocrites, and I have no intention of becoming one. That's my spiritual life."

"Kath, I didn't mean to…"

"Every time I talk with a Christian there's some guilt trip involved. People are basically good, not bad. You people don't get it. I mean, if people want sex outside of marriage and to have abortions, who are Christians to interfere?"

But she knew that her reaction came from her own feelings of guilt. She knew that what she loved about John, his character and decency, came from his upbringing and his faith. Still, she wasn't about to let him lay that stuff on her. She saw shock on John's face, and even though it quickly turned to a smile, she thought she had hurt him. Well, this conversation was bound to have happened. It was unavoidable.

Later, as their relationship started to grow more serious, she regretted her outburst. John's parents had moved down to Naples, and she knew his dad would put pressure on him to get back to church. She was right; John was under pressure, but not just for the reasons she supposed. John's parents had moved down because Jack had become ill and had to move to a warmer climate, and it was natural that he would follow his son to Florida.

Because his dad was sick, John lied and told him he was attending church and that everything was fine. He also told him nothing about Kathy, even though John had become good friends with Kathy's family; he played racquetball every week with her dad. John knew in his heart that his vagueness about his church life was not fooling his father, but he couldn't bring himself to tell his dad that he was very involved with a girl who had no interest in Jesus Christ. He just couldn't face his dad with this right now. For a while, everything was okay. Then one Saturday night, Jack called.

"You want to come to our church with your mother and me in the morning, John?" He spoke softly, hopefully.

As soon as he heard his father's voice, John put the beer he was drinking down on the coffee table. He hesitated, and it was fatal. "Er…I can't dad, I er…have to work."

It was lame, and it was a lie, and Jack's silence was both the prosecution and the judge. As his dad put down the phone, John stared at the beer, the taste of it now very bitter in his mouth.

By late 1984, John was well-established at Hole in the Wall. But country clubs at the time were releasing higher-paid staff and employing less-qualified people that they would train on the job. John felt threatened, so he started his own lawn service company, Agro Turf. This had been John's dream for some time, and he had a clear vision for his new venture. He was excited, and he spent all his spare time planning and working toward the success of the new company.

He spent hours distributing mailbox hangers, knocking on doors, and running around cutting lawns. Often, there was no response, or people were just plain rude, but John had his vision and refused to be disheartened. After a discouraging day, he would go right out and do it all again the next day with renewed energy. Kathy was amazed at him.

This quiet determination and inner strength was a side of John that she hadn't seen and hadn't expected. But John had suffered much more than rejection in his young life, and perseverance was just part of who he had become. She began to buy into the vision and believe that maybe she could step out of her comfort zone too and dream—think big. With John's help, maybe she could. Their relationship became stronger and deeper.

There came a time, inevitably, when John's parents had to meet Kathy. Jack and Jean were gracious toward her and accepted the situation, but John felt his parents' disappointment deeply, as if something were irretrievably broken or lost. He knew they had always assumed quite naturally that he would choose a Christian girl.

Kathy's attitude had softened as her love for John grew. She understood how difficult this was for him and she didn't want to force him to have to choose between his parents and her. John had supported her completely, so she decided she had to support him too. She suggested that maybe they should go to church. She really did mean it; the dark feelings of hopelessness and emptiness that plagued her were starting to come back. Why not try church? But John surprised her. No, he wasn't ready, and he would not discuss it. She thought he would appreciate her changed attitude, and she was hurt and shocked at his reaction. But the guilt he felt about deceiving his father weighed heavily, and for once, his endless patience ran out, and his temper snapped. It all ended up in a rare, bitter argument, and he would not go to church.

In fact, the first time they did go to church together was three years later, on April 25th, 1987. It was their wedding day. They were happy with their choice of church because they were not required to become members, attend special classes, or even spend time worshiping there. It was just a place to get married.

Leroy

Agro Turf had grown rapidly, and John eventually left Hole in the Wall to finally run his own business. Kathy had left the accounting firm, along with her boss, the president, and she was now working as his assistant in his successful new software company. As a married couple, with new careers, John and Kathy were working hard and playing hard, climbing the ladder and earning good salaries. They were living comfortably in a rented condo on the water in exclusive Naples Bay. They had not pressured each other at all to get married. They were partners, best friends, and inseparable, but saw no need to tie the knot. They enjoyed their independence. But one by one, their friends were getting married, and it just seemed like it was their turn. They both agreed, though, that children were out of the question. Freedom and independence to live their lives were very much on the agenda, but kids were not.

The next few years were a whirlwind of activity. Agro Turf went from being a lawn service company to a landscaping company with a staff of twenty-five. John was at full stretch to manage it. Kathy had grown in confidence and stature at work and was running the firm when her boss was traveling, which was often. They were both totally committed achievers, and they celebrated their success by buying their first home together.

Their social life was as hectic as their careers. John was always trying new things and constantly surprising Kathy. On their first wedding anniversary, a Friday, he called her at noon.

"Hey, you wanna go for pizza tonight, at my favorite restaurant? But you'll have to leave work a little early."

Kathy laughed. "John, you are so predictable. I just knew you would call and want to take me for pizza."

He laughed back. "Why?"

"Because you love pizza! Sure, I would love to, but if I'm leaving early I've got work to do. Bye."

In the car three hours later, Kathy frowned at him.

"John, where is this restaurant?"

He was smiling his shy smile. "Why?"

"Because we're headed for the airport."

"We're going to Chicago," he said.

"A restaurant called Chicago?"

"No. A city called Chicago. I said my favorite pizza restaurant. That's in Chicago. Oh, and we're spending the weekend there. Your suitcase is in the trunk. Hope I packed the right stuff."

She was speechless. He just smiled.

"Predictable, huh?"

Over the next few years they traveled all over the country to go water skiing, snow skiing, mountain climbing, and scuba diving. They went off to the Florida Keys on their newly acquired boat. They went to Disney World, rode motorbikes, sailed yachts, played golf, and both reached black-belt level in karate.

These were wonderful, happy times for Kathy. She wasn't good at many of these things, but John didn't care. In showing Kathy he only wanted to do them with her, he was expressing his deep love for her. She knew this, and she came to crave his encouragement and attention. It was all excitement, a constant high, a special time of happiness and intimacy.

But eventually, the excitement waned. Nothing was permanent. There was no purpose in all the fun, except fun itself. Kathy knew that no matter how high you fly, you have to come down. After their travels, her lingering depression and fear of isolation were always there to welcome her home. She dealt with it these days not by writing dark poetry but by listening to music, a strong influence since her early teens when she had played the flute. The radio became her friend.

At work, the sixty-hour weeks began to completely burn her out. Eventually, she had to concede that she just couldn't do it anymore. In March 1991, from a chance meeting, she was offered a management job with a new plumbing firm. They wanted her to set up and run the administration from the ground up. For Kathy, it was a cinch, and she took it. It was to be the start of not just a new job but a whole new life.

After six months, toward the end of 1991, the firm was established, and Kathy settled into a more relaxed routine. Most of the time she was by herself, and she liked it that way. She thought she was set for the next few years at least. She now had the time to focus on her marriage and on John's wants and needs. Kathy was acutely aware of John's continuing inner struggle, that he had left his faith behind somewhere, and that it hurt him and hurt his family too; there was still this distance between him and his father. Maybe she would talk to him again about going to church.

But she never did, and one day, her true feelings surfaced. Her friend Sherry came to visit. She had been to Kathy's wedding, and they were still very close. Sherry was bubbling with excitement, and she announced that she had something to tell Kathy.

"Kathy, I'm saved. I've given my heart to Jesus. I'm so happy." She waited for her friend's reaction, for her joy to be returned. But Kathy didn't know what to say, so she just looked back at her. Sherry continued, perched on the edge of her chair, tears forming in her eyes.

"I'm going to this great church, Kathy. It's incredible. Won't you come?"

Kathy sat in stony silence.

"Kath, you won't regret it. Just come and check it out. Please?"

"Let me think about it, Sherry. We'll talk, okay?"

For the next twenty minutes, Sherry talked about salvation and the love of Jesus Christ, while Kathy looked at her in silence, nodding here and there. It was awkward. They were both very uncomfortable. Over the next month, Kathy did not return even one of Sherry's many calls, and she spoke to her less and less, until eventually, they were not talking at all. Kathy just cut Sherry out of her life.

Work grew busy over the next few years. The company eventually had fifteen or so plumbers, and each morning, they arrived, collected their daily schedules, and took off in their vans for the day. They were gone before Kathy started at 8:00 a.m. and returned in the late afternoon, eager to put in their daily reports and be on their way home. But one man always seemed to hang around. His name was Leroy.

He was middle-aged, unassuming, and pleasant, and he liked to sit at Kathy's desk for fifteen minutes and chat. There was something about him that reminded her of John, and this intrigued her. When she discovered he was a Christian, she was disappointed, but she wasn't threatened. He didn't come across like an in-your-face Jesus freak. He was very comfortable in his faith, and when he talked about it, he related it to everyday life. He always managed to bring it up, no matter what the subject; but to Kathy, it was always interesting. He was never pushy, and she never felt uncomfortable with him. One morning, Leroy told Kathy that he and his wife were having problems with their teenage daughter, who was making poor life choices. Kathy leaned forward to listen; this could have been her own story.

"So what are you doing about it?" she found herself saying.

"Well," he replied, "we love her unconditionally. We don't feel that fighting and criticizing her will solve anything. The best thing, the only thing, is prayer. We have committed it to the Lord, and we pray for her every day. The Lord will fix this, by his grace." He smiled at Kathy and looked straight into her face. She could see he was completely at peace with his decision and absolutely certain that his prayers would be answered. Later that evening, Kathy sat and thought about this. She still didn't believe any of it, but Leroy had made her see Christianity in a different way. He wasn't judgmental and intolerant. He was completely humble. What would it be like to be able to believe like that, to trust something that much, to not have to worry?

A few days later, the two of them were talking about a local murder that was all over the news. Kathy said it was a terrible thing, and Leroy did his usual trick of bringing up his faith.

"It sure is, but you know, Kathy, that man could still be forgiven and go to heaven."

Kathy smiled. He'd gone too far this time.

"Leroy," she said, shaking her head, "that's ridiculous."

"Not at all," he came back. "The Bible tells us that if anyone turns from his sin in true repentance and believes that Jesus Christ died on the cross to save us and confessess that he is Lord, that person will be forgiven and will go to heaven."

"But he's a murderer," she said.

"Kathy, sin is sin. The Lord hates it. But he will forgive. He wants to forgive. He loves us that much."

"And the Bible says this?"

He leaned forward and looked into Kathy's eyes.

"Jesus said it in the Gospel of John. 'For God so loved the world that he gave his one and only Son, that whoever believes in him shall not perish, but have eternal life.' *Whoever*, Kathy." He leaned back, and smiled. "It's worth thinking about. You have a great evening."

She watched him walk out the door. She wasn't a murderer, but she believed she was a bad person deep inside.

Could that be true? Could she be forgiven and start over?

Christian Radio

She woke up one morning, and the darkness was back again. It always seemed to happen when she thought she had found some satisfaction, some stability in her life. She was happy at work, content with John, but back at square one with her depression. On the drive to work, she turned on the car radio to escape the silence. She needed the music to drown out the negative thoughts that would drive her to the pit of emptiness before noon. But today, all the songs on her favorite channel seemed to be about broken promises, lonely hearts, and tearful good-byes. She remembered another station she liked and searched for it. But as she turned the dial, she passed over a catchy, upbeat song, and she went back to it. She left it on, not really listening but enjoying the acoustic guitar and the beat, and it lifted her. As it ended, another one started, and she liked that one too. But then some lyrics took hold, and she realized she was listening to a Christian song. She was surprised that it could be so contemporary. It was cool.

She left the station on and listened to it later on the drive home. There were two very likeable young guys playing the songs, and in between, they talked about Christian stuff. But they were funny, and Kathy found herself smiling. A week later, she hadn't changed the station. It was called Praise FM. She looked forward to the songs, the phone-ins, the interviews—all of it. A month later, she had discovered other Christian stations and got to know all the top songs and artists.

Occasionally, she would flip over to the old stations but always ended up back at Praise FM, or one of the others. They were different somehow, fresh and clean. The jokes were funny, not raunchy, and the discussions and comments were always thought-provoking and positive. The message was about better things to come, that there was hope and joy, no matter what your circumstances, or how hopeless it all felt. Wow, did she need to hear that right now.

But this hope was all about a man called Jesus Christ. These young disc jockeys on the radio, the songs, the people who phoned in, they could not stop proclaiming their love for Jesus, how real he was, what he was doing in their lives, and their thankfulness that he had saved them. Kathy didn't understand how they were saved, how Jesus could be the Son of God, or how God could be their Father, but she felt a joy and peace in these people, just as she felt it so clearly in Leroy.

She craved that joy and peace, so listening to Christian radio became her secret passion. She told no one, not even John. Sometimes she heard a story similar to her own, or a song touched her deep inside, and she would sit in her car and cry. But they were tears of relief, of release. And although she didn't know these people on the radio, she felt them reaching out to her with their love.

Every morning when Kathy listened to Praise FM, they announced that at 9:45 a.m. there would be a special prayer time for listeners who called in with prayer requests. Kathy had never listened at that time because she was at work, but she often wondered about it and even thought about calling in. Would God answer her prayers?

One morning soon after, Kathy's boss burst into her office. He was breathless, running.

"Kathy, I need your car this morning. Mine's in the shop, and I'm late for an appointment!" He grabbed her keys and was out the door.

Kathy thought no more of it until he was back in her office three hours later with a big smirk on his face. He wasn't very subtle.

"What the heck are you listening to on the radio?"

She went cold. She knew instantly what had happened.

"Wh-what are you talking about?" she stammered.

"There was some guy praying on your radio. Praying!" He was gloating now and pointing at her. "Do you listen to all that Jesus stuff?"

Kathy swallowed.

"Don't be ridiculous. I guess the dial moved or something. Why would I listen to that?"

He gave her a long, searching look and then walked out, laughing.

Kathy sat staring at her desk. She was breathing deeply, her heart going crazy. She felt embarrassed, but worse than that, she felt dirty, as if she'd just betrayed somebody.

Some weeks later, in late November, 1995, she was sitting at home watching TV with John. She had done a lot of thinking since the incident at work. She was angry with herself. Why should she feel bad about listening to Christian radio? Why had she denied it? She had no intention of stopping. In fact, the whole thing had made her think beyond herself. If she could feel this bad about Christian radio, how must John feel about the rift with his father?

He had been brought up in a strict Protestant family, and he believed with all his heart that God had touched him and spared his life when he was a teenager. John knows Jesus. And now he is apart from him and his family, mostly because of her. They were comfortable, successful, and they lived a busy, active life, but inside, John must feel terrible. She had been so selfish. She knew she wasn't the easiest of wives, with her moods and her silences. But she loved him, and tonight, she was going to do something about it.

"John, I've been listening to Christian radio."

He swung his head and stared at her in shock.

"You what?"

She nodded and looked back at him.

"I like it. I like it very much."

She told him the whole story while he listened patiently. When she was done, she spoke softly, lovingly to him.

"I was thinking, maybe we should find a church. Just try it."

He smiled his shy smile back at her.

"Well, that's quite a coincidence because we've been given tickets for the Living Christmas Trees concert at a church called First Baptist. I'm told it's quite a show. So I was going to talk to you about going to church."

They went with friends, expecting to just have a good time, but for Kathy, it was one more tentative step toward Jesus. She was touched by the Christian message in the production and also by the invitation given by the pastor, Dr. Hayes Wicker, to come forward and accept Christ as Lord and

Savior. She didn't, but she knew that quite independently of each other, both she and John left the church that night knowing in their hearts that they would be back.

Discovery

I t was a Saturday afternoon. John had been playing tennis with some friends. When he got home, he shouted "hi" and went to shower. Kathy didn't answer. She was staring out the window in the spare bedroom. When she woke up this morning, black depression had hit her like a freight train. She had done nothing but think all morning, and for the past hour she had stared out this window, thinking. But her thoughts were not dark, confused and negative as they usually were when she was like this. They were clear, logical, rational, and far more scary. She recognized that she had reached the bottom of the downward spiral that had started way back in high school. Quite simply, her life was pointless and empty. Her career was a vain effort to find some purpose. Even her marriage was empty; she couldn't remember when she and John had last had a real fight. All the things they did together, the trips, the boat—it was all meaningless. Her entire life was overflowing with emptiness.

Kathy left the house and walked. She had no idea where she was going, but she knew she needed to be out of the house and away from John. She was overwhelmed by the clarity and depth of her thoughts. By the time she reached the lake at the Vineyards community three miles later, the sun was beginning to set. She found a bench, but instead of sitting on it, she sat on the grass with her back to it, legs drawn up and arms around her knees. There was no one around—just her, the sunset, and God.

As she stared at the last yellow-orange rays of the sun shimmering on the lake, the tears came —slowly at first, and then bursting into an unstoppable torrent. Soon, her entire body was being shaken by the intensity of the sobs that escaped from deep inside her. She lifted her head and cried out to God from the anguished depths of her heart.

"I don't know if you can hear me. I don't know if you care. I just want you to know that I'm done. I hate my marriage, my job, and my life. I don't want any of it anymore. I don't know what you want me to do or be. I don't know if you're sending me to heaven or hell. But I can't live like this anymore. If you're real, help me. Please, please help me."

In an instant, like a pressure valve releasing, all the hurt and pain evaporated, and she was enveloped in love so powerful and so pure she could hardly breathe. She knew it was Jesus, that he was there, and that he had heard her. She felt the reality of his touch in the deepest part of her, and she instantly knew, with absolute and complete certainty, that he was in control and that everything would be okay. The tears became happy tears, like a child's, and she cried unashamedly in gratitude for the answer that she had received.

By the time she reached home, she was completely calm. She sat on the patio and explained to her speechless husband that desperation had driven her out of the house and that God had just changed her life. God had responded to her cry and touched her heart. Now she had to find out who God is because his presence and the love she had just experienced was real. She had to find out about him, how she can know him.

John was completely stunned. Not just by Kathy's experience, which filled him with tearful happiness, but also because he had had similar thoughts since the Christmas concert, constant nagging thoughts of getting back to God and finding his faith again. When Kathy said their marriage was empty, that they never even argued, he realized he felt exactly the same way. They loved each other deeply, but something was missing. Was God saving Kathy and bringing John back to him at the same time? Yes, he was. They needed to respond to this. They needed to get grounded in faith. He would pray and he would fast. It had been so long, but now he would seek the Lord in earnest.

Part of the grounding process over the following months was the sudden realization that they wanted children. They had both agreed even before their marriage that their careers and their personal pleasures were more important than kids, but God was now showing them that his plan for them was quite different. Kathy had listened to a discussion on the subject on Christian radio.

Someone made the point that if Christian families are not prepared to raise the next generation, then who will fight for the cause of Christ? She immediately saw things differently. A child is a precious gift from God. How could she ever have thought that abortion was okay? Becoming parents was a subject they never discussed, but when Kathy tentatively brought it up, John was all over it immediately. He said he'd decided against kids because the world is a mess and he'd read that clubfeet could be a hereditary condition. He didn't want any child to go through what he'd been through. But the Lord had shown him recently that this was His decision, according to His will. John now saw that it was a Christian duty to raise Christian children. They had been married nine years, and Kathy was thirty already. They agreed to have children as soon as possible.

It took some time, though, to commit to a church home. They went to different churches but ended up back at First Baptist. John had resisted because although he had felt drawn to the church ever since his first visit at the Living Christmas Trees concert, it raised another issue with his father. The Reformed church followed infant baptism, and John had been baptized as a child. John felt that his dad would strongly object, feeling it was wrong to be baptized again, and Kathy knew it was a huge issue for him.

But in June 1996, they agreed that it had to be First Baptist. It felt like home to both of them. So on a sunny Sunday morning, John and Kathy went forward together. She publically affirmed her acceptance of Jesus Christ as her Lord and Savior, and he recommitted his life to Jesus. The Sunday after that, they were both baptized. They felt joyful and happy together, celebrating Kathy's rebirth in Christ and John's recommitment. They had something else to celebrate too.

Kathy was pregnant.

The months after Kathy's salvation were an incredible roller coaster ride for her. She was thirty years old and a baby Christian. She was a sponge, soaking in everything the church and her new faith could throw at her. She bought her first Bible, the same one the pastor read from during his sermon each week, and waited in service for him to say, "Please turn in your Bibles to Luke chapter four." But when he said it, she couldn't find Luke at all, and John had to come to her rescue.

Her first few Bible study sessions were even more stressful. The leader would go through a Bible passage and then say something like, "There are strong parallels here with the passage in Ephesians, where Paul tells us…" Kathy would panic. *What's Ephesians? Who's Paul?* It was a victory if she could get through the session without making eye contact with anyone.

But over the next few months, she read the Bible from cover to cover and learned key passages. She studied basic doctrine and tried to get to grips with the new Kathy, the one touched by God. Her introspective moments were sad and sometimes disappointing. Why had it taken her so long to find Jesus? She thought of her friend Sherry and how she had just cut her out of her life because she had become a Christian. How could she hurt her in such a callous way? She prayed for forgiveness and that Sherry was still a committed follower of the faith, wherever she was.

Then there was the startling realization that a few of her non-Christian friends were suddenly not talking to Kathy—no, not a few, many. She and John were not asked to dinner or invited to picnic at the beach. Was she angry? No, she wasn't. It was a strange separation, but she saw these people in a different way now. Some of them had shown genuine interest in Kathy's testimony, but most were not interested. Some were uncomfortable. A few told her straight out what many were saying; that it was one of Kathy and John's phases, like jet skiing or sailing, and would soon pass. One or two said church was a cult. How do you explain the joy of finding Christ to people who are so lost that they won't pick up a Bible but will sit up all night reading the latest best-selling novel? She knew they all needed to know Jesus Christ, and she knew that she had to learn how to convince these people of the truth and to do it with compassion, just as Jesus did.

After their daughter Kristen was born in March 1997, Kathy continued to work in the plumbing company for a while, and her boss saw her transformation as she grew in her faith. After the "Jesus incident," at work, and as her faith grew stronger, she would try to share her faith with him. One time, he came in to work looking very sad, and Kathy asked what was wrong.

"Oh, nothing much. My dog is very sick, he might die, and the family is all upset."

She looked him straight in the eye.

"I'm so sorry. Can I pray with you?"

He looked shocked.

"What? No thank you."

"Well, I'm gonna pray anyway. What's his name?"

He left her office in a hurry. Kathy allowed herself a little smile and enjoyed the irony of the moment. She had sure turned the tables on him.

As she became bolder, she also had to deal with a strange bitterness that she felt toward all the people in her life that she later discovered were Christians but hadn't witnessed to her. There were many. Was it necessary for her to go through all the pain of her teenage years and never know about Jesus Christ? She still had black days and bouts of depression, but she had Jesus and the power of the Holy Spirit living inside her. She was learning that Christ was greater than any human condition, and she could handle her depression. She was handling it. She drew courage from Philippians 4:13: "I can do everything through him who gives me strength."

Of all the people she knew, or later found out, were Christians, only two, Sherry and Leroy, had shared their faith. That was it. She resolved to be a bold and positive witness. As a new Christian, she was excited and had a great desire to serve. After all the years of feeling worthless, God himself told her he loves her, and she believed the Scripture when it said he had a plan for her life. She would just have to wait on the Lord's timing to find out what it was. But she was already feeling a burden to find the lost and bring them to Christ. They needed forgiveness and cleansing and a place in heaven.

Kathy went through her own cleansing. It was a bittersweet experience. In her quiet time of study, she came across David's song of praise in 2 Samuel 22. Verses five through seven record David's anguish before God rescued him from his enemies, which included his own king, Saul, who wanted him dead.

The waves of death swirled about me;
The torrents of destruction overwhelmed me.
The cords of the grave coiled around me;
The snares of death confronted me.
In my distress I cried out to the Lord;
I called out to my God.
From his temple he heard my voice;
My cry came to his ears.

As she read these words, Kathy saw in them stark images of her own early life. They described not just the events in her life, but her inner self, the deep, intimate parts of her soul that had suffered such torment. She vividly remembered the terrible snakes and beasts in her dreams and the poems and prose that were her feeble attempts to rationalize them and keep them at bay. These were the dark and lonely times she never talked about, when she wondered why she even needed to exist. As she read the Scripture, all these things were laid out bare for the first time.

Kathy cried out, wept, and let it all come out. She could do this now, even though she would never dare before, because she knew with all her being that the last part of David's song was as true for her as it had been for him. The God of the universe had heard her cry out. He had heard her, and he loved her. This was his assurance to her that he was with her and would always be with her. She cried for the release of the pain, the guilt and the memories; and she cried also for the privilege of knowing the Lord and in gratitude for his incredible grace in saving her when she did not deserve it. In her short Christian life, she knew it might be some time before she fully felt his joy, but right now, she knew his peace.

Nine months after Kristen's birth, Kathy stopped working at the plumbing shop to be with her. It was a precious time in Kathy and John's marriage. They were so happy with Kristen, but they also found a new level in their own relationship as a couple. John encouraged Kathy in her faith every day, and they read the Bible together, with John teaching her life lessons and deeper insights into Scripture.

He enjoyed pointing out things about her that had changed since her salvation. He called it the "before and after game." Some were obvious; she had stopped smoking and drinking. But others were so subtle that she had no idea of the change. She was more calm, more patient, and more thoughtful and forgiving. The Holy Spirit was at work. Kathy also discovered the benefits of Christian fellowship. Everyone wanted to help her, teach her, and love her. She was never more content than when she was around the church.

John had spent many hours on his knees seeking God, desperate to be close to him again. He knew in his heart that God had called him again because he had a plan and a purpose for him. He knew it with certainty. He was eager to begin his new walk with him.

It was at this time that Kathy first experienced the goodness and nature of God in her everyday life. Even though she had absorbed so much of the Bible in such a short period, and even with John's help, she felt inferior to so many of her new Christian friends, who seemed so well versed in the Scriptures. She still found it hard to take part in discussions in her Bible Life Group (or BLG, as the Bible studies were known at First Baptist Church), and it was frustrating because she wanted to contribute. Kathy was acutely aware of all the missing years.

But shortly after Kristen's birth, she was approached by the director of the preschool ministry and asked to consider becoming a teacher to a class of three-year-olds. She wanted Kathy to teach them Bible stories. Her first reaction was panic, but she found herself agreeing.

Over the next two years, she read dozens of Bible stories to her class, and she learned all of them as she taught them. At the same time, John had become a teacher in the youth ministry, a calling he felt as a result of his own happy experience in youth so many years ago. Kathy would sit in on his Bible teachings to the teenagers and soak it up. Often, she would hear one of her own stories, now told to these teenagers in a different way, with a deeper meaning. It gave her incredible insight.

It was at one of these times, in a youth class, that she suddenly realized that this was a gift from God. This was his answer to her learning dilemma. A crash course in the Bible. He was using preschool and youth teaching to make up all of her lost childhood years. Overwhelmed, she bowed her head right there in the classroom and thanked him. From that moment, she realized that God is always watching, always close by. She must stay close to him. She needed him.

BENJAMIN

"Even youths grow tired and weary,
and young men stumble and fall;
but those who hope in the Lord
will renew their strength.
They will soar on wings like eagles;
they will run and not grow weary,
they will walk and not be faint"

Isaiah 40:30–31

Darjeeling, India

Benjamin looked at himself critically in the mirror. It wasn't much of a picture, but then again, it wasn't much of a mirror. The crack that ran northwest to southeast gave two distinct images, and he had to sway like a drunken sailor to piece it all together.

The jacket he wore was borrowed from an uncle back in Calcutta. It was an old, dark-green tweedy thing that had seen better days. Two of the leather buttons were hanging by a thread. The breast pocket kept coming down, so he had contrived a fix with two old pieces of Velcro that seemed to do the trick. It was at least two sizes too big, but at least it was a jacket.

He had to look his best this morning. His faded white shirt was a good fit, although the points of the collar curled up with age. He had tried holding them down with his thumb and finger, but when he let go, they curled again like old parchment. Another uncle had provided the tie. The yellow paisley gave a touch of class, as long as the jacket was buttoned to hide the tea stain. His gray pants were in serious need of a press and were way too long. He adjusted them to cover the dirtier parts of his worn sneakers.

Benjamin frowned and focused on his face. He turned his head a little, lifted his chin, and pursed his lips.

"*Evan*gelist," he said smoothly, in his velvety Indian voice. He loved that word. It spoke to him of so many things, of his Lord Jesus, and his own vision of the future.

He was excited. He felt that this would be his day and that the Lord would give this day to him. For one whole year now, he had tried with all his heart to follow the calling that he felt so strongly. But church after church all over northeastern India had refused to let him preach. It was 1991, he was barely eighteen, with no formal training. His lack of height made him seem even younger, so no one took him seriously. Now, here he was up in hilly tea country, Darjeeling, West Bengal, looking to preach at a church in Jorebungalow that had a liberal pastor, or so he had heard.

"Evange*list*," he pouted. No, perhaps the first try was better.

For two years, he had wandered the streets of Kolkata with his cousin, Navin. Benjamin played a half-decent guitar, and Navin could sing like a bird, so they teamed up to sing songs about Jesus, the cross, salvation, and redemption. They sang and played in churches and in schools but also on street corners and train stations— anywhere that lost people could be found.

Navin was as tall as Benjamin was short, so people would accommodate this strange duo, thinking they would entertain. They sang in Bengali and Hindi mostly, but sometimes in English. Calcutta, a city of seventeen million people, has fewer than ten thousand Christians, although the British had introduced Christianity two hundred years before. Many evangelists would be discouraged at these figures, but young Benjamin saw only the potential. There were millions of Hindus and Muslims waiting to meet Jesus. How could anyone not see the vision?

They would play and sing, and Benjamin would proclaim the name of Jesus. He spoke with such passion and conviction about the living God that people began to listen. As he became bolder and more confident, he could see the Holy Spirit touching them, calling them, and saving them. And then, a year ago, the Lord had laid it on his heart to preach. The Lord wanted him to be a preacher. He had been on fire ever since.

He took one more glance at his reflection, picked up his guitar case, slipped his worn old Bible into the jacket pocket, and exited his room. The hotel was not great; the bed was broken, just like the mirror. But it was cheap and all they could afford. It was a cool Sunday morning, which was a blessing because they had a two-and-three-quarter-mile walk, mostly uphill. Navin, dressed in jeans and a tee shirt, gave him a strange look as they met outside, but said nothing. He was a young man of few words, which was yet another contrast with his little traveling companion. Together they took off west, past the bustling town market, which was busy even at 7:30 on a Sunday morning, and then out onto the winding road south.

They eventually saw the church, off the road and way up at the top of the hill to their left. It was an old wooden structure, but Ben noticed with a surge of excitement that it looked fairly large for such a remote place. It had a small steeple with a cross atop it. Navin was now carrying the guitar, as Benjamin was tired and sweating. He hadn't taken off his jacket, and for once, he hadn't been very talkative, as he was rehearsing his sermon in his head as he walked.

Fifty yards further on, a huge raincloud appeared above them. Benjamin looked up apprehensively. It was a month before the monsoon season, and sudden, soaking rain was a more frequent occurrence as the season approached. They walked faster, Benjamin upping the pace. They were almost there and could hear voices raised in joyous song when the heavens opened. For one full minute, there was a deluge of such soaking rain that Benjamin and Navin could barely see the church. Then, as quickly as it had arrived, it was gone, and the sun shone once more.

As they reached the church, Benjamin opened the door and peeked inside. He counted about fifty people in the congregation. Looking forward, he saw the pastor open up his Bible at an old, wooden lectern. He was old too, with silver, unruly hair. Suddenly, he glanced up and looked squarely into Benjamin's eyes. The pastor considered him for a moment and then began to march shakily down the aisle toward him. Benjamin closed the door, shook off his soaking tweed jacket, and turned to Navin.

"Praise the Lord, he hasn't started the sermon yet. How do I look?"

His cousin looked him up and down impassively. His eyes lingered over the legs of Benjamin's pants which now looked like twin sacks over his muddy sneakers, and at the steam rising from his jacket. Then he looked into Benjamin's ever-smiling face, his own face expressionless.

"You look ridiculous."

The door opened, and there stood the pastor. Benjamin turned, smiling, and saw that his silver eyebrows were as unruly as his silver hair. For an Indian, he had unusual blue eyes and wore a questioning frown.

"Can I help you? Who are you?"

Benjamin drew himself up to his full height. It wasn't a long journey.

"My name is Benjamin Francis. I am an *evan*gelist." As he said this, the Velcro securing his breast pocket gave up the ghost, and it flapped open. At the same time, a large bead of rainwater ran down the center of his nose and clung to the end of it, refusing to fall. This seemed to fascinate the pastor, who stared at it until gravity released its grip. Then he spoke up again.

"And what do you want?" he asked, puzzled. The eyebrows were dancing now. Young Benjamin saw his chance and dived right in.

"I have come to preach," he declared. Several conflicting expressions crossed the pastor's face until he eventually reached a decision.

"Well, you had better come in then."

Benjamin strode to the pulpit and pulled out his Bible, silently thanking the Lord that it was dry. He looked up to a sea of faces expressing everything from bewilderment to amusement. He didn't care. Smiling, he introduced himself, and directed them to 1 Samuel 13.

He launched into his sermon on spiritual warfare. The Philistines controlled the Israelite mines and their blacksmiths. So the Israelites, without weapons, were forced to have even their farming tools sharpened by Philistine blacksmiths. The Israelites were so oppressed by the Philistines that when the inevitable day of battle came, they had no weapons with which to fight.

Benjamin raised his Bible, and he raised his voice.

"This, the Word of God, is our mine, and the Holy Spirit, alive in each one of us, he is our blacksmith. The enemy has no control over them and no control over us. We are the people of God!"

He spoke for thirty minutes, and the congregation gave him a rousing response. He had forgotten to say some things and had mixed up some points here and there. It didn't matter. It didn't even matter that he was still soaking wet. He had preached, and they had heard the message. Later, as he played guitar and Navin sang, Benjamin closed his eyes and thanked Jesus for keeping His promise and giving him this day.

The Altar

Benjamin's father, Jagnarayn Ram, was named after the important Hindu god, Ram, worshiped in their village, situated in the state of Bihar, northeast India. His family had been Hindu for many generations, and it had been expected that he would become a witch doctor, as was his father, or perhaps a priest. Witch doctors were held in high regard by the villagers, who paid good sums of money to have sickness cured, gods pacified, and evil spirits banished. Benjamin's grandfather was considered a powerful witch doctor, and the people feared him.

But Benjamin's father instead took the twelve-hour train journey to Kolkata, or Calcutta, as it was then known, seeking work, and eventually found it in the telephone department of Calcutta city. He also found Jesus Christ after being brought back from the brink of death after contracting pneumonia, by a Christian doctor named Peter. He became a fervent Christian and changed his first name to Peter, in honor of the doctor, and his last name to Francis, as a symbolic gesture of his rejection of Hinduism.

He also met a Christian girl, Jayshri Singh, a teacher with a master's degree in theology, and they soon married. Nobody cared in Calcutta, but this union and his conversion to Christianity caused such a stir back home in the village in Bihar that Peter was completely rejected by them. He received death threats from surrounding villages. It was to be seven years before his family forgave him so that he could present his wife to them.

Ironically, within the Hindu caste system Jayshri was considered high caste, and eventually, Peter's family was celebrating his achievement in marrying her. The real achievement, given their colorful, recent family histories, was that they were even able to marry at all as first generation Christians—Peter's father being the celebrated witchdoctor, and Jayshri's father being a train robber from a noted family of robbers.

In June 1973, Peter and Jayshri had a son and gave him the strong biblical name of Benjamin. At first, things were good; Peter's career was progressing well, and he was active in ministry. But when young Ben was just five, disaster struck. His father was wrongfully accused of improper conduct with a woman, and although he was cleared of the charge, the church removed him from all ministry work. Shattered and embittered, Peter abandoned his faith in disillusionment and took a position in another city back in Bihar, leaving Jayshri to raise Benjamin alone.

It was the beginning of hard times. Jayshri worked and prayed, and struggled to feed and raise her son. Benjamin rebelled. He was a small, angry boy, growing up in a tough city, and trouble was never far away. One time, he saw a Tarzan movie, and the next day at school, he hung on his teacher's hair, dragging her screaming to the ground in front of the whole class. He hurt her so badly, physically and mentally, that she cut her hair short, and never grew it long again. He was an easy target for bullies because of his size and because he had no big brothers or father to protect him. But he had courage, pride, and a fierce devotion to his mother. He didn't care when the other kids taunted him for having no father or because he was poor. He didn't care when they insulted his mother's Christianity, but if anyone insulted his mother, he would fly into a rage and fight ferociously, regardless of his tormentor's size or age.

Jayshri was his saving grace. Her teacher's salary was never enough, so she had to take a second job, which exhausted her. A diminutive woman, she was a full four inches shorter than Benjamin, and frail. But she possessed an inner spiritual strength that belied her physical appearance.

She never missed taking Benjamin to church service. It took an age for her to walk the mile to church, as problems with her knees left her almost crippled. And she got down on those knees to pray several times a day. Benjamin would hear her praying by her bed in their two-room shack, and he would silently peek around the door in the dark and watch her cry as she prayed. He sometimes silently cried with her, his little heart breaking at the painful sound of her tears. He would watch for long periods, humbled by the scene before him, wondering to whom she was talking with such loving words.

Sometimes he drew near, careful not to disturb her, and he would listen and wonder why she was always praying for other people when they themselves had such troubles. And he often heard her pray for him with many tears. If he woke in the night, she was praying; and when he came home from school, she was praying. His mother's prayers had a deep and lasting impression on Benjamin. He learned from her that prayer is a special, important time with God.

Through his mother's unfailing commitment to prayer, even at his young age, he was able to grasp the power of the Lord and the reverence owed him. He also learned to forgive, and to love and pray for those who have hurt you. Benjamin didn't understand why his father had abandoned them, and he was angry that he and his mother were so poor, but through Jayshri's example he learned to find peace by giving it to the Lord. When he was a little older, he loved the times when he and his mother prayed together, because at these times, Benjamin became someone else. The wild boy would disappear, and another Benjamin took over—one that felt sorrow and love, one that wanted to know the Lord, just as his mother did. It was her influence that kept Benjamin from taking to the dark side of Calcutta, the side from which he would not have returned.

Jayshri sacrificed herself for years, working long hours and saving every rupee to ensure her son had a good education and a chance in life. Eventually, an organization called Compassion, and her church, Assemblies of God, took heed of her plight and magnanimously agreed to sponsor the last years of Benjamin's studies.

Benjamin stole food when they were hungry and told his mother he had been given it or had worked for it. He also stole cricket balls. Mr. Subramoney was a tall, thin gentleman, and he owned the general store. There was a whole world of goods in that store—food, clothing, fabrics, cleaning supplies, pots and pans, appliances, candy. And cricket balls. Benjamin and his friends made bats and wickets out of wood from old crates, but they needed a real ball to play.

So Benjamin, nine years of age, clothes ill-fitting and ragged, walked right in and marched up to Mr. Subramoney.

"I would like to see one of your finest cricket balls, please sir," he announced, displaying his most winning smile. Mr. Subramoney frowned down at Benjamin for some seconds, and then slowly and silently turned and fetched a ball from the display in the cabinet. Benjamin, lips pursed in concentration, weighed the ball carefully in his tiny hand.

"No," he said, putting it down on the counter. "This one just doesn't feel right. Could I see a different brand please sir?" The smile came on like a light bulb as he raised his head all the way up to meet the shopkeeper's impassive face. Another ball was patiently fetched, and then another.

This went on for some time until Benjamin said thank you, but he didn't like any of these. He smiled one last time and left the shop. Outside and around the corner with an expectant crowd of boys, he took a nice, shiny, red cricket ball out of his pocket and tossed it in the air. "Let's play," he said. They all ran off, screaming and laughing.

Years later, when he was eighteen, Benjamin remembered this incident, which he had repeated a few times. He went to the store, which looked exactly the same, walked in and approached Mr. Subramoney, who also looked the same apart from some gray streaks in his jet black hair. Ben smiled in greeting.

"Hello, Mr. Subramoney. I hope you are well, sir. My name is Benjamin Francis. I used to live in this part of the city as a child, and—"

"Yes," the older man interrupted, smiling. "I know who you are. You used to come in and steal my cricket balls."

For once, Benjamin was stuck for words.

"You know?" he asked, stunned.

"Of course. You were brazen but not a very good thief." Benjamin frowned.

"Why didn't you stop me?" he asked.

"Because your mother is the godliest woman I have ever met. As a Christian, she has taught me more about true faith and humility before the

Lord than any other person I have ever known. And I knew that if you were playing cricket, then you were not getting into mischief. That's worth more to me than seven cricket balls."

"Is that how many I took?" Benjamin's mouth hung open.

Mr. Subramoney nodded graciously.

"Well, I have come to apologize and to pay you for them," said Ben.

The older man smiled.

"Apology accepted, but no payment necessary. Consider it a fair trade."

As a teenager Benjamin lived something of a double life. He was streetwise and a tough little guy. He constantly felt the pull of Calcutta, and he needed to be part of that world to survive. But his mother had shown him something he began to feel he needed. He craved her peace and her inner strength, and she had shown him that he could only achieve this through Jesus Christ. He thought he had an understanding of what Christianity was. He read his Bible, and he thought he knew Christ. But it was at a Christian camp that he learned that although he knew about Jesus, he didn't really know him at all.

He was just seventeen and had been invited to the camp by a Christian friend.

"Will they be playing cricket?" Benjamin asked. They were, so he happily agreed to go. But he was completely unprepared for what he would experience. He met young men and women who were committed followers of Jesus, who lived their lives for him. They knew Scripture, just like Benjamin, but they really knew Jesus. They had a relationship with him that was obviously alive and fulfilling for them. Benjamin knew he was missing out on something important, something much bigger than he realized. It was what his mother had, and he wanted it. He yearned for it.

As the days at camp passed, he began to ponder who he was and where he had come from. His father's family had worshiped Hindu gods for generations, and his mother's family believed in no god at all. Now here he was, the product of a tentative Christian union at best. He knew he was not a fully committed Christian, but through his mother's faith, he had always felt God's pull. Had God orchestrated this for a reason? He felt that the Lord was trying to bless him through his mother's love, but that he had resisted. Was he now calling him?

By the last night of camp, Benjamin had clearly felt the Holy Spirit's touch, and on his knees, with tears flowing down his cheeks, he gave his heart and submitted his life to his Lord and Savior, Jesus Christ. He owned nothing, he had no prospects, but he had an education, and he knew that God could make of him anything he wished. He only had to trust. As he prayed, he felt the Lord telling him he would be involved in missions to bring the lost to the saving knowledge of Jesus Christ, and he resolved that night to follow that calling.

The next day, the last day, Benjamin got up early and walked out of camp. He had hiked a few days earlier with some of his group to a beautiful, desolate spot, with no sound but a gently flowing river and sweet birdsong. There was nothing there but God's peace, and in a rocky clearing, they had picnicked and read their Bibles before returning. Benjamin came back to this place that morning because he had a purpose. It was a two-hour journey, and when he arrived, he took off his backpack, ate the fruit he had hurriedly packed, and rested.

He then gathered the large, rough broken stones that lay all around that place. They were between six and nine inches in size and were sharp and heavy. When he tired, he rested and drank from the river, and he used the cool water to clean the small cuts that the stones had made in his hands and fingers to punish him for not being careful with them. After a couple of hours, he thought he had enough, and he began to carefully pile them up.

Soon, he had erected a large, very rough square of rocks that rose to a point. It stood almost as high as Benjamin's chest. He walked around it, adjusted some stones here and there, then stood back to admire it. It was an altar. Benjamin smiled, and then got to his knees to pray, to thank the Lord Jesus for saving him and to thank him for his grace and mercy toward him. He thanked him for his mother's love and guidance and for keeping them both alive. He thanked him for keeping him from the drugs, alcohol, and immorality that had surrounded him in Calcutta. He prayed for a long time, sometimes silently, and sometimes out loud, with laughter and with tears. Finally, he took one more drink, put on his knapsack, and walked back to camp. He was still smiling, completely at peace.

Benjamin told no one about the altar. It was between him and God. Others would find it, of course, and some may even figure out what it was. But only he and God would know what it stood for, and the love and gratitude that had flowed in Benjamin's heart as he had built it—an altar of acceptance, surrender, and thanksgiving.

This was not the only altar he was to build. He would find solace, humility, and comfort in building others. But why did he make them? These were deep, personal symbols for Benjamin. A part of a powerful address he was to make to Big Life leaders at a national retreat in Darjeeling twenty years later sheds some light on why building these altars has had such spiritual importance for him.

He spoke of God's great promise to Abram in Genesis twelve:

"I will bless you, he said. If you leave your country, and your father's house, and if you trust me, I will bless you. This blessing was extended to all of us, Abram's children, and this is why this story of the blessing is something the entire world needs to know. Abram built an altar of acceptance to receive this blessing, and when he moved east of Bethel he built another altar, to proclaim his obedience to the Lord's call. He was seventy-five years old at this time.

"You all have an altar in your life, at the place God called you. You met him at the altar of acceptance. But since you accepted the Lord's grace, have you sinned again? Or am I the only one here that has sinned? Abram did. In his life, he faced the same pressures you and I face today.

"When Abram lied to Pharaoh about Sarai his wife, and Pharaoh sent him away, he went back to Bethel to the altar, and cried out to the Lord. This great man, blessed by God, now kneels before the altar of repentance because of his lies. Just imagine if he had not repented. It would have affected countless people. And if we do not continually repent and make things right with him, generations will be affected. Every positive decision we make as disciples, to walk with the Lord and live a holy life, affects those who come after us.

"Abram understood that the altar is also a place of unity. All peoples will be blessed, the Lord had said. We come from different backgrounds, and many diverse cultures, but we are Christians, and we come together to submit and worship in unity before God.

"Later, when Abram separated from Lot, he showed great character by allowing the younger man to settle on the finest looking land, while he set off in the opposite direction. As Abram led his people away from the fertile land, they must have wondered where he was taking them. But the Lord said to Abram, 'Lift up your eyes. Everything you see before you I will give you forever, and your offspring will be like the dust of the earth.' Abram clung to the Lord's promise, and he built another altar, an altar of promise, and later of gratitude.

"Today," Benjamin concluded, "we come to the modern day altar to remember that our Lord Jesus paid for all our sins."

To Benjamin, the altar was the place of communion with God on many levels, a reminder and a covenant that the Lord was always to be at the center of his life.

So it was 1990, and Benjamin was saved. The camp was a watershed in his life, and he would never be the same. But he was seventeen, he was poor, and he had to go back to the jungle that was Calcutta. He quickly found work, which was a blessing for him and his mother, and life in the city simply swallowed him up. He became so busy with the practical business of life that all his great godly plans and dreams suddenly seemed unattainable. He began his work in the church and taught Sunday school to young children, but the Lord's constant pull on his heart told him there was something else the Lord would have him do.

He became convinced that the Lord was calling him to preach. He prayed about this constantly because he now saw Calcutta as a city of lost and damned souls in desperate need of salvation. The city was full of temples and idols, and great old churches, but nobody seemed to care whether someone was Christian, Hindu, Muslim, or anything else. Survival was the important thing, and surviving took all of one's energy, resources, and time. It changed one's needs, perspective, and morals.

He searched for Christian friends and found them, mostly teenagers who came from poor backgrounds, just like him. They would hang around teashops, sometimes until the early hours of the morning. They praised Jesus, sang about Jesus, retold the great Bible stories, and they practiced preaching to each other and to anyone who cared to listen. These were great formative years for Benjamin, and as he honed his preaching skills, he knew that he had been born for this. He felt the Lord working powerfully within him; the anger he'd felt as an abandoned child was being channeled into a passionate and urgent preaching style. He loved to proclaim the Word of God, and his friends loved to listen to him do it. Many who visited the teashops for a late-night soda or snack had no idea that their lives would be changed that night, but it happened often. This was such a strong band of friends that Benjamin remained in touch with all of them. Even though they were eventually scattered all over the world, they remained strong Christians, and most have prospered. It was from these nightly gatherings that Benjamin and Navin began their evangelistic music ministry around Calcutta that culminated in his first preaching opportunity in Darjeeling.

He became a youth counselor at his church. He met plenty of girls, but although many of them were at the right dating age for him, he respected his position and found he had many "sisters" and few dates, although many were drawn to his personality. The lack of a girlfriend frustrated him, as his friends were all dating, but he was prepared to be patient. He knew that God would show him the right one.

Benjamin progressed in his career. His confident and extroverted personality made him a natural salesman, and with Panasonic, he progressed over the next four years from sales clerk to sales manager. He was in the best financial position of his young life. This success helped put to rest a lot of the demons that plagued him, such as the hardship in his upbringing, the absence of his father, and the taunting at school about his height and his family. It also became a burden because he felt that constant pull from the Lord, and he knew in his heart that he would never be content or find fulfillment without absolute submission to Jesus. Studying his Bible one night, he was convicted by Jesus' words:

I am the light of the world. Whoever follows me will never walk in darkness, but will have the light of life.

John 8:12

He asked himself if he had the light of life, if he was following the Lord with complete surrender? "Follow me," Jesus told Matthew, and Matthew got up, left everything and followed. Could Benjamin follow and deny himself, deny his newly found success? It was painful to admit it, but he really didn't know.

But the Lord wasn't finished with Benjamin. With Jesus' command to follow constantly tugging at his conscience, soon, another of the Lord's commands began eating at him. It was *go*.

> Therefore go and make disciples of all nations, baptizing them in the name of the Father, and of the Son and of the Holy Spirit, and teaching them to obey everything I have commanded you.
>
> Matthew 28:19–20

The Great Commission, Jesus' last command and a call for his church to be extended to all nations by obedient believers. Go.

So Benjamin went. On weekends, he visited villages north and south of Calcutta. He sang and played gospel songs and hymns, preached, read from the Bible, and shared about Jesus' presence in his life. He was amazed at the hunger these people had for the truth. For a while, he was happy with these spiritual vacations. He would return home uplifted and satisfied that he had brought people to the Lord, that he was serving him. But eventually he had to admit what he knew to be the truth all along. He was making a deal with God. He had become a part-time evangelist—an effective one, but not a fully committed one. God wanted more from him, and God intended to have it.

Witchdoctor

arly in 1995, Benjamin was struck by an urge to visit his father's village in Bihar. It was a lawless state, a dangerous and dark place, known as the graveyard of missionaries. For years, many had tried, and some had died trying to bring the gospel. There were no churches out there. Benjamin had heard that his father was working in the north of Bihar, so he wouldn't see him, but he would get to see his grandfather. He was excited. He traveled the long train journey with Navin for a weekend there and prayed earnestly that it would go well and that they would be accepted so that he could tell his Hindu family about Jesus.

It was life-changing for Benjamin. He discovered so many things about the village and village life that he had been so ignorant of. One was that there were over 2,500 people living there, and in one way or another, most of them were related to him. They accepted him immediately, particularly his grandfather, the witchdoctor, who was so happy he wept for joy. He had wild, gray hair, and a long, silver beard. Benjamin loved him.

They worked in the fields in the day, and in the evening many of the people gathered in the center of the village to eat and socialize. Traditional music was played, and Benjamin and Navin joined in with both song and guitar. When they were invited to play, they sang simple Christian songs and hymns in Hindi and Bengali. They didn't introduce them as Christian songs, they just sang. The villagers laughed and clapped at the stories they contained. It was joyous.

On the second night Ben began to play and sing something else in Bengali. Navin quickly joined him.

"How great is our God, sing with me
How great is our God, and all will see
How great, how great is our God…"

The people were silent as Ben and Navin sang the verses, listening to the words and swaying to the music. As they reached the chorus again, some joined in. Ben nodded his encouragement as he sang, "Sing with me…" Soon many were quietly singing to this God they did not know, caught up in this precious moment. As Ben looked out at them, at their wide, shining eyes reflecting the flickering firelight, and their open smiles, his heart went out to them. He could see and feel their need and their hunger for Jesus. Soon he and Navin were singing through happy tears. *What a blessed time this is*, Ben thought, *and how different from Calcutta.*

Later, he was able to talk about Jesus to many who approached him, eager to know about this 'great God.' He was cautious and discrete, careful not to offend, but they had many questions, and soon, he had a crowd. Before retiring to his bed in his grandfather's house, he sat alone on a rock, picking at his guitar. He was deeply affected by what had happened tonight. After a while, he stopped playing and looked up at the heavens—breathtaking diamonds on a black velvet cloth.

Yes, the Lord had spoken to his heart tonight. This village—no, all these villages—they all need to know Jesus. How many villages? Thousands. How many souls? Millions. It was incredible to even think about. As he looked at the countless twinkling stars, he prayed and wept silently, knowing that it was God's purpose that he was here.

"Follow me."

Yes, Lord.

"Go and make disciples."

I hear you, Lord. Thank you, Jesus, thank you.

On the train home, Benjamin had much to think about. This was his father's village, his grandfather's village. But it was also his village. His family lived there and even in the neighboring villages. They were his people. Was he so much different from them just because he was born in Calcutta? In every hut there was an idol that they worshiped, prayed to, and relied upon because they had never heard the name of Jesus Christ. He pulled out his worn Bible and found Romans 10:12–15:

> For there is no difference between Jew and Gentile-the same Lord is Lord of all and richly blesses all who call on him, for, 'Everyone who calls on the name of the Lord will be saved.' How, then, can they call on the one they have not believed in? And how can they believe in the one of whom they have not heard? And how can they hear without someone preaching to them? And how can they preach unless they are sent? As it is written, 'How beautiful are the feet of those who bring good news!'

The message was clear. It was a huge task for Benjamin, but not for the Lord. He had no plan, but the Lord did. He had no resources, but the Lord's were limitless. He wasn't sure he had the courage, but he was certain he had the Lord. As the train swayed its way slowly back to Calcutta, Benjamin had a dread feeling that he was headed in the wrong direction.

His intuition was right. Within a week, he was swallowed up again by life in the city. A month after that, when he wasn't working long hours, he was serving wherever possible—back at church, witnessing on street corners, addressing school kids at morning chapel. He had even been invited to preach at a large Calcutta church, as people were beginning to talk about his sermons. He was grateful and accepted. But inside, he struggled because his mind kept taking him back to the villages in Bihar. He thought of the apostle Peter when asked by Jesus the third time, "Do you love me?" What would Benjamin answer, knowing that Jesus knew his heart better than he did?

Three months later, he felt the decision had been made for him. He resigned his job and went back to Bihar. His church didn't understand, and his colleagues at work thought he was crazy. But for Benjamin, it was a huge relief. This was the Lord's will.

This time, he stayed not for a weekend but for over a year. He preached in the village every week, distributed Bibles, and soon started a Christian fellowship. There was talk in the village. Could this Jesus be the one true

God? The Bible says Jesus performed miracles, and the people were healed by faith, by their belief in him. Benjamin taught them how to pray, and where there was sickness and hardship, to pray for restoration with expectancy. There were healings, and he gave the glory to God. Soon, the name of Jesus was on everyone's lips.

But there were those who were alarmed that Benjamin had arrived, bringing his Christianity with him. The surrounding villages were angry. He was low caste. Who did he think he was, preaching to Hindus as a low caste Christian and bringing other gods to Bihar? Benjamin received death threats, just as his father had years before. The village took the threats seriously; some huts on the edge of the village were burned. They had to protect Benjamin—he was family—and they were honor bound to him. Everywhere he went he had to be escorted by a couple of dozen men; if Benjamin were killed, it could start a blood feud between tribes that could go on for generations.

Benjamin felt no fear. The Lord was blessing his very own village, and he was in a fever of activity. He even started a school, including morning chapel and Bible-teaching as part of the curriculum. He was close to the Lord, doing his work, bringing souls to him, and the fellowship was growing as the Spirit moved in the village.

Emerging from the schoolhouse one morning, Ben saw his grandfather striding across the village square towards him, accompanied by a man he hadn't seen before. But they clearly knew each other, because they were laughing and chatting as they walked. As they reached Ben they fell silent, the old man grinning and the other man now wearing an uncertain smile. Ben was a little taken aback, but as his gaze took in both their faces, he was struck by how alike they were.

"Hello Benjamin," the man said, very softly. Ben frowned, and then realization set in.

"Father?" He whispered incredulously. The other man's eyes filled with tears as he slowly nodded. Then Benjamin, overwhelmed with emotion, wrapped his arms around the father he had not known since he was five years old. Soon three generations of Francis men were embracing each other in their home village. It was a precious, blessed moment for Benjamin. His father tried to apologize for abandoning him all those years ago, but Ben would have none of it. After much prayer, he had long ago forgiven him, and over the years he had developed an aching desire to know him. His joy was complete when his father told him he was walking with the Lord again. They spent two glorious days together, and they laughed and cried and prayed together as if they had never been apart.

Benjamin was always aware of the presence of his grandfather as he preached and taught about Jesus in the village. The old man could have stopped him at any time. After all, he was still a Hindu and a powerful and influential man in the village. But he didn't do or say anything to hinder Ben's progress. He was always around, in the shadows, watching and listening as Benjamin shared about Jesus.

One balmy night, nine months after his arrival, Ben was sitting under the stars with his grandfather. He listened, fascinated as the old man recalled what a scandal it had been when the village found out that Benjamin's father had renounced his religion and married a Christian.

"They were horrified, scandalized, until they discovered that his new wife was a higher caste than anyone in our village," he went on, chuckling. Then he became more serious. "And now here you are, his son, bringing not a wife, but your Christianity to our village."

Benjamin smiled but said nothing. He was grateful that his grandfather had allowed him to do his Christian work here, and although it was always his intention to share Christ with him, it had to be at absolutely the right moment. They lapsed into silence, lost in their own thoughts, and Benjamin tried to lighten the mood.

"So, grandfather, you are a rich old man. How does it feel?"

His grandfather looked up at the stars.

"It feels empty," he replied.

It wasn't the answer Ben expected. He tried again.

"I mean, tell me about some of the good times you have enjoyed in your mystic religion."

The reply was full of sadness and regret.

"There are none. My gods have given me no fulfillment."

Benjamin was shocked. He hadn't expected this at all. He turned to the old man and spoke softly.

"You seem to be telling me that you have wasted your life."

"Yes, I believe I have," came the sad reply.

"You should have given your life to Jesus Christ," Ben said, without thinking. There was a silence between them. Benjamin was suddenly fearful that he may have caused offense and was wondering what to say next. And then there was a strangled sound, and he turned to see the old man crying. Soon, he was sobbing like a baby. Ben stared at him, incredibly moved, as the tears disappeared into his great gray beard.

Ben shuffled closer and put an arm around his bony shoulder. The old man's arm came shakily over Benjamin's. Then, quietly, he led his grandfather in a prayer. The most feared man in the village, and for many villages around, a man who was believed to have the power to communicate with Hindu gods, power to heal or harm, prayed to Jesus Christ for the forgiveness of all the sins of his long life. He asked Jesus to come live inside him, and he accepted his free gift of eternal life.

Gillian

enjamin had to go home. The fellowship was thriving, particularly since his grandfather's conversion. The school was doing well. Perhaps he should have continued and gone to the next village with the good news. But the risk of violence to his home village was always there, and after much prayer, he felt the time was not right. He also missed his mother terribly. He had never been apart from her, and it had been over a year now. He must go back to Calcutta. But even as he prepared to leave, he rejoiced in the sure knowledge that this was a beginning, not an ending. The Lord had shown him something important, and he had grasped it, been alive to it. It was his purpose, his calling.

It was wonderful to be home with his mother again. She was so proud of him, and even though she did not know village life, she understood that something special had happened there, and to her son. He was changed, but it was no surprise to her because she had prayed for him for twenty-three years.

But Benjamin was back in Calcutta, and he needed a job. He prayed, "Lord, if you are going to give me back my tomorrow, then please give me a job for today."

The Lord provided. He found work almost immediately through a Christian friend. It was in an agency that sold credit cards and services for Standard Chartered Bank. He found instant success, and after a little while, the bank approached him to work for them directly. He soon slipped back into his old life and was welcomed back by the church.

Before service one Sunday morning, the pastor called for Benjamin to come to his office. There he handed him a note. It was handwritten:

My Dear Benjamin,
    It grieves me to tell you the bad news that your grandfather has passed away. I want you to know I am so proud and happy that you brought him to the Lord. The fellowship you started is doing well, and the grand old man never missed a service. I pray you can take comfort from this.
                                          I love you son,
                                                Dad

Benjamin swallowed, nodded to the pastor, and went to the prayer room to be alone. There he read the note again then fell to his knees. The tears fell freely, but they were not sad tears. He praised and thanked the Lord for his love and grace, for saving his grandfather. Lifting his head, he said aloud, "He has not passed away, he has passed into glory. He is with God, in heaven. Praise the Lord." As he left the prayer room, he quietly uttered one more thing.

"I love you too, Dad."

He was making a sales call at a large company. Benjamin approached the reception desk and asked the girl there if the vice president was available. She looked up from her computer and smiled at him. She was unusually pretty. An unfamiliar sensation swept over Benjamin; he was suddenly very nervous.

"Do you have an appointment?" she asked brightly. She spoke excellent English, with just a hint of an Indian accent. It was perfect.

"Yes, I do," he replied, shyly. *Shyly?*

"Just one moment." She looked at him a little longer than necessary, smiled again, and called the vice president. Benjamin was uncomfortable, and he had the distinct impression that she was enjoying it. An hour later, he left the building smiling and with a sale. But he had more than that. Her name was Gillian. She was raised in a Catholic family, and she loved Jesus Christ. And yes, she would love to go to his church next week.

The annual church Christmas musical drama was a grand affair. They always used an American arrangement and gave it an Indian flavor. It was like Bollywood. Benjamin had always loved being involved. Sound, lighting, cameras—there was so much to do. The program included a one-hundred-person choir, an orchestra, singing and dancing, and was very well-known in this part of Calcutta. People paid to attend, but it was truly a ministry, and many would find salvation as they learned the true meaning of Christmas, watching the drama and being swept away by the music and the nativity which was always the finale. Benjamin just loved it.

By late November, he was putting his considerable organizational skills to good use as co-director. "Praise the Lord!" would ring out as he worked, and his infectious laughter was everywhere. Benjamin was especially happy this Christmas, 1998. They had asked him to star in the production, "The Gift," as a father of three, and Gillian was cast as his wife. It was a fun, up-lifting play. It was a blessed time, a time of true joy, because as they acted their roles to a delighted audience, Benjamin knew every time he looked at Gillian, that she was the woman that God had set apart for him.

But 1998 had also been a year of disappointment. Many young Christians in India had a strong desire to study overseas, to complete their biblical education in order to serve the Lord in the mission field. Benjamin was convinced, after his Bihar village experience, that he would be a missionary to a country that God would show him. Hadn't he started a church in a Hindu village? A Christian school? Wasn't he a gifted organizer? He believed he had confirmation of this when he was granted a full scholarship to the William Carey School of World Missions in Durban, South Africa. He had grand visions of doing great work for the Lord, but he was devastated when he was refused a visa. It was an agonizing time for Benjamin. He prayed constantly, seeking the Lord, pleading with him for answers, for direction. But the Lord was silent. He had to wait. It was a time of testing, and he struggled. He was confused, not understanding God's purpose. For a while, he thought the only true, real thing in his life was Gillian.

She was from a different culture, from an Anglo-Indian background. Her family spoke English and were practicing Catholics, but Gillian became born again in 1995 when a friend took her to a Baptist church and bought her a Bible. She soon found she needed a personal relationship with Jesus. After that, she had developed a heart for missions. This desire prevented her from becoming serious with men, as she waited on her call from the Lord. She prayed often that when the time was right, the Lord would lead her to a true man of God. And then she met Benjamin. She was taken by his strong personality and gentle nature and his unstoppable confidence. She was drawn to him very strongly.

Their dates were unusual. She stood on street corners while Benjamin preached fiery sermons. She leaned against lampposts while he witnessed to strangers passing by. They drank soda and ate fast food while he explained Bible passages to her. But she loved all of it. She learned so much from him spiritually that her own walk with God became a real, deep, and precious thing.

Benjamin made it very clear from the start that he was certain that the Lord had put them together, and this put Gillian in a quandary. What about her missions plans? Was she not being disobedient in even considering Benjamin at this stage of her life? She clung to her life verse: "'For I know the plans I have for you,' declares the Lord, 'plans to prosper you and not to harm you, plans to give you hope and a future'" (Jeremiah 29:11).

Was Benjamin her hope and her future? He was out of work the night that he proposed, but he took her hand, looked her in the eyes, and told her he loved her deeply and passionately.

"Gillian," he said, almost in a whisper, "I have nothing to offer you but the promises of God. If we stand together on these promises and live by faith, I know the Lord will bless us." It was irrational, but all her doubt and confusion melted away in happy tears. She saw Jesus in him. There was no way she could refuse.

A year later, in 1999, the South Africans once again offered Ben a scholarship, and once again, Benjamin's expectations soared. *This time*, he thought, *I have my answer.* This time he would go. But once again, he was disappointed. Several sets of circumstances conspired to prevent him raising the necessary funds. The chance was lost and would never come again.

He was invited to apply at another missions college in Minneapolis, Minnesota. They accepted him, but this time, he could not find a sponsor. Benjamin was heartbroken. He had given up his job at the bank because he was certain he would go overseas, and now, his world was upside down. The

Lord had shut the door. Benjamin devoted himself to prayer and fasting. He knew he could do nothing without Jesus, and he prayed for the Lord's presence, his leading in his life. He was evangelizing in the streets, at train stations, and bus stations. He brought dozens to the Lord, then he brought them to the church, and he discipled them. This was all good work, but it was also unfocused and frenetic. Inside, he was in turmoil.

But as he prayed, he began to feel the Lord speaking again, and he knew that He had never left him. Over the next few months, God broke Benjamin and showed him that what had happened in the village had been His work, not Benjamin's. It had been God's good pleasure to use him.

Most importantly, Benjamin learned that from God's perspective there was no bigger mission field than the subcontinent of India. Benjamin had decided that God needed him in some far-flung place, but the Lord had said no. God was not holding him responsible for his work in Tanzania or Timbuktu, or anywhere else, but he was making him responsible for bringing his own countrymen, his brothers and sisters in India, to the saving grace of God through the sacrifice of his Son, Jesus Christ.

Benjamin finally understood that the door to his international missions dream was closed. But the Lord would open another door, and Benjamin would have to watch and wait for the Lord to show it to him.

JOHN

"…To obey is better than sacrifice…"

1 Samuel 15:22

Obedience

I t was the summer of 1996. Agro-Turf was growing, doing really well, and John and Kathy were actively serving in the church. They had joyfully gone forward together and committed their lives to God and had been baptized. For John, baptism was not an easy decision. He understood why he must do it from a scriptural perspective, but he had been given to the Lord as a child. How would his father take this? John was convinced that his father would not just disapprove, he would be deeply offended and take it as a rejection of all that he believed. It would be nothing less than a betrayal. John felt guilty, and it troubled him so deeply that he didn't even discuss it with Kathy. In the end, unable to face his father, he didn't tell him he had been baptized.

When they visited Jack and Jean to tell them of the pregnancy, their joy was tempered by the terrible news that Jack had been diagnosed with cancer. Two weeks later, on a Saturday afternoon, John was sitting on the patio with his dad. As he stared out at the tall pine trees in the backyard, Jack asked his son a question.

"John, are you going to get involved with church again?" Jack continued to look out at the trees.

John knew it was coming. He also knew he had to let his dad know that he was walking with the Lord again. It was important to him, and the shocking news of the cancer had now made it imperative. He hadn't planned on telling his dad anything specific about his church, but now he really had no choice. He took a deep breath.

"Kathy and I have been going to First Baptist Church, Dad. We like it there. We've made friends…"

Jack slowly nodded. He continued to stare into the distance. As he looked at his profile, John was shocked at how much older his father looked.

"Did you join the church?"

"Yes, we did."

John took another deep breath. He knew what the next question would be. His dad turned to look at him for the first time. His eyes were tired, but his gaze was strong.

"And did you get baptized?"

"Yes, Dad, I did."

Jack stared at his son. John held his stare. He was waiting for the explosion, the rebuke. But then his dad's eyes softened, and John saw nothing but deep sadness in them.

"Why didn't you tell us?" It was a whisper, not an explosion.

John didn't know how to reply, where to begin.

"Dad, I—"

But Jack continued, his voice cracking a little.

"We would love to have been there. We would have been so proud of you, son."

John felt as if he had been slammed in the stomach. He was instantly swamped by guilt and shame. He tried to explain, and Jack said it was okay, that he understood. But John knew it wasn't okay. He had let his father down, misjudged him, and hurt him. He had been cowardly and deceitful. And worst of all, he knew now that he had no grasp of the depth of his father's love for him. Later, alone as the tears came, he prayed for forgiveness, for a way to make it right. But there was no way to make it right.

By early November, Jack was fading fast. He said he wished he could hold on just long enough to meet his grandchild. John and Kathy rushed to have an ultrasound, to discover if they had a boy or a girl, to put a name to this little life. It was inconclusive. They begged the doctor to do one more, to try again, and he told them to come back in a few days. They prayed, went back, and discovered their child was a girl. Back in Jack's hospital room, John wept at the joy in his father's face as he told him her name would be Kristen.

The family took turns to be at Jack's bedside for the next two days. John and his brother Jim took an hour's break to have dinner, and while they ate, John was taken by an overpowering feeling of dread. He looked up at Jim, who was already pushing back his seat. At the hospital, they were informed that Jack had died thirty minutes before.

Kristen's birth in March 1997 was such a blessed event. John wondered how they could ever have thought of not having children. She was a little miracle from God, and he gave thanks for her. After his father's death, John wanted to be more active in the church, and he began serving in the youth ministry while Kathy served in preschool.

That summer, he agreed to be a counselor at high school camp. He thought it would be a neat thing to do, teaching and having fun with a bunch of teenagers at camp, but it was to be a profound experience for him. The theme of the camp was obedience, and as the days passed, John realized through the Scripture studies and discussions that complete, submissive obedience to the Lord was something he had never been taught or exposed to before. He had accepted Jesus as Lord and Savior because he believed in him with all his heart. But complete obedience, no matter what? He, and so many others he knew, regarded salvation very simply; as long as you believe, you get to go to heaven. But he was learning here that obedience involves submission, nothing less than dying to self and handing over control of your life to Jesus.

On the last night the youth pastor challenged everyone. He told the story of the rich young man in chapter nineteen of Matthew. "This man claimed to be obedient. He told Jesus that he had kept all six commandments that related to others. But-

"'Jesus answered, 'If you want to be perfect, go, sell your possessions and give to the poor, and you will have treasure in heaven. Then come, follow me.' When the young man heard this, he went away sad, because he had great wealth'" (Matthew 19: 21–22).

"This was hard. The young man could not give away his wealth, not even for the promise of treasure in heaven. What if you were that young man? Could you give up everything for Jesus? "

Could John give up everything for Jesus? His house, car, or even his business? This rocked him. He really didn't think so, and he hoped he would never be put to the test. He was pretty certain he would fail.

The following January, John was ordained as a deacon. It was a proud but poignant moment, walking in his father's footsteps. He was so sad his dad was not there to see it. He also became involved in a five-man accountability group. Two members were Pat Stuart and Jim Powers, both of whom would have significant impact on John's life in the years ahead. John was happy. His faith was growing, his prayer life was vibrant, and his marriage was revitalized after Kathy's salvation three years earlier. Kristen's arrival had just cemented it. His business was booming. Life was great. And then health issues brought it all crashing down once more.

Before Kathy was pregnant with Kristen, John had begun developing acid reflux, which worsened until it eventually ate away the wall of his esophagus. The doctor prescribed a drug that was meant for short-term use, but that they said John would have to take for the rest of his life. He was a human guinea pig. In the end it seemed ineffective, so they operated to wrap his stomach around the esophagus to create a valve to protect it.

When the doctors went in, they found that the drug had begun to heal the esophagus but the scar tissue had welded it to John's stomach, which in turn had been welded to his heart. So instead of performing a fairly routine laparoscopic surgery, they had to cut John's stomach away from his heart. He woke up in screaming agony, pleading with the nurses not to touch him as they transferred him from the gurney to the bed.

Later, the doctor commented that John's esophagus looked like it had been through a cheese grater and that he had the stomach of an eighty year old. A second surgery followed to correct issues with the first, and then a third. Thankfully, neither of these was as painful as the first, but the end result left John with continued problems. He wasn't yet forty. He had to sleep on a recliner for many weeks because he could not lie down.

The doctors thought that the stress of running his business had brought on John's condition. They strongly advised him to slow down. Fortunately, one of John's managers, Art, a long-term employee, had stepped up over the past year and was helping him to manage the business, so John was able to pass on more responsibility to Art in 1998 and step back a little. It was just as well because 1999 was to be quite a year.

Perfect Life

I n January, John and Kathy became involved as lay leaders with a ministry at church called Prayer Partners. The purpose was to get people together for a regular weekly time of prayer. It was a time of spiritual growth for both of them as they sought the Lord in their prayer ministry and in their personal quiet time. It was a deeply satisfying experience, capped for them by the news in early February that Kathy was pregnant once again.

One night, John and Kathy were lying on their living room floor with Kristen. A gospel CD was playing their favorite song. John stroked Kristen's hair with one hand as she played on the carpet, and stroked Kathy's tummy with the other. They talked and joked about whether they would like another girl or a boy.

John said if it was a girl, she had better be good at baseball, and Kathy laughed and said, "Well, then it had better be a boy." They agreed, of course, that it didn't matter. It was all up to the Lord. As John lay there looking up at the ceiling, a feeling of great contentment flowed right through him. He felt on top of the world.

"God is so good, Kathy. Look how he's blessed us. We have a great marriage, a beautiful daughter with another little one on the way, a great church, a nice home, a successful business that I'm semi-retired in—"

"Yeah," Kathy agreed. "The Lord sure has blessed us."

John smiled.

"I think we have the perfect life. Just perfect."

But even as he said it, it sounded a little hollow. Just for a fraction of a second, like a quickly passing shadow, he felt that he didn't quite believe it. Something was missing, like a piece of a puzzle.

But the Lord had all the pieces, and he was building the puzzle piece by piece. March brought Bill Elliff to First Baptist Church. A powerful and knowledgeable preacher of the Word, Pastor Elliff of Little Rock, Arkansas, led revival conferences around the country and brought thousands of people to an examination of their personal walk with God. The conference was scheduled for four evenings, but it actually had to be extended into the following week because of the response. Hundreds of people attended. John was interested because it sounded like something he could learn from. He had no idea what it would do to him.

Booths had been set up around the sanctuary and even outside it, and the pastor explained that these should be used as cry rooms, places to go if needed. John thought this a little extreme. People might need to use them, but why so many?

Pastor Elliff was a man with a big presence, but when he spoke, it was in a humble, calm voice. His love for God and his people shone through his preaching. As he worked his way slowly and carefully through the fourth chapter of the book of James, John was riveted. The pastor described Christian life as outlined by James with such insight that John felt that the pastor's words, and the words of James, were being addressed directly to him.

Over the next seven nights, Pastor Elliff showed that everything flows through the presence of Jesus Christ. Through his endless grace, we can submit to him, resist the enemy, stay close to him, and continuously repent of our sins so that we attain complete surrender to him and instantly obey him. *There it was,* John thought, *surrender and obedience again. It's all about obedience.*

One night, Pastor Elliff talked of wronging people. At the end of the evening, he asked everyone to pray about people they had wronged, either in word or in deed. He asked them, if they felt led, to find those people, confess their wrong, and ask their forgiveness. Slowly at first, but then in a flood, people rose and were soon confessing and forgiving. John and Kathy were amongst them. It was a great release, a cleansing of guilt and shame. The cry booths were busy.

Later, the pastor turned to Luke 19, the story of Zacchaeus, a wealthy tax collector in Jericho. After his encounter with Jesus, he was saved and declared that if he has cheated anyone, he will repay four times the amount.

"Is there anyone that you owe a debt to? Have you cheated anyone?" asked Bill Elliff.

On the drive home, John and Kathy began to remember things they thought they had forgotten. Like a time way back when John was working at the golf club in Chicago.

"Kath, it's incredible. Until tonight that incident has never once crossed my mind. I worked until 3:00 a.m. one night and I put in ten dollars of gas from their pump. It never ever occurred to me to pay it back. I feel like a complete fraud." There was no reply from Kathy so he turned to her. She was staring through the windshield, lost in her own thoughts. She shook her head.

"You know how much stationery I've taken from work over the years? It's stealing. I'm a thief! We have to fix this, John. Right now."

The next morning, John sent a check to his old employers for forty dollars, along with a baffling explanation and apology. In the end, they sent a couple of dozen checks and letters. But a much bigger issue was soon to surface in John's mind.

Jim Powers, Pat Stuart, and the other men in John's accountability group were attending the revival, and they all were deeply stirred by it in various personal ways. They met the same evening of the "Zacchaeus" lesson, and they had all reacted the same way John had, all deeply convicted of many things. But then one of them said, "Hey, guys, what about our businesses?" There was silence as each of them considered this.

For John, the silence was deafening. Conviction slammed into him, as he recalled a business contract that suddenly worried him. He had bid on a large job, and the purchasing officer, a good friend, told John he was not the lowest bid. But he took out some of the bid requirements and awarded John's company the contract at the higher price. There was no bribery involved, but the bidding rules were broken because of John's friendship with the employee. This was wrong. John estimated that he had benefited twenty-five thousand dollars for work he had not completed. How could he have allowed business to become that important? Why did he not realize this was wrong? Before the revival was over, John went to see his friend.

"You want to do *what?*" he said, a look of complete amazement on his face.

"We have to come clean here," said John. "I reckon I owe your company twenty-five thousand dollars, and I have to pay it back four times, which is one hundred thousand."

He stared at John in complete bewilderment.

"Four ti—John, are you completely crazy? Nobody's telling you to pay it back, and besides, it will lead to an investigation, and I will be fired. Forget about it."

"I'm not crazy, I'm a Christian, and someone *is* telling me to pay it back. Look, I won't get you fired. But I have to pay this back. We need to think about it."

His friend was still looking at John as if he had just told him he was an alien from Mars. He shook his head.

"Do you even have one hundred thousand dollars?" he asked.

"No, I don't," John replied. "But I will find it, and I will pay it back."

Back at the office, John pored over the contract, his invoices and his time sheets. After some investigation, he was stunned to see that the value of the remaining work on the contract was exactly one hundred thousand dollars. He didn't need to check it again. He knew that the Lord had orchestrated this by his grace, and he was humbled and grateful that he was being shown an answer to the problem in such a way. He bowed his head right there in his office and thanked the Lord for this chance to make it right.

John completed the contract and did not send in one invoice. It was never queried and never questioned. At the end of the contract, John didn't rebid, although the company had indicated that they would like to retain him because of the high quality of his work. He walked away. He told his accountability group the story and was not really surprised to find that they had all had their own issues and had all struggled to correct gray areas in their business lives after the revival. God had told each of them that these were unacceptable.

A deacon meeting was scheduled on Saturday, and Bill Elliff attended. He was introduced by Pastor Wicker, who asked what the men thought about the revival so far. The replies were enthusiastic and positive, many commenting that it was a great spiritual experience.

After the meeting Pastor Wicker brought Bill Elliff over to John.

"While the guys were talking about the revival I noticed you were pretty quiet, John," he said. "How are you feeling about it?"

John's answer was immediate. "I feel as if I've been run over by a truck," he said. "I've seen areas of my life that I have not even begun to submit to the Lord. It's the most painful experience of my life." As he said this, John began to get choked up. He really meant it. None of his surgeries could even compare to the pain he had felt this week.

Bill Elliff smiled gently, and put his hand on John's shoulder. "Forgive me John, but I'm delighted to hear it. Brokenness is often the beginning of the Holy Spirit's true work in a life. Stay close to the Lord, John, and let him have his way with you. You will be blessed more than you can imagine."

But the most painful evening was to be the last one. Pastor Elliff asked everyone to write a letter to his or her father.

"Just tell him about your life. If your father is here, just bring it over when you're done and read it to him. If your father is not here, I want you to go home and mail it; and if your father has passed on, just give it to the Lord, and he'll make sure it gets delivered."

John bowed his head and thought about what he would write. He wanted to be positive, to tell his dad that he was so glad to be walking with the Lord, just as he had taught him—how successful his business was and what a great Christian marriage he had. He wanted to reassure him that Mom was holding up well, even though she had missed him so much these past three years, and how Kathy and Kristen spent so much time with her.

Kristen. He suddenly thought of Jack lying there, two days from dying, and how he had smiled when they told him his granddaughter's name was Kristen. He had leaned over to kiss Kathy's tummy. "I love you, Kristen," he had whispered through the pain. John wanted to tell him how beautiful she was and that Kathy was pregnant again.

And then, he just let go. All the years of bottled-up pain, guilt, and regret, he just let it go. He wanted to bring his dad into this great church, show him how proud he was to be serving the God he loved, and somehow make amends for not having his dad at his baptism. He wanted to tell him that if their new baby was a boy, they would name him Jack, after his grandfather.

He wanted to tell him how deeply it hurt him that he never even got to hold his grandchildren. He wanted to tell him how sorry he was for the thousands of times he knew he had disappointed him. And he wanted to look into his face and tell him how much he loved him. But he couldn't because it was too late. It was too late. John couldn't write because his hands were shaking. He couldn't see because he couldn't control the tears.

Completely overwhelmed, he ran for the nearest booth. It was full. So was the next one—full of people crying and praying. When he found a place at last, he sank to his knees and prayed for the Lord to come to him now and help him. As he prayed, his heart filled with the stark reality of just how much he missed his dad and how much he really meant to him. "Lord," he cried out, "I can't do this. It's too hard. Help me." Suddenly, the presence he sought was there, and he was enveloped in the love that only his heavenly Father could bring. *It is okay to grieve*, he told him, *it's okay*.

It took a few days, and more tears, but John did write the letter. He thanked his father for being a great, great dad, and he told him he loved and missed him. He thanked him for raising a family that stuck together, even though they were taught independence. He thanked him for the incredible financial sacrifices he had made, both for John's medical problems and for putting him and his brother and sisters through college. Most of all, he thanked him for raising his family in church and for the strong roots he and John's mom had given him. John promised to be a good father, husband, and son. Lastly, he told Jack he was proud of him and the way he had lived his life. He thanked him with all his heart and said he will tell him face-to-face when he sees him in heaven. It was a happy, positive letter. He folded it carefully and put it in the drawer of his desk. Then, on his knees, and with many happy tears, he gave it to the Lord to deliver, just as Bill Elliff had said.

The conference broke John. His dad had been a tough guy, a man's man, and John had tried to grow up as the strong one, the one who could handle hard things in an unemotional, resolute way—a rock. But the Lord had shown him that whole week that he could do nothing without Christ. He needed the Lord's strength, not his own. Both John and Kathy had gone into the revival looking forward to a mountaintop experience. But at the end of each day, they were a raging river of battered emotions and painful conviction. They realized how far they truly were from the Lord, how sinful their lives had been, how dependent they needed to be on him in every aspect of their lives.

They both felt the Lord telling them that if they would submit to him fully, he had a plan for them. They would pray and wait on him to show them where he wanted them to be, to join him in his work.

They wouldn't have to wait too long.

Unveiled

It was a Wednesday night, and John and Kathy were leaving church to go home after an evening with the Prayer Partners group. As they neared their car, the new secretary of the missions ministry approached them. She was a pleasant woman but pushy and very committed to missions. She got right to the point. "Hi guys," she said with a smile. "I was wanting to talk with you. As you are leaders of the prayer ministry, I thought you might be interested in becoming involved with the new missions Committee?"

John didn't like this at all. Although he had prayed and thought long and hard about serving more since Bill Elliff a month ago, getting involved with overseas missions was not on the list. He had no desire to be involved with missions—period.

"If you're asking us to add missions to our ministry prayer list, we would be glad to. But we are way too busy to be on any committee."

She smiled. "I see. Are you familiar at all with our work in missions?"

"Not really," John replied curtly. He wanted to go home.

"Well, maybe I could get you to read this. You might find it helpful. Something to pray about." She was holding out a slim book. John took it, smiled back, and walked on, hoping he hadn't been rude. When they got to the car, he opened the door and threw the book onto the back seat.

Tuesday evening at 8:30, two weeks later, John was sitting in his study. He was reading a Bible commentary, but for some reason, he couldn't focus. He was restless tonight. Then the missions secretary came into his mind, and then the book, and he realized it was still in the back of his car. He would look foolish if Ms. Missions approached him again, and he hadn't even looked at it. He went to fetch it and sat back in his chair. *Unveiled at Last* was the title. He started to read.

As he read, John found himself gripped by Bob Sjogren's book. It described the Bible as a unified work that clearly shows that it is God's unchanging purpose to bless his people so that they may pass on the blessing to everyone on earth, for God's ultimate glory. He read of the critical and urgent need for Christians to spread the gospel of Jesus to every lost and unreached people group around the world. Around the world. John had never even thought this big. It rocked him.

John read that the Great Commission was in fact first given to Abram by God:

> I will make you into a great nation and I will bless you;
> I will make your name great, and you will be a blessing.
> I will bless those who bless you, and whoever curses you I will curse;
> and all peoples on earth will be blessed through you.
>
> Genesis 12:2–4

These words were familiar; he had read them many times. But it was as if he now understood their true meaning for the first time. "All peoples on earth." That's everyone. How can it be possible to reach all peoples on earth? But this was God's plan. Earlier that night, he had been reading Jesus' words in John 10:16:

> I have other sheep that are not of this sheep pen. I must bring them also. They too will listen to my voice, and there shall be one flock and one shepherd.

He pondered and prayed. He read Isaiah 6:8:

> Then I heard the voice of the Lord, saying, "Whom shall I send? And who will go for us?" And I said, "Here am I. Send me!"

Send me! John had never even considered such a thing. Wasn't that for missionaries, people who are trained to do that stuff? He read on and discovered facts that jolted him. For every dollar put into the offering plate in the United States, only four cents goes to missions, and of that three and a half cents goes to areas that already have churches. Less than one cent goes to reach the unreached peoples of the world. Only 10 percent of the foreign missionary force is going to totally unreached areas. Is this completely obedient to the Great Commission? Does it glorify the Lord?

He read that in these places one person dies every second without hearing the name of Jesus even one time in his life. John stopped reading. That's one person every time his heart beat. He picked up a calculator and worked it out. Over 80,000 people per day were leaving this world without knowing Christ. Ordinary men, like him. Women, like Kathy, and children, just like Kristen. Suddenly, he thought he had a clear vision of how this must break the Lord's heart, and he found himself crying for these lost people. He cried out, "Lord, what can I do about this? What are you showing me?"

As he read on, he found himself increasingly convicted. He came to a sentence that really shook him. He read it over and over.

Are you leading a little life in your own little world? He recalled lying on his living room carpet with Kathy and Kristen just a little while ago. They had talked smugly about their perfect life and how they'd been so blessed. Now, he felt ashamed. Their life wasn't perfect; it was as shallow as a puddle of rain. Oh, they had been blessed, but what had they done about passing on the blessing? They were serving in their local church, but what were they doing about serving the nations? Saving the nations? Nothing. It was all selfishness, all about them. John was completely convicted. He closed his eyes, and told the Lord he didn't want to lead a little life. He wanted to live a big life.

As he went back again to this one line, this question that had so convicted him, a bigger question jumped into his mind. A challenge.

Are you leading a little life in your own little world? Are you willing to lead a big life, a life with a big kingdom impact? Yes, he was.

John realized how patient the Lord had been with his dullness toward others. Look how he had brushed off the missions secretary even as she had handed him this book. Had he been blinded all these years? With everything that he and Kathy had experienced and explored since her salvation, they had not discussed missions at all. Not even once. He got to his knees to pray again, to beg forgiveness, and once again, the Lord broke him. He cried out for the Lord to make him understand more, to give him wisdom in this. He cried because his heart was so far from the Lord's. He cried for the unsaved, for the souls of billions he would never know.

"Lord, can you use a nobody like me? Why is the Scripture so clear right now? What are you showing me? Lord, please give me a heart like yours. Give me a heart that breaks for the things that break your heart. I want to be obedient. Please show me what you want me to do, Lord. Show me how to leave my little life and live a big life, for your kingdom and your glory."

Another Scripture passage quoted in the book jumped into his head and convicted him: "I urge you to live a life worthy of the calling you have received" (Ephesians 4:1).

John did not understand the call yet, but he knew the Lord had spoken to him tonight. But it scared him too. *If the Lord used me in some way,* he thought, *how would it affect my family? God said he would bless Abram's family because of his obedience. Will I have the courage to follow him if he wants us to make big changes? Will this eagerness fade in a few days?* He thought of things he could do right now—prayer support for missions, help with funds, paying for others to go on trips, buying Bibles—but no, this was not his decision. It was the Lord's.

So he would pray, fast and wait on the Lord.

He finally got off his knees and looked at the clock on the wall. Almost 3:00 a.m. No matter, he would wake Kathy. She had to read this book, and they had to talk.

He woke her.

"Kath, you have to read this book."

She woke up in a panic and quickly switched on the bedside lamp, thinking there was something wrong. Then she was confused. He woke her up to read a book? But as John stumbled through an explanation, she heard the trembling excitement in his voice, and she knew that something important had happened.

"It's okay, John, It's okay."

She got up.

By the middle of the following day, Kathy put the book down. She was also completely convicted.

One section told a true story of missionaries in Mali, Africa. They had an opportunity to show *The Jesus Film* to hundreds of Muslims at a wedding. They traveled hundreds of miles to get there, and as they were setting up the old projector a windstorm blew it over, wrecking it. No film. But later, in the middle of the traditional dancing, one of the missionaries began an impromptu dance, acting out the crucifixion and resurrection of Christ. All eyes were on him and there was absolute silence as he danced. The ending was greeted with an explosion of questions. Why did he die? How can he live after death? They made the missionary dance it again. And then they clamored to know the full story of Jesus. The evening became the morning of the next day. The gospel was shared. Some weeks later, as the missionaries prepared to leave, they heard that the Messiah dance was being danced and the story of Jesus told in every village in the region. Kathy was amazed at how the Lord works.

As they talked about all this the next day, John and Kathy saw missionaries and mission work in a completely fresh way. They had seen it as too difficult, a work too complex to attempt. It was a pointless exercise for individuals, like spitting into the wind. Now they saw clearly how narrow-minded and selfish they had been. The Great Commission is a command, not an option. They read that in Matthew 24:14, Jesus says: "And this Gospel of the kingdom will be preached in the whole world as a testimony to all nations, and then the end will come."

The end, of course, is the second coming of Christ. Like all Christians, John and Kathy looked forward to that day. And then they read 2 Peter 3:12: "As you look forward to the day of the Lord and speed its coming."

They talked this over, and they realized that God has a clear objective and a time line here. When the gospel is preached over all the earth, Jesus will return. By being obedient to the Great Commission, they realized that they can influence this, have a share in it.

Suddenly, they understood that missions were not for other people, they were for all true Christians to embrace. This was God's work, and his purpose. They had to get involved in some way.

Possibilities

The missions secretary called the following week. She certainly was persistent. There was a missionary family coming in from Turkey. She asked John and Kathy if they would like to meet them. Yes, they would. Over lunch they got to meet Chris, his wife, and their three kids. He was an engineer from Texas, and when the Lord had called him to missions a couple of years earlier, he had walked away from his job, joined the International Missions Board, and moved his family to Turkey so he could minister to the Muslim population. The conversation was mainly about the terrible earthquake that had just devastated the city of Duzce, east of Istanbul. Early estimates had put the loss of life at 30,000, and maybe as much as 40,000.

John and Kathy's reactions to the lunch could not have been more different. Kathy was completely in awe of these people. They had given up everything to move to Turkey—the entire family, including three children. Who would do that? Who would *do* that? And they all seemed so nonchalant, normal, and happy.

John could not believe the scope and destruction of the earthquake. He felt the same emotions that Chris felt as he described it. John was excited. He wanted to get involved.

"Just think about it, John," said Chris, "Thirty thousand people just died without hearing the name of Jesus."

John just looked at him. He didn't know what to say. He glanced away, and as he turned back, Chris was staring hard at him.

"Let's go," he said.

"What? Go where?" John was stunned.

"To Turkey. They need Jesus. We can get a plane tomorrow and go."

John didn't even have a passport. But he could see that Chris was dead serious. He could leave this lunch, and in less than a day, he could be in an earthquake disaster area in Turkey. It was incredible.

Suddenly, missions work seemed like the new frontier, and missionary people were frontiersmen, pioneers.

The third approach from the missions secretary was to ask John to go on a prayer walking trip to Turkey. John liked the idea of praying for Turkey after the terrible earthquake. "No, she said, we are going to the eastern border, to pray for the people of Iran." John was confused.

"Why not just go to Iran?" he asked.

"Because Christians are not allowed in Iran. We'll pray for them along the Turkish border."

Wow. John didn't know that. He didn't know that Iran was closed to Christianity. He agreed to talk to Kathy and pray about the Turkey trip. Soon, he was excited, and when he was asked to lead the trip, he became very excited. John asked his two friends, Pat Stuart and Jim Powers, to go; when they both agreed, they started to pray and fast in earnest. John was convinced this was the start of something important.

The missionary, Jerry, who trained them for prayer walking in Turkey a few weeks later, was intrigued that they kept talking about Iran and how closed it was.

"If you did some kind of sports camp, you could get into Iran," he said.

John didn't believe it. He'd done his research. Iran was closed. But he went along with it.

"Well, we could do a baseball camp."

"Yeah," Jerry nodded. "They play baseball in Iran."

John smiled at him and glanced at Pat and Jim. *Is this guy serious?*

"Okay. You get us invited into Iran, and we'll do it."

The three of them paid it no more mind and continued to pray about the Turkey trip. Ten days later, John got an e-mail from a man called Aaron Roberts. It said he understood that John and his partners would be willing to conduct a baseball clinic in Iran. He, Aaron, could make that happen. John couldn't believe it. He read it three times and still didn't believe it. It was an adrenaline rush. They could get to go where no Americans get to go—where no Christians get to go.

Aaron was an interesting character. Unlike the classic model of a missionary, he found the Lord relatively late and in unusual fashion.

He was twenty-three and in his fifth year of college because he had changed courses midstream. Aaron was good-looking, athletic, confident, smart, and arrogant. On weekends, he drank, chased girls, and studied when he had to.

He was relaxing with a soda on a sunny day on campus when he was approached by a pimply high-schooler carrying a clipboard.

"I'm doing some research on Christianity on campus. Could I ask you some questions?" Aaron smiled. Christianity? Sure. A girl at the gym suddenly flashed into his mind. She was strikingly attractive, but she was a Christian. He had tried asking her out several times, but she kept switching the conversation to Jesus. It was ridiculous, and it irritated him that he could make no headway with her. Now this guy wants to talk about Jesus. This should be fun.

"Fire away," he said pleasantly.

"Who do you think Jesus is?" the young man read from his sheet, pencil ready.

Aaron launched into a self-opinionated diatribe of Jesus and the Bible, outlining its antiquated ideas that are so out of touch with the character of our fast-moving modern world. He mentioned some Bible stories to illustrate his point. He spoke for two or three minutes, enjoying himself immensely, until he stopped listening to his own voice and looked into the kid's face.

The young man wore a slight smile over his pimply face and was nodding gently, patiently. But his eyes looked right through Aaron's façade, and he pitied him. Or was he mocking him? Aaron had stopped speaking. Suddenly, he felt foolish, a sensation that he didn't like at all. He also realized that his questioner had not written a word of what he'd said.

"Have you ever actually read the Bible?" the young man asked brightly.

Aaron, stunned, was stuck for words. He just stared back at him. The kid thanked him and moved on. The episode so affected Aaron that he hardly slept that night, and the next day, he went to the bookstore.

"What version do you want?" smiled the pretty sales assistant.

"What? There's versions?" replied Aaron, stupidly.

She took him to a wall of Bibles. He was completely lost, but with her help, he walked out with a New International Version with the words of Jesus highlighted in red. Two days later, he had read Genesis to Leviticus, and the entire thing had gone completely over his head. He was frustrated. But then he recalled that the question the young guy had asked was about Jesus, so he left the Old Testament and turned to the Gospels.

Aaron was smart. He had A's in logic. He'd studied philosophy as elective subjects. He was liberal and tolerant to a point that if someone claimed the moon was made of green cheese, he would say, "Hey, that's fine. You're entitled to your view. I respect that." But this was all just to cover his guilt and avoid uncomfortable criticism about the way he was living his life. By the time he'd read the book of John, the red words of Jesus had utterly convicted him of his own sin. He had never felt good about his lifestyle, but it was all too easy to not think about it and enjoy the pleasure, or to point to others who did worse things, at least in his opinion.

The next few years were a whirlwind. As a new believer he started to seek out Christians on campus, including Rachel, the girl in the gym, who happened to be the daughter of a Baptist pastor. Six months later they married, and then an old high school friend that he had lost touch with called to say he had been thinking of him and just felt he had to look him up. He happened to be a Christian now, so they started a Bible study. They would pore over Scripture every week, and Aaron's faith grew astoundingly.

And then one Sunday, he was listening to his pastor preach in church, and he heard the word *go*. It was like a light switching on. He knew the Lord was calling him to leave his comfort zone. It was 1994, he was thirty-four years old, living an easy life in Minneapolis, and now he felt the Lord calling him to overseas mission work. He didn't know how to tell his wife and parents, but over dinner one Sunday, Aaron said to his father-in-law, "So how does someone become a foreign missionary?"

He expected a stunned reaction, but he glanced over to see the sweetest smile on Rachel's face before her dad answered, without missing a beat.

"Well, we can get hold of one of the missions boards, I guess."

The Lord opened all the doors. Two weeks later, Aaron and Rachel were interviewed by the International Missions Board and were accepted. They now had to sell off and become debt free in order to join them. They had no idea where to begin, but Aaron's employer unexpectedly decided to scale down operations and gave him an equally unexpected severance package that covered all their debt. They prayed for their house to be sold, and they sold it to the first family that viewed it, at the price they had prayed about. As they were packing to leave for the airport, a man showed up with cash to buy their truck.

Aaron's college sports background enabled his new employers to use him in recreational ministry in areas where a seminary-trained pastor could not go. So they were sent to south Asia. The IMB had pioneered recreational ministry work by offering sports development to non-Christian countries. They had a registered sports development company that approached countries like Iran to offer expert coaching, camps, clinics, tournaments, training in sports medicine, and so on. They were the Red Cross of sports, with funding coming from grants, donations, and sponsorships. Because the cost to them was minimal, the countries approached would normally accept the offer, and the IMB would begin opening up channels for their personnel to set up evangelistic and discipleship programs on the back of the sports programs.

By 1999, there were basketball, volleyball, tennis, and track and field programs active in Iran, and they were soon to host an international basketball tournament, which included a US team. There was interest in a baseball program as it was soon to become an Olympic sport. No other nations in that part of the world played decent baseball, so if Iran could win a few games, they might make the Olympics. Aaron used his contacts, and John, Jim, and Pat were on the fast track to the Olympics.

They were galvanized about Iran. They prayed, fasted, and met to discuss formally starting a ministry. They were convinced it was not a one-time deal. They were going to be among the first to evangelize in Iran through baseball. The energy was amazing, and when the trip was confirmed, John could hardly wait. Visas for Iran were unobtainable in the United States, so they were to fly to Frankfurt, Germany, where they would go to the Iranian embassy to pick up their visas for Iran, then off to Tehran.

With the trip a couple of weeks away, John began to have doubts. It was unknown territory for him and for Pat and Jim. It was a dangerous place. John was assailed with thoughts of *What if this happened? What if that went wrong?* And then amidst all this was the unexpected reaction to the trip from some people in their own church. When word got out that the three men were going to Iran, several friends approached them to object. Some were very vocal, telling them they were plain crazy to go to such a dangerous place. One woman, a church employee, grabbed John by the arm and shook him as he and Kathy were entering church one Sunday.

"What are you two thinking?" She was angry, her voice raised. "Isn't there enough work for you here, without worrying about the other side of the world?"

John and Kathy just stared at her, completely lost for words. Shocked, John went to see the pastor, certain that he would find the encouragement he needed. Dr. Hayes Wicker was loved and revered by his congregation for his wisdom and strong biblical preaching, but also for the compassion that shone through everything he did. He was a friend and a counselor.

They talked for some time. John explained how the opportunity arose and how they planned to evangelize to the young people of Iran. The pastor was delighted that John was taking such a bold step in the service of the Lord. He had also felt John's calling, particularly after the Bill Elliff revival. But then his smile faded, and his expression became stern as he asked John a pointed question.

"John, is Kathy on board with this whole idea?"

"Sure, we've talked it through." John was hesitant, a little taken aback at the sudden change of mood.

The pastor looked at him hard. He spoke to him hard.

"I mean, is she completely on board? If this thing takes off, if it becomes bigger, or if it becomes dangerous, is she completely committed?"

John didn't reply. He was thinking about Kathy, and danger.

"John, you are going on the front line for the Lord here. Satan will be all over you. You will have a big bull's-eye on your back and on your family's. Are you ready? Is Kathy ready?"

John left that meeting feeling anxious. Even as the two of them had prayed, he felt uneasy. But the pastor was right. This was not a game; it was war. In all the excitement and fervor to serve the Lord, he hadn't really looked at it as ruthlessly as that. He sat in his car and thought. *Did he really have to do this?* He bowed his head and sought the Lord. Five minutes later, he knew. Yes, he absolutely had to do it. He started the car and drove home.

Ten days before they were to travel, non-refundable flight tickets in hand, they received an e-mail from the Iranian Olympic Committee telling them that the trip was cancelled. The baseball players were having their final exams at college the week of the trip. The three men were stunned. How could they do this? John wrote to Aaron, asking what to do now. He wrote back to say there was an opening in Turkey, right where the earthquake was. They were looking for someone to work with displaced kids in the Duzce area. He said it would be a good opportunity for evangelism, but they would have to be careful since evangelizing to children is illegal in Turkey. So, after declining the prayer walking trip, they were going to Turkey anyway.

Dangerous or not, there was little opportunity for evangelism on this trip. The interpreters were scarce, so John, Jim, and Pat tried to teach baseball in 120-degree heat to kids who for the foreseeable future would have only inhospitable shipping containers to call home. Duzce was completely demolished, with few buildings standing. Rubble was everywhere, hampering even the Red Cross efforts to distribute food, blankets, and other necessities. Each session, they would pray before baseball began, but the children understood nothing and just wanted to get on with the game.

From a humanitarian perspective, the three of them felt good about what they did, bringing some joy and temporary relief to people whose lives had been devastated in forty-five seconds and whose suffering was far from over. They had also seen the situation firsthand. The heat was unbearable. It touched John's heart to see people suffer this way. Although there had been little opportunity to witness, John felt he had personally gained much.

The good news from Aaron on their return was that the Iranian Olympic Committee had now reapproved their trip. Ten days later, the three of them were at the airport with their wives, trying to find a way to part on a positive note. They were going to Iran, where no Christians go, and none of them had any idea what to expect. With just a few minutes left before the men were to go through security, they prayed, and then all stood silently in a circle, trying to find right words to say. It was pretty somber.

"Well," said John at last, "I guess we had better get moving."

"Yeah," said Kathy. Kristen was getting fidgety in her arms, starting to get upset. She wanted Daddy. It wasn't helping.

"So," said Jeanette, Pat's wife, "you're off to Iran."

The men nodded and looked at her solemnly.

"You know, I wouldn't send the three of you to the grocery store together, never mind Iran."

It helped relieve the tension, but John was still apprehensive as he walked toward the gate, Kristen's forlorn howling ringing in his ears.

Baseline Sports

When they reached Frankfurt, it started to seem real. The taxi dropped them at an old house that the driver assured them was the Iranian embassy. Inside, exhausted, they stood in line with a few dozen Asian people. Eyes were on them constantly. Why would these three be coming to Iran? At the window, John was relieved to find that they were expected and that their visas were ready. Back to the airport, and then, at last, off to Tehran by Iran Air. The plane was full of Iranians who were more than curious about these three. They were not hostile but not friendly either. It was surreal.

The flight arrived at midnight. Suddenly, not knowing what to expect, John felt a stab of insecurity as he stood in line to get through passport control. He had no idea who was picking them up or even where they were going. But some movement caught his eye, and as he looked up to the second floor, he saw an arrival area with two dozen young guys smiling and waving like crazy at them. It had to be the Iranian baseball coaches and team. He gave a huge sigh of relief. Soon, they were hugging and taking pictures in the parking lot and loading up the mountain of baseball gear they had brought. At the hotel, they sat up all night in the lobby just talking. John was pleasantly surprised that several of them could speak English. They were educated, friendly young men, eager to know all about America.

The next nine days went by so fast. The training that John, Jim, and Pat had undergone had taught them that they would be constantly watched, their hotel rooms and telephone would be bugged, and that they should be cautious when evangelizing. They told everyone that asked them that they were Christians, and they were able to share their faith one-on-one many times. They cemented important relationships, found the Iranians to be useful baseball players, and paved the way for further trips.

They also discovered that their hosts' view of America and Americans was just as skewed and naïve as their own was of the Iranians. They went to a party at a house that had an illegal satellite dish and a basement full of illegal alcohol. The TV was showing old reruns of *Dallas* and *Miami Vice*, and while half the Iranians kept the Americans entertained, the other half slipped downstairs to drink. The Iranians were bewildered when the Americans refused anything stronger than soda because they thought all Americans were hard-drinking, gun-toting womanizers. The Americans were just as surprised to learn that all their new Muslim friends had satellite dishes, just like the one at this house, and that they all kept their stash of alcohol in their basement.

At the end of June, John, Jim, and Pat were back home. They had made progress, and the baseball was great, but they had not achieved enough to even think about this being a ministry yet. Even so, John felt the Lord urging him to continue in some way, and he knew he had to go back to Iran. He was trying to be obedient, one step at a time. He also had to be patient and wait for the Iranians to approve and schedule the next trip.

In July, 1999, Kathy gave birth to the little boy they'd prayed for, and they named him Jack, after John's father, as they promised they would. Jack's arrival, and heavy commitments in the business, kept John and Kathy occupied until the end of the year. Kathy maintained her preschool duties and John stayed busy with his church ministries, but the fire that had been awakened in him by *Unveiled at Last* remained as strong as ever. He had forgotten none of the things that had gripped him when he first read it.

Are you leading a little life in your own little world? Are you willing to lead a big life, a life with a big kingdom impact?

John, Jim, and Pat were determined that this future ministry would be a reality. It was all they talked about, and their prayers told them it was God's will. They also gave it a name. It would be called Big Life Ministries.

The second trip to Iran was scheduled for March, 2000. In preparation, they registered a company, Baseline Sports Tours, with a website that showed a group of guys who loved sports and travel and had a desire to bring sports to the underprivileged.

This trip really built on the first. Relationships were cemented, and local and official interest in baseball grew. Familiarity with the players and coaches led to friendship and trust and more opportunities to witness. John was surprised to discover that many Iranians believed that all Americans were Christians and that they were forced to be Christians, just as the Iranians were pressured to follow Shia Islam. But as far as he could see, most of those he met did not follow the Muslim faith by choice at all.

There were Christians in Iran, but they totaled less than half a percent of the population. Most had fled after the Iranian Revolution in 1979, fearing persecution from the Ayatollah. Conversion from Islam to Christianity was forbidden, and in some cases, punishable by death. Americans were not officially welcome, due to their support of the pre-1979 monarchy, but the Iranians John had met did not hate Americans. On the contrary, they were extremely curious about them.

For John, Pat, and Jim, the mission field was ripe. These people were open and searching for truth. They needed Jesus. But for now they were happy to be connecting with the Iranians through baseball. They had a relationship of sorts with the Iranian Olympic Committee, and although they always had to wait on them, they hoped that their work would gain momentum.

In the meantime, John was surprised to hear from a South African missionary he had met. He was working in Turkey, and he invited them to join him. John and Jim leaped at the opportunity, and this time, Kathy and Jim's wife, Nancy, agreed to go with them.

They went in November, and once again, the trip left John disappointed and frustrated. There was plenty of humanitarian work to do, but the four of them were treated as visitors, not as coworkers. On the plane back, John was morose. When would he find his place, his purpose?

Aaron contacted him to say he was coming home to the States and would like to meet with him for the first time. They met at John and Kathy's house in February 2001, and their friendship was cemented immediately. While Kathy listened in they chatted and laughed about ministry, baseball, Naples, and of course, Iran. John was so grateful for Aaron's part in his progress there, and it was a real pleasure to be able to thank him face to face.

Aaron's cropped hair and trendy glasses gave him a youthful appearance. He had an easy manner, and as they talked John could see smiling was a pleasurable activity for him. Eventually the talk became more serious, and Aaron got down to the real reason for his visit.

"You know John, there's a position opening up in recreational ministry. It's based in Cyprus. We think we can use sports to get into some countries in the Middle East and part of Asia. With what you've achieved and learned in Iran, it might be perfect for you." He smiled, and glanced over at Kathy. She looked straight back at him, and then at John.

For a moment, apprehension and then excitement gripped her as she saw herself as a true missionary, just as she had viewed Chris, with her husband and two kids serving in some foreign land. They had prayed so hard about this, and they had agreed that they would serve the Lord in any country He wanted to send them. She was so happy to be part of what God was doing with John that she would follow him to Cyprus, or anywhere. She saw elation on John's face, and she thought he was going to accept on the spot.

But then a strange thing happened.

John responded with a smile. "It sounds fantastic, Aaron."

Aaron nodded his approval. "Great. I guess we…"

"Did I tell you about the ministry that the guys and I have talked about?"

Kathy frowned at John. He seemed far away, nor even aware that he had interrupted Aaron. What was he doing?

"What ministry is that?" replied Aaron.

"We believe God is calling us to begin a ministry that will be effective in bringing Christ to places that need to hear about him for the first time. There are whole nations to be saved, Aaron, and we have to respond."

"You mean through baseball? Aaron asked, a little taken aback.

"If we can reach the world through baseball, or some other sport, then yes," he replied. His voice became louder. "But we have to think God-big, and we have to have big kingdom, global impact. Why can't we have Baseline Sports working in every country in the 10/40 Window?" He stopped and stared at Aaron, almost challenging him. Aaron frowned, silently assessing John.

"We don't even know what this ministry is yet, but we've named it Big Life."

Kathy just stared at John. It was so unlike him to open up like this, when he had no clear idea of his plans. She had never seen him so emotional.

Aaron continued to frown at him. John broke the awkward silence, talking around his shy smile.

"You think I'm crazy don't you?"

Aaron shook his head. "No, I don't think you're crazy. I think you need to find out what God's up to, because he's certainly up to something. Let's put Cyprus on hold while you figure it out."

Before he left that night, after they prayed, Aaron quietly turned to John.

"John, this ministry of yours…"

"Yeah?"

"If you do it, if it works, and your plans become international, you can't manage it over there. You will have to stay in the U.S. It won't work any other way. And John, think carefully and pray earnestly about this vision of yours."

It was to be prophetic advice.

May 2001 was marked by two major events. Pat Stuart accepted a ministry position in Texas. John was pleased for Pat but sad for himself. Pat was a great friend and partner. They agreed to continue to be partners in whatever Big Life would become. But then Aaron's long-awaited e-mail arrived, telling him that the Iranians wanted them back again. It seemed that they had plans to start seriously considering baseball for the Olympics.

So now it was just John and Jim, but that was okay. Well, it was okay until they arrived in Tehran and were told that this time they were to be separated, each man running a separate baseball camp. Jim was sent into the desert and John to a resort area. Their passports were taken away, as they had been the previous two times. It hadn't bothered them before, but this time, with their separation, it seemed more sinister somehow.

Despite their unease with this change in plans, it ultimately did afford them two of the best witnessing opportunities they had with the baseball players. Jim's group was sitting at lunch when one of them started asking about the Garden of Eden. Why were Adam and Eve thrown out? Jim spent hours explaining to a captive, fascinated audience the whole story of sin and how Jesus Christ is the only way for man to get back to the garden.

There was a heat wave, so John's group took a two-day break. Some of the players took him on the eight-hour drive to see the Caspian Sea. There were seven squeezed into the car, and one of them slipped a cassette into the tape deck. It was Michael Bolton singing Christmas songs. All the guys knew the songs, and they loudly sang along as they drove. John could only smile; Michael Bolton singing Christmas tunes in June. "Do you know what the songs are about?" he asked.

"No," was the reply, "but we just love Michael Bolton. What are they about?"

John explained the songs and asked if they knew the real meaning of Christmas. They all shook their heads.

"Well, these songs are about the birth of Jesus Christ," he explained. "Jesus is the Son of God, and he came to earth as a man to save us from our sins."

"He did?" one of them asked.

"Yes he did," John went on. "He came to teach us to love God above all things, and to love each other as we love ourselves."

"What do we need to do to be saved from our sins?" asked another.

"If you believe in Jesus, he will forgive your sins."

They were curious. For the next two days, with the beautiful Caspian Sea as a backdrop, John was able to tell them what the birth of Christ meant to him, and to the world.

John had just pitched his umpteenth ball at batting practice. He wiped the sweat from his brow and walked the few steps to his water bottle. Taking a mouthful, he turned, to find the guys had all gone over to third base.

They were sitting on the ground fully focused on a man who was standing addressing them. He wore a flowing, tailored black coat, a black hat, and was obviously a man of some importance, a cleric maybe. As John was looking, fascinated at his long, black beard, the man turned slowly to look back at him. His expression wasn't friendly. John held his eyes for just a second, then he busied himself with his water bottle and didn't look again. But he was sure he could feel the man's eyes boring into him. He felt uncomfortable, intimidated. After ten minutes, the man left, and John continued practice.

But he was back again the next day—black coat, black hat. This time, he sat on the bench in the dugout. John noticed another man dressed in a suit, standing close to him. They watched the practice for a few minutes, and then the suit man waved for the players to come over. John was a little irritated, but this turned to unease as the suit man stared at him and John realized the summons included him.

The cleric didn't rise but motioned for John to sit a little way from him on the bench. The team sat on the floor at his feet, just like the day before. But instead of addressing them, the cleric turned and spoke to John.

John understood nothing. He was alarmed now. *What is this?* He focused on calming himself and then looked up at the suit man as he spoke to him in English.

"Good morning."

So the suit man is an interpreter. The cleric had come to talk to him. John studied him. He wasn't old, early fifties, John guessed. His face was unsmiling, and his demeanor was hard. He smelled pleasant, like expensive soap. John smiled and returned the greeting. He relaxed, guessing the cleric wanted to ask some questions about baseball. He was wrong.

"Are you a Muslim?"

What? John's mind raced. *How do I answer this?* He was suddenly afraid for the first time. He hadn't met anyone like this before. Then he remembered his trainer, Jerry, telling him, "If they ask you if you are a Christian, say yes. You are what you are. A father, a husband, a son. You are a follower of Christ. You love your wife, your kids. You love pizza, football, and Chevrolet. Never, ever deny Christ."

"No, I'm not a Muslim. I'm a Christian," John replied evenly, addressing the man in black. John saw, as if for the first time, his deep, intelligent brown eyes. The cleric listened calmly to his interpreter, and then he spoke again, moving his hands gracefully, making the sign of the cross. John saw manicured fingernails.

"Are you Catholic?"

"No," John replied carefully. "I am a Protestant."

John saw the question coming as the cleric shrugged his shoulders.

"What is the difference?" he asked. "There are so many different kinds of Christians. What is the difference? Is one better than the other?" He seemed to smirk. John knew he had to be careful.

He shook his head.

"I can't answer that. All I know is that I have a personal relationship with Jesus Christ, and that is what is important to me."

The cleric stared at John intently. His intelligent face betrayed no emotion as he weighed up John's words. John was feeling cornered. *This is an important man, cultured and educated. What does he want with me? Am I even safe here?* He silently prayed, seeking the Spirit's calm and guidance. After what seemed like an age, the cleric spoke again.

"What do you mean when you say 'personal relationship with Jesus Christ'?"

John breathed deeply. Here goes.

"Well, I spend time with him; I talk with him, and feel his presence. In all aspects of my life, I am totally dependent on him. He is my Savior and my Lord."

For the next hour, with the baseball team listening to every word, John was assailed with questions about Christianity, the crucifixion, the resurrection, and about this personal relationship with Jesus. Suddenly, fear gripped him anew. As he glanced at the players, all of them riveted by this interchange, he realized he had witnessed to most of them. Was this a trap? If someone had reported him, how much trouble would he be in? Could they harm him, maybe even kill him?

But as John answered his questions, he sensed a softening in this man. Obviously deeply religious, he was perhaps only showing a genuine interest in a foreign religion that had profound historical roots with his own. John began to relax and realized with some ironic satisfaction that in answering his questions he had been unconsciously witnessing to him and to the players.

Suddenly, the cleric got up and abruptly left. The players rose instantly, bowing slightly as he passed, the interpreter close behind. And then he was gone, without a goodbye or a backward glance. The players all looked to John. He took a deep breath, scratched his chin, and resumed the practice.

That evening, before sunset, he was looking out of the window of his hotel room. The streets were full of people. Tonight, John was melancholy. He had been genuinely afraid today for the first time, and although he had stood the test and proclaimed Jesus' name to several Iranian Muslims, including an important one, he was strangely subdued. What's going on? And then it hit him, and he knew he was feeling terribly, awfully lonely. Today had made him realize just how alone he was in this place. He missed Kathy and the kids so much, but apart from a "Hi, how are you," he couldn't talk because *they* were listening. *They* had his passport. *They* were watching, questioning, and assessing him. He felt like a prisoner.

As he looked out at the people crowding the streets, it struck him that they were prisoners too. In the evenings over the past eight days, he had been amongst these people, walking their streets. Each day at the prescribed times, the mandatory "call to prayer" rang out, but most ignored it, going about their business. It was like background noise. In Turkey, the instant response was for the men to leave their work and go to pray. Everything he saw made John doubt that most of these people were true Muslims.

Two days ago, he had been standing outside the hotel waiting for his ride to practice, and some kind of anti-American demonstration was passing by, followed by TV cameras. They were burning a US flag. When they saw John, two of them came running over and excitedly asked in English if he was American. When he nodded, they smiled. "What is the US like? Are you a Christian?" John pointed to the burning flag in bewilderment, and they said that was nothing, they had been paid to do that.

When he was picked up each morning for practice, the players were full of questions about Christianity the moment the car door was closed. If he got into a taxi, there were questions about Jesus as soon as he sat down. They weren't just curious, they were hungry—hungry for truth. They were hungry for Jesus Christ.

Suddenly, John was overwhelmed with grief for these lost people. He stood at the window with tears streaming down his face, and soon, he was on his knees, praying and crying out to God.

"Lord, help these people see truth. Help me to help them, Father. They have nothing, nothing to cling to, and all they need is you. Please, Lord, save these people. Save them, Father. Show me how I can serve you in this. I am not doing enough. Show me the way, Lord, I beg you. Please help me. I don't even know where to begin. Give me direction, Lord."

John was desperate to hear from God and feel his presence, hear his voice. He was far from home, swamped by discouragement and loneliness, and all he had was the Lord. He was completely broken, dependent on the Lord. He had never felt so utterly helpless.

At 10:00 p.m., the telephone rang. John was startled, but then he got off his knees to answer it. It was the interpreter. The Imam would like to meet him at a park a short walk away, at midnight. It wasn't a request; it was a directive.

Imam

I mam? He's an Imam? An Islamic leader? And he must meet him in a park at midnight. Were they going to kill him? It seemed preposterous, but John had to consider it. His heart raced. What if he refused to go? It made no difference; he had nowhere else to go. If they wanted to harm him, they could have done it already. They could do it at any time. He prayed and placed himself in the Lord's hands. At 11:30, he picked up his little pocket Bible and turned to Deuteronomy 31:6: "Be strong and courageous. Do not be afraid or terrified because of them, for the Lord your God goes with you; he will never leave you nor forsake you." He closed the Bible and slipped it into his jacket pocket.

Walking east toward the park, he was surprised to see people everywhere. It was more like 8:00 p.m. than midnight. As he neared the park, it became even busier. All along the brightly lit streets shops were open for business. Men were sitting at tables outside cafés, talking loudly and drinking coffee. Couples were strolling the sidewalks, chatting and laughing.

Crossing the road to the park entrance, John saw the interpreter looking for him. He had no greeting for John; he just motioned him to follow. They walked some way into the park, and soon, the crowds thinned out. John grew anxious again as the false safety of the swell of people and of the busyness back there evaporated, but as he walked he prayed.

Then he saw him. The Imam was alone, sitting calmly on a bench. Head down, hands together in his lap, John thought he might be in prayer. He was dressed in black, as he had been earlier, although he now wore a softer, less formal hat. He appeared to be deep in thought and only lifted his head when the two men stopped in front of him. He silently looked up at John and invited him to sit with an elegant wave of his hand.

The light was not bright here but sufficient to see. There was no one around. The meeting place had been well chosen. The interpreter stood facing them, glancing up and down the path, looking ironically just like an FBI agent. John's heart pounded in his chest as he waited for whatever this was to begin. When it did, he was taken completely and utterly by surprise.

The Imam seemed to search for his words, and then he spoke very quietly.

"I would like to talk to you further about this personal relationship with Jesus Christ."

John swallowed. Did he hear right? This was the last thing he had expected. He licked his lips. *Calm, keep calm.*

"What would you like to know?" he replied.

"We followers of the Muslim faith pray five times a day. How many times do you pray?"

John was praying right now. He knew there were ways to speak to Muslims about Jesus, and he knew none of them. He prayed for the Holy Spirit to help him, speak through him.

"I can pray to Jesus as many times as I wish. I can pray to him whenever I need him."

"What do you mean? Where do you go to pray?"

"I can pray anywhere. I have been praying since I left my hotel room."

The Imam stared at John as he considered this.

"How do you know he hears your prayers?"

"I know because I feel him. He lives inside of me."

The Imam looked away. When he turned again, his eyes burned into John's.

"He lives inside of you? You believe he inhabits the Christian soul? This is your Christian theology?"

John frowned and swallowed. This was important. He had to get it right.

"No. I mean he lives inside of *me*. He does live inside every other Christian, but I experience him uniquely. It is a personal relationship between God and me. Jesus is my Lord. He is first in my life. I trust him completely, and I have given my wife and children to him. I pray constantly for his will and direction in my life. I feel the joy of his presence always, and I live my life in obedience to him."

It was the Imam's turn to frown.

"How do you achieve this? What do you have to do?"

"You don't have to do anything—just believe that Jesus Christ died on the cross to save you from your sins. It is a free gift of grace from God that you receive by faith." John pulled out his Bible and asked if he could read from it. The Imam nodded his assent. John turned to Romans 10:9: "That if you confess with your mouth, 'Jesus is Lord,' and believe in your heart that God raised him from the dead, you will be saved."

"Saved from what?" asked the Imam.

"From the penalty of your sins." He flicked a couple of pages back to Romans 3:23.

"'For all have sinned and fall short of the glory of God.' Do you remember this morning," John went on, "that I described Jesus' death and resurrection? The sacrifice that he made on the cross in atoning for my sin allows me to have a personal relationship with God the Father."

The Imam looked away again, agitated, then back at John once more.

"You see God as your Father?"

John turned to Romans once more, and read chapter 8, verses 14–16.

"'Because those who are led by the Spirit of God are sons of God. For you did not receive a spirit that makes you a slave again to fear, but you received the Spirit of sonship. And by him we cry, 'Abba, Father.' The Spirit himself testifies with our spirit that we are God's children." John finished reading and looked up at him.

The Imam looked away again for some time. He was clearly in turmoil. As he turned back, he involuntarily edged nearer to John. They were now quite close. He raised his hand for emphasis.

"Are we not really worshiping the same God? Is it not that we see him differently?"

John slowly shook his head.

"There is only one Creator, one heaven, and one way to reach it." Without opening the Bible this time, he looked straight into the Imam's eyes. "Jesus said, in the Gospel of John, chapter fourteen, verse six, 'I am the way, and the truth and the life. No one comes to the Father except through me.'"

The Imam went curiously silent for some seconds then spoke quietly, almost to himself.

"Mohammed died, and no one truly knows if he reached paradise or not."
At this, the interpreter interrupted forcefully. John looked up, startled.
He had been so focused on the Imam, and waiting to hear his next words,
that he had forgotten that the interpreter was the one speaking.. The man
spoke to the Imam in his own language while glancing sharply at John. It was
clear that there was love and trust between the two, and he was just as clearly
cautioning the cleric. John ignored the interruption and continued, raising
his voice a little. He couldn't stop now.

"I have the absolute assurance, through the Word of God, and through
his Spirit that lives in me, that when I die, I will go to heaven to be with
Jesus. He died for me, he loves me, and he wants me to be there with him."

The Imam was silent, head down, but there was high emotion here. The
air was charged. John was breathing hard. He had to go on. He leaned very
close to the bearded man and almost whispered.

"I can feel the Lord here, right now."

The Imam nodded very slightly then sighed. He replied without looking up.

"I can feel him too. I have felt him since yesterday morning." He turned
to John with moist eyes. "Will you pray with me?"

John's heart soared. Then he was shocked as the Imam took his hand,
not because he took it, but because it was shaking uncontrollably. John
prayed with him, for him, slowly and earnestly. The words did not need to
be interpreted. The Imam wept quietly and gripped John's hand tight. John
wept too, for the soul of this man. He felt such love for him, and he didn't
even know his name.

The Imam reached into his pocket and pulled out something. He held
it out, and as John reached for it, he let it drop into his hand. It was a string
of beads.

"My prayer beads. I won't need them anymore. I wish to pray for Jesus to
live inside me and be my Savior."

John led him in a prayer of salvation. It was beautiful, but it was bizarre,
because although he faithfully translated the words, the interpreter was
disconnected from the emotion of this moment. When it was over, he seemed
furious with John. In between his continued furtive glances up and down the
path, he ranted at him.

"You have no idea how important this man is. Do you realize what they will do to him if he is discovered? Do you know what they will do to a man in his position if he is found denouncing Mohammed? *Do you?*"

John looked up at him sharply, but he could see in his anguished face that he was torn between his love for the Imam and his own Muslim beliefs, and he felt incredible compassion for him.

The Imam seemed removed from all of this. He was joyous, full of the Holy Spirit. He held John's hand for some time, wiping tears from his cheeks with the other. Eventually, the agitated interpreter convinced him that they must go. John promised to stay at the Imam's home on the next trip, and he gave him his Baseline Sports business card, promising to stay in touch. As they shook hands, John smiled his shy smile and handed him the small Bible.

"You gave me your prayer beads. Please accept my Bible."

Then he was gone.

John was awoken early the next morning by the ringing phone. He reached over, thinking of Kathy, but it was the interpreter. He said the Imam wished to thank him for his help and advice with the baseball camp, and he looked forward to future progress. They must stay in touch.

John knew of course exactly what this meant. The interpreter would be very well aware that the telephone and the room were bugged. John replied that he hoped the Imam would continue with his interest in baseball in Iran, gave the Imam his very best wishes, thanked him for his call, and promised to stay in touch. Two hours later, he was reunited with Jim for their long journey home.

Back home an email awaited him, sent from an unrecognizable address. The Imam hoped he got home safely, and had a few more questions about Jesus. It was the first of dozens sent over the next nine years. John read and answered every one, engrossed in tracking the progress of this man trapped in worldly circumstances as he found spiritual freedom in the embrace of the One who never fails us.

Two weeks after John returned home, Aaron wrote to say the Iranian Olympic Committee would like to arrange a national competition in October. This was great news. They suggested teams to be chosen from promising players in nine different regions of the country and a tenth team to be comprised of Americans. From the tournament the final Olympic team would be selected. They wanted Baseline Sports to be involved in all aspects of this as the organizers and hosts. There was even talk about starting a Little League system in major cities.

John was over the moon. Within two weeks, he had commitments from ten college players, all Christians. He needed eight more. Plans were just falling into place. Best of all was that the tournament was to be held at a closed resort, Kish Island, so the Americans would be rooming with all the other teams for two weeks. It would be a fabulous witnessing opportunity. Donations came in, which eased the burden on John's company that had paid for just about everything so far. He was sure this must be God's will.

But it wasn't. On September 11, 2001, John and Kathy watched their television in disbelief and dismay as the two jets exploded into the Twin Towers in New York. Some days later, President Bush made a speech denouncing terrorist extremists and the countries that harbor them. Iran, Iraq, and North Korea were named. John watched with concern and outrage, agreeing with the sentiment along with all Americans. But he had no way of knowing how disastrously this would affect his fledgling ministry.

Three days later, the Iranian Olympic Committee wrote a terse email to Baseline Sports. They were no longer invited to host the tournament and were no longer welcome in the country. Their visas had been withdrawn. The IOC was severing ties with immediate effect, and no further correspondence would be entered into.

John was crushed. He wrote back, but the IOC did not reply. He spent several days emailing everyone he could think of —Aaron, the players, even the Imam. Eventually, he realized that he was not getting back into Iran. It was over. His prayer life became a constant crying out to the Lord, asking why this had to happen. He could not see the future because he could not see past his anger. The last two years were suddenly a complete waste of time and money.

The service at First Baptist the following Sunday had a missions emphasis, and when John arrived at church, he was met by his close friend, Forrest Head, with a message that the pastor wanted John to close the service with a prayer for missions. It was recognition and encouragement from him for John's work in Turkey and Iran. How ironic. It was the last thing John needed right now.

It was a difficult prayer. John took the microphone and found himself praying for the nations, praying for the Lord to use missions everywhere to reach the lost. But as he finished the prayer, he felt an unexpected, uplifting surge of insight. The excitement and passion of his journey up to 9/11 suddenly came back to him. He realized he had shared Jesus with maybe fifty people, including the Imam. Who knows what the Lord would do with that? Humbled, he realized he must trust the Lord and remain obedient. Back in his seat, calm and still, he prayed another brief prayer, for himself.

"Lord, it is your purpose and your plan. It's all about you. Help me, Father, to listen, hear, and obey so that I can follow you and do your work. Give me patience and wisdom, Father, so that I can be used in your service and for your glory."

Epiphany

Three days later, John received a surprising email. A missionary in India, working as a businessman, had seen an article in a Kolkata newspaper that said India was considering raising a national baseball team. They were hopeful of making the Olympics. The missionary had recently corresponded with Aaron, who told him about Baseline Sports, John, and Iran. He had approached the Indian Olympic authorities, and they were very receptive to US help for this project. Would John be interested in taking baseball to India? It was a unique witnessing opportunity.

John leaned back in his swivel chair and stared at his computer screen, lost in thought. *No*, he thought, *I don't think I would*. He searched the Internet for Indian missions and missionaries. William Carey, the father of modern missions, first traveled to India in 1793. Christianity had become established, and today, there are thousands of churches in India situated in most regions of the country.

John was unimpressed. What would he achieve in going to India? The country was already an established mission field. How many missionaries do you need there? Iran had excited him because it was fresh ground. Christianity was virtually non-existent because there was restricted access, but look what the Lord had done with the Imam. It was a great challenge, and that is what he wanted. He didn't want to go to India. Even the man who was inviting him was a missionary there.

He spoke to Kathy, and she wasn't excited either. Jim and Pat felt the same way about India. They didn't want to go. They all agreed to pray about it, but in the end, John declined the offer. The Lord had continued to financially bless his business and had freed him up to spend time seeking his ministry, but after the Iranian door had been slammed in his face, the only alternative seemed to be India. It just did nothing for him.

But it wouldn't go away. He was surprised to receive a second invitation and a note from the missionary saying the Indians were really keen to do this. Please reconsider. He did; but again, he declined. None of them felt good about India. But a week later, John began to think differently. Perhaps he was being negative. Perhaps a visit to India would be the wise thing, even if it was to confirm that his initial feelings were right. But he had declined, so he let the thought pass. Then, two weeks later, the persistent missionary wrote again. He felt he should ask one more time. John was so surprised at him that he accepted on impulse. He immediately regretted it and was convinced it was a mistake.

The next evening, sitting in the study, he was in a sour mood. He could not think of one positive thing that could possibly come out of this trip to India. Why had he agreed? Kathy walked in, wanting to talk.

"I don't feel good about this trip, John. I don't want you to go," she said bluntly. John frowned at her.

"Why, Kath?"

"I don't know. You know I've supported you in everything. I was even okay with Iran, but I just don't feel good about India."

John sighed.

"We should pray."

They prayed. Thirty minutes later, they lifted their heads, opened their eyes, and looked at each other.

"I think I have to go, Kathy. I gave my word."

She nodded and gave a small smile.

"I know."

There was a beep from the computer. John pressed a key on the keyboard, and there on the screen was an email from the missionary. Everything was organized. The Indians were looking forward to meeting him.

He was on his way.

John sat on the plane arguing with the Lord. *Going to India doesn't make sense, Lord. I need to go back to Iran. Believers are being persecuted there, jailed*

and killed. What am I doing, Lord, going to India? The whole Baseline Sports organization was geared for Iran, not India! He made up his mind right there that after these nine days were done, he was going to find a ministry back home. He wasn't cut out for this. He wasn't a missionary. He would find some other way to serve the Lord and be where he could use him—somewhere he could make a difference.

He arrived in Kolkata at 5:00 a.m. and was picked up and driven to his hotel. He was tired and morose, and he had made up his mind to get this whole thing over with. By 10:00 a.m., he had met the officials and team management and was out on the baseball field with the team, setting up practice. He went back to the hotel for lunch and then back to the field for afternoon practice. The team managers met him for dinner in the evening before he went to bed, exhausted.

It was like this for three days. John had no interest in walking the streets as he had every day in Tehran. He did invite some of the players for dinner but was told that was not allowed. How ironic—there had been no such restrictions in Iran. The players there would be knocking on his hotel door at 7:00 a.m. to come down to breakfast, and he had spent every evening with them until late.

One evening after practice, John saw one of the players headed in the direction of his hotel, and he ran to catch up to him. But he had barely said *hello* before some officials came to separate them. They had followed him. Then he noticed that there were officials around the field, officials in his hotel lobby, officials everywhere. It was clear that they were suspicious of his motives and that he would have no opportunities to share about Jesus. It made him angry.

John called Kathy several times a day, complaining about everything. He missed her and Kristen and Jack terribly. He was incredibly lonely and wanted to come home. She didn't know how to respond, other than to count down the days with him.

He was amazed at the interest the press showed in the baseball program. "Baseball comes to India!" There were different reporters at every practice, and television cameras recorded several sessions. He was interviewed every other day, and soon, tired of being asked the same questions. He found it ironic that in Iran he was closeted away, and here in India, he was treated like a celebrity. He was informed that after the final practice, there would be an official press and TV conference and he would be asked to report on the team's progress.

After dinner on the fifth evening, he finally went for a walk. His empty hotel room was driving him crazy, and he needed to have people around him. He was certain he was not coming back, so he felt he should try to at least get a feel for Kolkata. He turned right out of his hotel and walked. He was immediately overwhelmed by the mass of people on the street. Beggars and cripples lay on mats on the sidewalk, urgently holding out their begging bowls. Vendors screamed out their wares. Smells of spices, sweat, and street trash wafted through the air. Traffic filled the roads, the incessant wailing of their horns jangling his nerves. A man carrying an impossibly large drum tied onto his back shouting, "*Chai!*" stopped just long enough to pour some tea from it in exchange for two rupees. Filthy, malnourished children constantly mobbed him, pulling at his clothes, begging for money. Noise, activity, crowds, and dust pervaded the entire scene.

By the time he'd walked the six blocks back, he was once again overcome with the stark realization of how hopelessly lost these people were, just as he had been in Tehran. He'd read that as much as forty percent of Kolkata lived in abject poverty. That's almost seven million people. There were so many people just trying to survive. Were they Hindu or Muslim? Did they care? Back in his room, he prayed for these people wandering lost and without hope in a city that offered so little to so many. He found himself going out each day after to walk among the people. He always felt safe and always touched by their hardship and hopelessness.

The media conference arrived soon enough, and John was blown away by it—ESPN Asia, CNN Asia, national newspapers. It was a big deal. Where the Iranians had been so understated, the Indians were way over the top. He was bombarded with questions about the baseball team, the preparation, their prospects, and the Olympics. Cameras flashed incessantly, and microphones crowded the desk in front of him.

John wasn't completely comfortable in the spotlight, but when a reporter asked about his Olympic baseball coaching experience, he had to hold back a smile when he answered that he had coached the Iranian team. It was just what they wanted to hear. An hour later, he was able to retire to the final reception in the hotel.

He was sipping orange juice and chatting to an official when a young Indian man approached him, dressed in an expensive suit. John remembered that he had asked a question at the conference. He thought he was a newspaper reporter. The young man smiled as he shook John's hand, and his English was impeccable.

"Mr. Heerema, you must be tired of questions, but I have one more for you."

He seemed pleasant enough.

"Fire away," John replied.

The reporter edged closer.

"Are you a believer?"

John eyed him carefully. There was something appealing about him, an openness.

"Yes, I am," he replied.

The young man's smile widened.

"So am I. Would you like to go to church tomorrow morning?"

John was leaving for home the next day, Sunday. But church was just what he needed. He'd walked past some magnificent old European churches here, and he wanted to experience at least one, because he still had absolutely no intention of returning to Kolkata.

"Yes, I would."

They agreed to meet outside John's hotel at 7:30 the next morning.

They took a motorized rickshaw to the outskirts of Kolkata. It was a long journey, to what was clearly a poor part of the city. The reporter had said the church was near his home, which John found strange given his cultured appearance. They stopped outside an ancient brick building that had been whitewashed a hundred times and was in need of another coat. John took a few steps inside. It was gloomy, and he stopped to let his eyes adjust. He saw it was a large space, like a community hall, with high ceilings, but dark and oppressive, with small windows and poor lighting. There was no flooring, just red dirt, the same as out on the street. The walls oozed damp, and it didn't take long for the strong musty smell of it to invade his nose. This was no church, although the old wooden desk up front would obviously serve as some kind of altar. A rough, wooden cross, about ten feet high, towered behind the desk. John guessed it was an abandoned building being used as a church. This was a long way from being the church he thought he was visiting today.

Where was he? What was he doing in a place like this? It was like no church he had ever been in, and he was regretting coming here. There was no seating, apart from some old plastic chairs toward the back. It appeared they were a little early, and people up front were tuning Indian instruments. Thirty or so people had congregated there and were raising their arms and intoning prayers in Bengali. Most of them wore traditional Indian dress, loose-fitting saris, dhotis, and lungis tied at the waste. But their clothes were old and ragged, and many of the men were bare-chested. Red dirt seemed to cover everything. John gingerly took a seat on the aisle at the back, first checking to see if the seat was clean. He felt uncomfortable and dirty in this place, and although he was committed to worshiping this morning, he hoped he wouldn't have to endure this for very long.

More people came in, and his discomfort grew into alarm. As the only white man in the place, he was quickly noticed, and he became the center of attention. Locals were talking loudly to him in Bengali, pointing at him. He couldn't understand them, and he was intimidated, wishing they would leave him alone. There was no aggression, just curiosity, but John was way out of his comfort zone here.

One filthy man took his hand, and John recoiled at the feel of the sticky hand gripping his own. He stood and faced forward stiffly, trying to ignore these people. Then he heard a shuffling to his right, and he turned his head to see a beggar dragging himself down the makeshift aisle. John saw with shock that he had no legs, and he was pulling himself forward with agonizing slowness, his hands and his fingers struggling to find purchase in the dirt. But this man didn't look right or left; he was completely focused on something up ahead. Following his gaze, John saw that it could only be the cross. John felt an urge to help him as he struggled, but he couldn't bring himself to move. All he could do was stare and wonder at the determination on the wretched man's face.

After him followed a limping woman with open sores over her face and arms; half-naked children in rags; two crippled men clinging to each other for support; and a blind man being led forward by a tiny girl. One man turned to him and smiled. As his mouth opened in a wide grin, John was appalled to see that the man had no teeth and no tongue. He froze as each terrible image passed by and was replaced by another. These were the untouchables, the lowest caste, who have nothing and no reason to ever hope for more. The more John saw, the more he desperately needed to leave this place. But he couldn't leave because he couldn't move. He was rooted to the spot.

As the room began to fill, and the morning wore on, the heat became claustrophobic, and John struggled to breathe with the damp and the dust swirling from the constant movement of the people. The noise level increased, and in amongst the prayers came wails and screams, the shouts of people desperately crying out to God. John had never heard such cries, and his alarm grew to panic. He closed his eyes, trying to focus on his journey home later and being with his family tomorrow. He had to get through this nightmare and get out of here.

Soon, the room was full of people standing, sitting, lying, and milling around. John had maybe 200 people ahead of him. They were excited and expectant. Suddenly, a smiling young woman appeared at the cross, wearing a bright-red sari. There was instant silence. Raising her arms and her eyes to heaven, she addressed the congregation in Bengali. The swell of response became an overwhelming flood of praise. The name of Jesus was proclaimed everywhere, and for the first time, John looked all around him in amazement at these people. The musicians started to play, and the woman began to sing. Her voice was beautiful, and even though he didn't understand the words, John was captivated by her.

As she sang, people began to sing with her. She nodded her encouragement, and soon, everyone was raising their voices, looking up, reaching for heaven, adoring and praising the Lord. John was speechless. He looked around again, in awe of these people. The infirm, the hungry, the downtrodden, and the hopeless were singing their love for Jesus as if they didn't have a care in the world. Suddenly, John realized that he knew this song. They were singing "Because He Lives," the old Bill Gaither song.

Because he lives, I can face tomorrow,
Because he lives, all fear is gone;
Because I know he holds the future,
And life is worth the living,
Just because he lives.

John was suddenly confronted with the realization that these people had absolutely nothing but Jesus Christ, but in him, they had everything. This wasn't just a worship song for them, it was a description of the hope of their lives, and it completely overwhelmed him. A million miles away, on his knees in his study, he had wept, asking God to show him what breaks his heart, and here, he was swamped by it.

As he was filled with the Holy Spirit, he tried desperately to keep control. He looked down, holding back the tears, and saw his own shaking white knuckles as he gripped the plastic chair in front of him. He felt the Lord telling him, screaming at him, that these people had lived in poverty like this for hundreds of years. *They don't need things; they need me.*

He kept his head down as the tears came, not trusting himself to look around, but then he felt the slightest touch on his arm. Still bent over, trembling, he turned his head and looked directly into the eyes of a child. It was a small, perfect face, like a doll's face, and the eyes were perfect too, deep brown and round. It was a little boy, no older than seven or eight, dressed in pitiful, filthy rags. He held John's gaze as if he were made of rock. The tiny hand that had touched John's arm reached out to him as if to wipe away all his tears. He smiled. Then in a high, soft, Indian voice, he spoke tenderly to him in broken English.

"It's okay, mister, he lives."

It took a second to register, and then John broke down completely. Collapsing to the ground, his knees and hands in the red dirt, he wept uncontrollably. The Lord was still screaming at him.

Look at these people and listen to me.

As the singing continued, he climbed to his feet and staggered to the open door. He leaned against the doorpost, breathing deeply, head down, sobbing, and when he finally looked up he was confronted with the mass of humanity passing by. *Look at these people.* A few hundred yards up the road, a Red Cross truck was offloading large sacks of provisions. *They don't need things; they need me.*

Stumbling into the street, he walked and walked, completely lost, trying to regain control, until he found a taxi to take him to his hotel. In the quiet of his room, he took off his red stained clothes, and wept until there were no more tears. The terrible images of the people he had just been with played out in his head like a horror movie, and as he ran it and then re-ran it, he prayed for these poor, wretched, incredible people.

He prayed to thank the Lord for showing this to him, and he asked forgiveness for his selfishness and his disobedience. This whole trip had been a poor response to God's leading. John wanted to go to Iran. John wanted to be where no one else could go. John didn't want to go to India. John had the perfect plan. It was all about John.

There are incredible Christian organizations in India, bringing food to the hungry, medicine to the sick, and education to the poor. There are great churches, hospitals, and orphanages. Iran had none of these—it was true. But God was in control, and it was all about him and no one else. God had a plan for Iran, and for Big Life, and he would let John know about it in his time. John vowed to listen and to be obedient.

Then he realized that the Lord had helped him today. He had spoken. The people of India need God. John would be back. Big Life would be back.

As he traveled to the airport, he thought about the reporter for the first time since that morning. John could not remember speaking with him, or even seeing him after he took his seat in the church, and he certainly hadn't been around when John had staggered out of there. Come to think of it, he couldn't remember his name, or even what he looked like, no matter how he tried. How strange is that?

Back home, his Bible Life Group had its Christmas party at a local Naples restaurant. Everyone wanted to know about the trip. John gave an emotionally charged account of the events surrounding the church visit, and the whole group became emotional, tears flowing freely. They all encouraged John and Kathy to continue.

The next trip was planned for March 2002. It was to be John and three others, two baseball players and an umpire. The plan was to keep going with the baseball camps and see where the Lord led them. But once again, the Indian officials prevented all private contact with the players. In April, he returned, this time with Jim and three baseball colleagues; and again, all doors to evangelism were firmly closed by the Indian authorities. It was hard to see the way forward, hard to continue like this.

In spite of the frustration, the baseball camps were highly successful. The Indian players were not as naturally talented as the Iranians had been but were improving steadily. All the media attention began to have an effect too, and suddenly, plans started to come together for bigger, more extensive camps, and travel to other cities. It was building into a national project.

Before returning home, there was the inevitable media conference. Possible future plans would be announced. It was all exciting stuff. An Indian liaison officer had been assigned to the American group to assist with organizational issues. John would meet him at the media conference.

John tried hard to be positive at the conference, but his real purpose was lost in all of this. He drifted off, wondering how the ministry was ever going to take shape. Even though the Lord had spoken so clearly such a short time ago, it was hard to listen to his voice when he was running into brick walls. He felt a stab of doubt once more that if even being here was the Lord's plan. He would have to get home, regroup, fast, and pray.

Someone was talking to him. He turned to find a smiling Indian face looking up at him. He smiled back. He hadn't seen this fellow before. He was short and obviously friendly.

"Mr. Heerema, good day to you, sir. Let me introduce myself. I am your new liaison. My name is Benjamin Francis."

KATHY

"I wait for the Lord, my soul waits,
and in his word I put my hope."

Psalm 130:5

Marking Time

How could she help? How could she be involved? Kathy felt like a spectator on the sidelines while the big game was played out in front of her. No, this was worse. She couldn't see the plays; she could only see the results. She had gone to Turkey with John, and it had been disappointing. They had worked hard, done what was required, but it wasn't enough. They hadn't made much of a difference. The only consolation for Kathy was that they had done it together.

She supposed she was gearing up for when John would announce that they were off to another country on mission somewhere, and she wanted John to know that it was okay. She would go; she would support him. She would go anywhere. He was the big vision guy, and she would follow him and be part of that vision. But after the meeting with Aaron, that all changed. Aaron made them see that uprooting the family may not be best and may not even be God's will.

So the game had changed, and Kathy had to be content with staying home with Kristen and Jack while John went to Iran to run baseball camps and try to find his purpose. It was tough for her. She missed him terribly, and the phone calls only made it worse because she couldn't talk to him without being overheard. She knew he had arrived, was alive, was coaching, and that was it. She strained to hear his inner voice, to hear if he was making progress with the ministry. She felt his frustration and loneliness, and she could only try her best to uplift him.

When he came home, he was always quiet, thoughtful, and moody. She learned not to push but to wait until he was ready to talk about the trip.

When he did, she felt his frustration with the slowness of his progress, the lack of opportunity. But Kathy began to see other things. When John had talked about the Iranian people, how willing and hungry they were to learn about Jesus, it was with passion and feeling. It broke his heart, and with each trip, Kathy saw this passion grow deeper. The incident with the Imam had deeply moved John and had convinced him of God's purpose in that country. Kathy saw that God was preparing her husband for a purpose too.

After the June trip, he was so excited about the national tournament. It was perhaps the breakthrough he was waiting for. John was in a fever of activity, enlisting friends to help with the organization, contacting Christian players, forming a prayer group to meet weekly. And then it all came crashing down on September eleventh.

When the opportunity for India arose, Kathy thought it was a bad idea. She didn't even have a good reason for her reaction. Maybe she'd had enough of seeing John disappointed, or maybe she was tired of not having him home. Maybe it was that no one wanted to go with him. But she didn't like the idea of India at all. The night he flew, Kathy had sat crying in the swivel chair staring at the computer in the middle of the night, wishing she hadn't let him go. When he arrived there, it was just more frustration, and he intended to stop going. And then that visit to the old church had affected John so deeply. Kathy saw a new determination and inner peace in him after that trip. It was huge.

But she wanted to do something now, to be more than just a spectator, sitting at home with Kristen and Jack while John was running a baseball camp and hunting down his vision. She wanted to show John she could do what he's doing, to support him in some solid way. When the opportunity to go to Russia came up in February 2002, she thought she would have one more go at this.

She went twice to Russia, in February and then again in April. She managed a Vacation Bible School for the children of missionaries who were attending a three-day conference, and she assisted in wheelchair distribution to needy people. She felt out of place and in the way on both occasions, and apart from experiencing the very different culture, she felt the trip was a failure. Kathy feared that missions was perhaps not for her, and she prayed fervently, *Lord, what is your plan for me?*

JOHN

"If any of you lacks wisdom, he should ask God, who gives generously to all without finding fault, and it will be given to him."

James 1:5

Upside Down

Nothing much changed, as far as baseball was concerned. The Indians controlled everything; access to players was still denied outside of scheduled practice, and the Americans were closely watched. John would have run out of patience and turned his back on India, but he didn't, largely because of Benjamin Francis.

He was the first Christian that John could communicate with inside the Indian baseball network. That fact allowed him some relief from the frustration. They would meet for lunch and talk about Jesus, their faith, the U.S. and India. Toward the end of the March 2002 trip, Benjamin invited John and his baseball colleagues over to his house to meet Gillian. It was a wonderful evening, and they worshiped together, singing old hymns and new songs to Benjamin's guitar. Ben taught the Americans some Christian songs in Bengali, making fun of their clumsy attempts at the language. It was a worshipful, fun time.

John was fascinated by Benjamin. He was positive and intelligent, with a deep knowledge and understanding of the Bible. He had a way of making the Word come alive, and his love for the Lord became ever more evident the more John got to know him. He was amused and constantly surprised by Ben's effusive and extroverted personality and his impulsive sense of humor.

Benjamin had arranged a lunchtime for John to speak at a school. They finished morning practice in sweltering heat, and John raced to where Ben was waiting with a taxi. John was trying to change in the back of the taxi, but the sweat made his clothes just stick to him. While John struggled, Ben chuckled.

"You're not helping, Ben," John said as his shirt stalled half way over his head.

"I'm sorry my brother, but this is just so funny!" Now he was laughing in earnest.

They raced into the school hall just in time for John to address the school children, dripping with sweat. It was crazy, but John loved it. Through Benjamin, he was finally talking about Jesus in India!

Toward the end of the April trip, John took the short walk from his hotel to the big church on the corner. He had walked past it on his nightly mingle in the city, and he noted the times of service. Although it was only 8:30 in the morning, it was hot and humid, and he started to sweat as soon as he left the hotel.

The church was impressive. Built to resemble a classic medieval English church, it was clean, and air-conditioned. Inviting, but empty. There was room for maybe 500 souls, but today, John counted fifteen. He heard English and German accents close to him, so he guessed that most of the congregation was tourists. But there was not one Indian person. The pastor was American, spoke only English, and gave a classic western service. John could have been back in Naples.

As the closing hymn was being sung, John slipped to the back of the church, where a smiling Indian attendant was stationed at the entrance. John asked him where all the local worshipers were, and he was led out of the church and then to an outbuilding on the property. It was dark and dingy, in stark contrast to the church. He opened the door just a crack and peeked in. He couldn't believe his eyes. The place was crammed with people, sitting or down on their haunches, listening to a Bible-waving Indian pastor give a sermon in Bengali. They numbered perhaps 300, all in stifling and oppressive heat. A couple of them looked his way, but the rest were engrossed in the sermon. He quietly closed the door, walked over to a bench under a big, old, shady tree and sat down with a sigh. In front of him, the flower-lined path wound around to the entrance of the church. It was impressive, grand. John shook his head.

This made no sense. It was upside down. This magnificent church was made to glorify God, but instead, it made a mockery of the reason for its very existence. It should be full to the brim with Indian believers and other Indians searching for the truth that can only be found in Jesus Christ. Jesus' name should be proclaimed in Bengali there with a worship service designed and dedicated to bringing more Indian souls to him. But the local people were next door in a hot, uninviting building that was way too small to house them in any kind of comfort.

John was confused and angry. He walked past hundreds of people every time he ventured out of his hotel, and the masses of lost humanity tore at his heart. *Every second, one person dies without hearing the name of Jesus.* That statement had shocked him back home, but here in India, it completely overwhelmed him, just as it had in Iran. His baseball ministry was a beginning, a foot in the door, but how could he witness to the masses? He had no idea.

John believed that the Lord had given him a vision, the Big Life vision. He didn't doubt it for a second. Even in times of crushing discouragement he still felt that small flame burning inside. He needed wisdom and guidance to fan it into a raging fire for the Lord. He prayed for that wisdom, that the Lord would reveal his plan, so that John could follow in obedience. *Where are we going, Lord? Please show me.*

BENJAMIN

"And we know that in all things God works for the good of those who love him, who have been called according to his purpose."

Romans 8:28

Revelation

He had been patient. The disappointment of finding that his plan was not the Lord's plan was a thing of the past. He still loved Jesus, was on fire for him, and he would continue to be patient and wait on him. He had continued his street evangelizing, and it was always tough and challenging but always a real blessing. The saved ones needed support and discipleship, so he started a small church in a hotel room. It started out with four souls, and after just a couple of months, it had grown to eighty. Benjamin borrowed a hall from a friend each week, and he became their pastor, preaching to his congregation every Sunday.

Benjamin and Gillian were married at last in September 2000. Friends paid for the wedding, and many others gave generous gifts. The Assembly of God offered their magnificent church for the ceremony. It was a tangible sign of how the Christian community felt about Benjamin, and he was touched by their love and kindness.

Word had spread, not just within Kolkata, but all over West Bengal, and even as far afield as Nepal, of Benjamin's powerful preaching. He was invited to preach at churches all over Kolkata and at rallies, retreats, and Christian gatherings everywhere. He took every opportunity, seeing them as appointments from the Lord. Benjamin was particularly enthusiastic when speaking to young people, and he was as energized addressing kids at chapel as he was preaching to thousands in some great church. It was teenagers that he sought when he roamed the streets and train stations at night.

Benjamin was so certain that the Lord had a plan for him that he refused to resume his career when he returned from his father's village. He knew he had left not just a lucrative job with the bank but long-term security. He had no regrets, and he wasn't going back. He was in the Lord's hands, and he had to be ready when the Lord's call came. Through his contacts, he found part-time work teaching economics at the Assembly of God school. He also met a missionary who gave him work, and it was through him that Benjamin was employed as the liaison attached to the American baseball coaching team.

Benjamin had met many missionaries. He respected them and enjoyed working with them in Kolkata, but John was different. He had this quiet determination and a restlessness that seemed to drive him. He was always asking questions, learning about Hindus and Muslims and Indian culture. Benjamin saw that he was seeking, searching for something that the Lord would have him do, and he would not stop until he found it. Benjamin understood this because he felt that too. He was intrigued by John and touched by his clear burden for the lost.

John came back to India three more times before the end of 2002, and he and Benjamin became close friends. Benjamin saw his frustration and discouragement with the baseball camps and tried to encourage him, introducing him to other believers whenever he could. As they spent more time together, the trust between them grew, and they began to open up to one other. John told Benjamin about his visit to the church.

"Ben, I don't understand this. Why do the Western churches insist on trying to reach Indians the Western way?"

Benjamin shook his head slowly. "It saddens me too, John. So many empty churches."

"I mean, it's like the early gentile Christians having to become Jewish before they could be called true Christians."

Benjamin could only shrug. "The westerners paid for and built the churches. They also built hospitals and schools. The people needed these badly, so they accepted the churches. They just don't attend them."

When they met again in September, John finally shared with Benjamin his growing vision for Big Life.

"I don't want to do baseball camps, Ben," he said. "I want to see a church-planting movement started where Indians can embrace Christianity as part of their culture."

Benjamin became excited. He had been pondering the same dream lately.

"Yes," he replied. "I agree; it would be wonderful. But John, it's not just the cities but the villages that must be reached. This is where most of the people are. You must experience the villages."

He went on to tell John the emotional story of his year-long visit to his father's village—the hunger of the villagers to hear the Word. He described how the Lord had started not just a fellowship but also a school and that he had the privilege of bringing his own Hindu grandfather to Christ. He had word that the fellowship was still meeting weekly in the same house and had grown in numbers.

John was fascinated with the story, and as Ben talked, ideas began to form in John's mind. Could there be an outreach in the villages where believers were trained to reach out in turn to other villages and teach their converts to reach out to others? It was a daunting task. Was it even possible? Of course it was possible; all things are possible with God.

The December trip was a watershed. Their time together was spent in exhilarating discussion and prayer for a ministry that would evangelize to the hundreds of thousands of villages in India and the rest of Asia. And there would be a way to enable discipleship, to empower Asian believers to spread the good news in their own culture and in their own language. By the end of John's trip, they hadn't found the way, but two things had become crystal clear to John. The first was that he had done more kingdom work in India in his time with Benjamin than with all the baseball camps; and the second was that he needed to know much, much more about the villages than he knew right now. He had to see them and meet the people.

He made up his mind. He was coming back next year. And there would be no more baseball camps.

JOHN

"…if God is for us, who can be against us?"

Romans 8:31

Ani

It was a strange thing, but John's worst times were often when he returned home. He would have overwhelming feelings that he was wasting his time, money, and energy on the other side of the world. Sometimes he felt as if he were lapsing into depression. At these times, John met with Pastor Wicker. He needed his encouragement and his feedback. He had achieved so little, and he felt as if he were grasping at straws. He told the pastor of his vision to reach the villages in India and of his frustration in not finding a single handhold to begin climbing this mountain. Pastor Wicker reminded him that he was under spiritual attack, and it was not likely to diminish while he was on the front line in God's army. He encouraged John to be persistent in prayer and to persevere, just as the apostle Paul did. He was certain that John's efforts would bear fruit.

John was so grateful for his home church. It was solid, his home base. He felt so much love and encouragement there that he longed for it and relied on it. He grew close to Forrest Head, senior associate pastor, who had taken a very personal interest in Big Life and everything John was doing. They spent hours together in discussion and prayer, and Forrest gave encouragement through real, practical, biblical advice.

Advice was also always available from his old friend back in Chicago. He spoke to John Van Proyen for hours on the phone, pouring out his frustrations, unloading his deepest burdens. It was a special relationship that John cherished with all his heart.

John's accountability group was a real blessing. Their constant prayer and support uplifted him. His partner, Jim Powers, shared John's vision and was not just a ready and willing partner on many India trips but a constant source of inspiration and encouragement.

Benjamin called with the great news that Gillian was going to have a baby. She was fine, and they were excited and thankful. John and Kathy were delighted and prayed with them over the phone. John promised to celebrate with Ben and Gillian on his next trip.

John's return to work was, as always, a little strained. Art had been running the company well in John's absence, and although he was always gracious in having John around and bringing him up to speed, it was clear to both of them that Art was steering the ship. The company continued to be profitable, and the baseball trips had been a manageable financial burden. This was a blessing as far as John's India trips were concerned but a source of guilt for John personally. As a fully-committed man by nature, he was not comfortable as an absentee owner.

Just before he had left for home in December, John connected with an American missionary working in Kolkata. He wrote that the next time John was over he would take him to some villages. After Benjamin's earlier advice, it sounded like an offer John could not refuse. In February 2003, he flew out to Kolkata once more with Jim Powers. It was to be an amazing, eye-opening trip.

They drove for hours to reach villages that had never seen westerners before. At first, the villagers were hesitant, not knowing what the white men wanted; but after the interpreters introduced them, the villagers just came out and surrounded them, curious and eager to see them. John and Jim stayed for hours, sharing about Jesus and the Bible. The people loved the Bible stories, and as each one ended, they asked for more.

One of the interpreters really captured John's attention. He captured everyone's attention. His name was Ani. He was about thirty, with an easy, smiling manner and a gentleness about him that endeared him to everyone. His English wasn't good, but he understood John well enough, and although there were more fluent interpreters there, John found himself using Ani all the time. He could see that this young man was full of the Holy Spirit, and when he spoke to the villagers, he spoke so powerfully and with such authority that his words seemed to charge the atmosphere.

The people's eyes never left Ani. When he spoke the name of Jesus, it was with such love and reverence that John felt completely humbled. At one Muslim village the people were particularly hostile to hearing the Word, and reacted badly, but Ani took charge. He not only calmed the situation, he turned it around and spoke for some time. John didn't understand the language, but Ani was clearly witnessing, and the people were clearly listening.

Ani took John to a village fellowship that he had started. Fifty people were gathered, and they sang praise songs to guitar. Then the pastor, a village leader, read and taught from the Bible. Later, John was able to get Ani alone, to talk to him. He spoke slowly, trying to overcome the language barrier.

"Ani, why do you have a pastor here?"

Ani nodded his understanding, and pointed off into the distance. "If I am far away, the fellowship must be. I train the pastor for to lead it. I am here once a month to see all is okay. I disciple him, encourage him. Then I go to start another fellowship for Jesus, over there." He pointed into the distance again, but in another direction, and his face lit up into a huge smile.

Yes, thought John, *he's completely right. What an incredible, simple way for one man to grow existing fellowships and be available to raise up new ones.*

John nodded, and smiled back. He couldn't help it. Ani's smile was completely infectious. For some seconds, John was lost in thought, and then he spoke up again, pronouncing his words carefully.

"Ani," he asked, tracing a circle in the air with his finger, "How many villages are in this area?"

Ani's face split into a huge grin once more. "Sixteen hundred," was the immediate reply. They both laughed together. John decided he liked Ani very much.

John was always sorry to leave the villages. The women gave John and Jim their babies to hold, and they wanted to know all about the faraway place that they were from. He was touched by these visits and by the openness of the villagers, and on the final long, tiring drive back to Kolkata, he thought constantly about how God had screamed at him to look and listen. *They don't need things; they need me.* He was looking, and he was trying hard to listen.

He thought of Benjamin, how he had urged John to do this. He now understood Ben's excitement about these villages, how they need to hear the Word, how open their minds and hearts were to Jesus. A recurring thought entered his mind: *Could he and Benjamin work together to begin a ministry?* For a second, John was excited; it made all the sense in the world after these village visits. But then the difficulties of such an idea invaded his mind as it always did. *What would it cost? How would he fund it? The cost of the trips was beginning to be a burden on the business. How would Ben be paid? Would Ben take such a chance? Would it even be fair to ask him with his baby on the way? What about John's own family?* No, it was just too risky.

But then one simple, mind-blowing thought encapsulated all his thoughts and emotions at that moment. One and a quarter billion of God's people inhabit the subcontinent, and most of them live in villages just like the one he was driving away from. John's concerns about financing Big Life were real and frightening. But the way the Lord had shown him his heart for these people—that was real too. He needed to have courage and commit to find a way to reach them. He knew God knew the way. He would pray and ask Him to show it to him. He would pray for courage.

A BIG LIFE
Photo Section

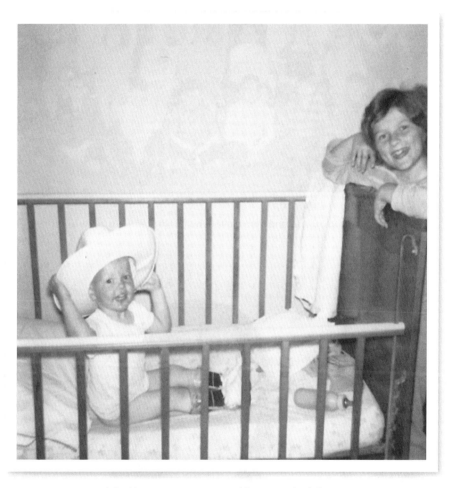

John Heerema at two years, with casts on both legs.

John (front row, second from right) in his fourth grade class picture.

Kathy Lacke at age fifteen.

A rare treat for nine year old Benjamin Francis,
all dressed up for a studio picture.

A typical street scene in Kolkata-incessant traffic and masses of people.

Jim Evans and John Heerema caught in a traffic jam
on the road from Siliguri to Darjeeling, September 2003.
"There's God everywhere, John. Can't you feel it?"

Benjamin prays before approaching a village near hilly Darjeeling.

John outside the first Big Life offices in Kolkata.

Benjamin makes his point in an informal
Big Life leaders meeting, early 2006.

Village children listen to stories about Jesus as
they eagerly await the showing of *The Jesus Film*.

The Jesus Film. Here, the film is shown on DVD on a screen,
replacing the old reel-to-reel format.

A Big Life medical camp, South 24 Parganas district.
Ani opens the camp with prayer.

New believers receiving their first Bibles at a fellowship in a village near the region of Bashirhat, North 24 Parganas district. This man had been a Muslim Imam in this village for sixty years before coming to Christ. He now leads the Big Life jamat in his home.

A young woman is baptized in a village pond in North 24 Parganas district.

A typical village fellowship in South 24 Parganas district.

Kathy Heerema learns crafting techniques from the village women.

Benjamin preaching at First Baptist Naples
on his first visit to the United States, April 2007

John Heerema addresses the 2000 strong audience at First Baptist Naples.

The dramatic setting for Benjamin's first preaching engagement in the United States. '21600' represents the number of people around the world who statistically would have died during this three-hour event without ever having heard the name of Jesus Christ.

Praise and worship at the third
"Women of the Word' retreat in Kolkata, 2007.

Kathy prays with one of the attendees of the 'Women of the Word' retreat.

Ani witnesses to a young cleric training
to be an Imam in the Sunderban Islands area.

Some of the Big Life group at the June 2009 training conference in Darjeeling.
Left to right- Robert, Naresh, Karma, Raju Chetri, the author,
Benjamin, Prem, Sam (on the van), Sunderam, Raja,
Mr Mondal, Ani, Madan Rai (front), Amit, Partho and Saiful (rear).

Ben and Prem lead praise and worship at Darjeeling.
Left to right- Sunderam, Saiful, John, Benjamin, Sam, Prem, Amit and Ani.

Rajesh leads praise and worship at Darjeeling. Left to right- Raju
(from Nepal), Benjamin, Rajesh, Raja, Sam, Madan Rai and Ani.

Tapan preaches at a fellowship in a village close to the Bangladesh border in January 2008, two months after the murder of his wife.

John and Ani take a break on the journey to Darjeeling, June 2009.

Our medical camp party boards a Nowka to get to Chota Seari village,
where cyclone Aila wreaked such devastation. Dr Singh has just boarded the boat.

The village square at Chota Seari, completely under water.

The 'Man of Peace' Ashosh Mondal,
who allowed a fellowship to begin at Chota Seari.

KATHY

"The kingdom of heaven is like treasure hidden in a field. When a man found it, he hid it again, and then in his joy went and sold all he had and bought that field."

Matthew 13:44

"Do not let your hearts be troubled. Trust in God; trust also in me."

John 14:1

Sacrifice

John was home, but this time he was quiet for way too long. Kathy was concerned. It was almost two weeks, and it wasn't just that he was silent about the trip. He was just silent. Then one Saturday afternoon, sitting on the patio, he told her about a baptism he had witnessed in a small village pond. She could see his emotion as he described it.

"Kath, when this man came up out of the water, he was glowing. *Glowing!*" He drifted off into the memory of it as the tears filled his eyes.

"That's so beautiful," she replied, smiling at him. She thought that the effect it had on John was beautiful too. But his next words rocked her.

"Kath," he went on, breathing deeply. "Kath, I think we have to sell the business."

She was shocked, unable to reply. *Sell the business? Did she hear right?*

He leaned forward and looked into her eyes.

"Kath, if we are to do the Lord's work, we need to commit everything, our entire existence, to him. Right now, I'm not doing India well, and I'm not running the business. Art is. We can sell it to him. If Big Life is going to get off the ground, it needs one hundred percent of our commitment and money."

She frowned, trying to frame her thoughts. Trying to stay calm.

"So we sell the business. That means we will have no income, only the money from the sale of the business, right?"

John nodded slowly.

"John, you don't even have a ministry started yet. How much will it cost?"

John shook his head and replied calmly. "I have no idea."

For a second, fear came like a knife in her gut. *What if?*

"What if the money runs out?"

They stared at each other in silence as the question hung in the air. When John replied, it was a whisper.

"It's God's money, Kath. And he will provide. He will."

She took a deep breath, then nodded. Of course he will. Trust and obey. She didn't hesitate. Screwing up her nose, she pointed at him. "You better get a good price, mister."

He laughed and then became serious again. He wasn't done.

"There's one more thing. You have to go, Kath. You have to see what I've seen. You are my wife, my partner. Whatever Big Life will be, we will be in it together."

Kathy felt a surge of excitement and emotion. She smiled and nodded, not trusting herself to speak. This was incredible. *Thank you, Lord.* John thought a women's trip would be best. She could go with supportive friends, just as he had. He had already discussed it with the missionary in Kolkata, and they had planned it for November.

She was ecstatic, full of joy at this, and she hugged and kissed him. She hadn't told John what this meant to her, of her frustration and her earnest prayers, but now she could contribute, not just be somebody in the background. She couldn't wait to see India, meet Benjamin, and experience the things that had changed John so much. She could really catch his vision, and she could support and encourage him in the future with understanding. She could not wait to go. *Thank you, Lord, thank you for your answer to prayer.*

As they settled down to pray, she gave him a sideways look.

Well, John Heerema, she thought, *after two week's silence, you certainly let it all out, didn't you?*

Art was also ecstatic. He agreed to purchase the business immediately. They had an independent valuation, which was a little less than John expected, but he accepted it. He was happy for Art, who had been a loyal employee and good friend for so many years. He deserved his chance.

It was a strange time for John. He was sad to leave Art and the business, which had allowed him so much freedom, but now he felt a new freedom. He was content to be totally and utterly dependent on God for everything.

Kathy had nagging moments of worry, but at these times, she would pray. As she felt His peace, she knew the Lord would provide, just as he had promised. She would support John, support his vision, and believe in God's purpose. She prayed for Big Life constantly, and she felt the Lord was with them. And a week later, she was able to turn the tables on John, surprising him by announcing that she felt they should sell their home and buy a more modest one.

JOHN

"…let us run with perseverance the race marked out for us."

Hebrews 12:1

Confrontation

The next trip was in June, 2003. John spent a pleasant two days in Kolkata with Benjamin and Gillian before traveling out to the villages. Ben was excited that John was exploring village life, and he was full of ideas, encouraging him to keep on.

John was disappointed to find that Ani wasn't available on this trip. He had been looking forward to seeing him and discussing his ideas with him again. This time, the missionary took him in a different direction, but the results were very much the same. He was greeted with silent, probing stares, but the stories of Jesus soon broke down barriers.

On the road back, John casually asked the missionary when they were going back to the first villages they had visited in February. He was eager to see the results of their visits, and he hoped that maybe they had started fellowships. He'd thought about this non-stop on the plane. *No*, was the surprised reply, *we don't go back; there's too many other villages, too much other work to do.*

John was completely stunned, as if he'd been slapped in the face. It had never occurred to him that there would be no follow-up. Surely starting some kind of ongoing fellowship was their purpose in going to a village in the first place? Even the first missionary, Paul, went back to the churches he raised.

Back in Kolkata, he was introduced to an Indian interpreter, Mina, a former Muslim who became a Christian and was now working with Western missionaries to facilitate introductions to Muslim villages. He was working where John needed to be, and John was full of questions, eager to learn everything he could from this man. The haphazard, shotgun approach of the missionary was leaving him frustrated and impatient. It was no way to make measurable progress. But with Mina, he felt he was on more solid ground. He was driven, just like Ani. The pleasant Indian offered to take John to a former Muslim village where Christians were established so he could see how they worshiped and conducted their fellowship.

Mid-afternoon, two days later, John was traveling in an old van on a bad road west of Kolkata. He was with Mina and two other men. They pulled off at a bend in the road at the top of a small hill and climbed out. John could see thickly treed hills rolling off into the distance. Mina pointed to a nearby one, just over the valley, off to the left.

"There's our village," he announced. "We'll have to walk from here."

John squinted in the punishing sunlight and took a long pull from his water bottle. He saw habitation, buildings, and huts dotted here and there among the trees. The more he focused, the more he saw. Then he glanced right. There was another hill, a little further off. John saw huts there too.

"What's that?" he asked.

"That's a Muslim village," Mina replied.

John reacted immediately.

"Let's go there. We can go to the Christian village later. Tomorrow. Let's go." He hitched his backpack and set off.

"No," said Mina firmly.

John stopped and turned to look at him.

"What do you mean *no*? Mina, I've come halfway round the world. This is what I have come to do. I want to talk to those Muslims about Jesus Christ."

He turned to go and was startled to see Mina walk ahead then turn to face John, stopping him in his tracks. Mina looked straight at him, a troubled frown etched on his face. There was a moment of tension before John spoke.

"Is it my safety—is that what you're worried about? Don't be, I'm fine."

"No, not your safety."

"Then what?" John didn't understand.

Mina stared at John for some seconds, then he spoke evenly and powerfully.

"John, I have been evangelizing in that village for months. I'm very close to starting a fellowship there. I am a former Muslim, and I have converted to Christianity for reasons that I may make them understand, but you won't. If we go there together, I will be seen as a western puppet. I will be rejected, and all my efforts will be in vain. I don't need you, and I don't want you there. I'm sorry."

John stared stupidly back at him. He was right. Of course he was right. But how could John be so wrong? As they trudged off to the Christian village, John tried to think this through. He was confused, shocked, and angry that his thinking could be so wrong. As they reached the village, he had to put it out of his mind. He would pray about it later.

Later, at his hotel, he was on his knees. He prayed for forgiveness for his own rashness, impatience, and stupidity. For weeks, he had been crying out to the Lord to help him to listen for his direction and for wisdom. Today, he realized that the Lord was talking, but he was still not grasping it. He had been critical of the big churches here for trying to westernize the worship practices of the people of Kolkata, and here he was about to stomp into a Muslim village and ruin the carefully laid plans of a knowledgeable brother who was doing it exactly right.

John recalled that in John, chapter 4, Jesus arrived with his disciples at Sychar in Samaria. No self-respecting Jew would go there or talk with an 'inferior' Samaritan. But Jesus did, and he spoke not to a man, but a Samaritan woman, a woman of ill repute. He witnessed to her, and she went back into the town. The scripture says, "Many of the Samaritans from that town believed in him because of the woman's testimony." (v 39) The woman's testimony, not Jesus' testimony.

This was the same situation: Mina's testimony, not John's.

Jesus was illustrating perfectly how we are to spread the gospel to other cultures. Mina was right. He was far better equipped to approach these villages than John would ever be. John was humbled. He needed to think differently and carefully and always with Jesus as his guide.

Ten days later, he was sitting in his new office back in Naples, lost in thought. The office had been offered to him by a good friend, Jim Evans, eager to help John with the ministry. It was a spare office, and Jim was right next door if John wanted to talk or pray or just hang out.

This last trip had really gotten to John. He knew the Lord was talking to him, showing him his will. It seemed to him that the only times he was listening was after he'd messed up. Well, maybe that wasn't quite true. It was when he stopped trying to do it his way that he heard the Lord speaking. And it was when he was broken, as he had been in the church in Kolkata, that he heard him loud and clear. Yes, God had certainly spoken again on this trip. What was that phrase that came into his head on the flight home? "Empower and equip"—that was it.

Benjamin, Mina, Ani, and all the other Indian believers he had met were solid Christian men. He would trust them with his life. But they were from a different culture. Western missionaries had largely ignored this fact and attempted to impose western thought on these people. But Jesus said, "All nations." So-empower and equip them. Don't change them.

He had to go back soon.

"Hey, Jim," he called.

"Yeah," came the reply from the other side of the wall.

"Come in here a second."

He looked up as Jim came through the door.

"You want to go to India in September?"

Jim and Betsy Evans had moved to Naples in 2001, and soon met John and Kathy at First Baptist. Jim was fascinated that their new friends had started a ministry to the Middle East and then Asia on the back of baseball camps, of all things, and he was amazed at John's perseverance. Just the thought of getting all the equipment through the airports filled Jim with dread. He thought John must be some special kind of guy.

Even so, Jim was very careful not to get involved. He hated baseball as much as he hated missions. They both bored him to distraction. But in spite of this, he couldn't help becoming interested in what was going on. John and Kathy were driven, searching for a way to carry out the Lord's Great Commission in a really meaningful way. They were completely committed, and as Christians, Jim and Betsy could only admire them. Even when it made no sense, like when the door to Iran was shut, they just kept on going, trusting the Lord, and believing in him. When John told them about the

Imam, they were astounded. It wasn't just a great story; it was really heady stuff. And then they went and sold their business to raise the money to do this full-time. When John started going to India, Jim was always there when he returned, interested to know what had happened, how the Lord had moved. Little did he suspect at the time that the Lord's plan would involve him too.

Eventually, he knew he had to go, and when John asked him that day, it was no surprise. At home early the next morning, as Jim and Betsy sat together to read Rick Warren's *Purpose Driven Life*, their current devotional, he told her about John's offer. They discussed it a little and decided that they would give the decision over to the Lord in prayer after their reading time.

It was chapter thirty-eight, "Becoming a World-Class Christian." As Jim read it aloud, the words just seemed to come alive.

> The best way to switch to global thinking is to just get up and go on a short-term mission project to another country!…Quit studying and discussing your mission and just do it! I dare you to dive into the deep end. I urge you to save and do whatever it takes to participate in a short-term mission trip overseas as soon as possible.

They were stunned, humbled, and then excited. Their prayer was answered before they'd even prayed it. The only prayer needed was one of thanks. Jim couldn't wait to go. It would be a great trip.

Part-Time

The trip was a complete disaster. John had asked the missionary to arrange for them to return to some villages, to think about new visits to villages that were predominantly Hindu or Muslim, to meet with Mina again, and to think creatively about progressing some kind of ministry direction. But when John and Jim arrived, the missionary greeted them with a question.

"So, what do you guys want to do here?"

Nothing had been arranged. They visited Benjamin and Gillian, and as always, the little man's personality and excitement about their coming baby lifted John's gloom. But only for a while. He was boiling over with frustration. John was touched to receive an invitation to the Muslim wedding of one of his old baseball players. Ben organized for the Americans to address morning chapel at a school. They prayer walked and witnessed briefly to Muslims outside a mosque.

These were worthwhile, but not the purpose of the trip. He felt like a tourist, like he was back to square one. They walked the city, saw the poverty, the broken, hurting people, but were unable to contribute anything. They couldn't speak the language or even understand the street signs. Benjamin suggested that the two of them take a trip to Siliguri, a twelve-hour train journey north. Ben had connections there and could arrange visits to villages. It would at least be a chance to show Jim village life. Maybe they could go up to Darjeeling and see the town. Ben would love to have gone with them, but the baby was due at any time, and he didn't want to leave Gillian.

John and Jim got off the train at 10:00 a.m. to 110-degree heat, and their rented van had no air conditioner. John decided to travel straight to

Darjeeling. It was a mistake. Traveling up the steep hills toward the town, they were soon at a standstill, caught in a single-lane traffic jam. The heat was relentless, and they climbed out of the van to find relief under some trees. John was quiet, completely deflated. He told himself that this was it; he was not coming back to India. This was all a mistake. He glanced at Jim. His friend was uncomfortable, sweat pouring down his face. He had been gulping down water like crazy. John felt awful. He looked away, trying to find the words to apologize for bringing Jim here on this wild goose chase, taking him away from his family. But Jim spoke first.

"John…"

John could barely look at him.

"John, this whole thing. Everything you're trying to do here. It's got God all over it. It's huge, John. I'm just completely blown away."

John turned and stared at him through the heat haze.

"What? Jim, you don't have to say this. I know it's been a complete disaster…"

"No, it hasn't. There's God everywhere. Can't you feel it?" His eyes blazed as he continued. "You don't need the missionary. Forget him. You need to do this another way. These people need to know God, and God will show you how this must happen. It will be incredible."

John continued to stare at Jim.

"You're on the right track, John, that's what I hear the Lord saying. You have to persevere."

John turned and looked down over the shimmering hills leading back to Siliguri, hills covered with village huts, as Jim spoke again.

"Seems to me your vision is right in line with Benjamin's. Maybe the Lord wants you to do this with him."

He prayed. All the way back to Kolkata, he prayed. Was Benjamin his man? Could they do this?

"Lord, this is your ministry. You know all things, and you know I am committed to it completely, Father. Please help me. Forgive me for being impatient and so easily discouraged. You have shown me the harvest field,

Lord. Give me the tools and show me your workers, and we will work together for your glory."

He prayed for clarity, for divine guidance, and to thank the Lord for bringing him friends like Benjamin and Jim Evans.

He met with Benjamin, and John poured his heart out. They talked for hours, and John let out all his frustration. The lack of fruit after so many trips, the wasted time, the wrong turns. Benjamin responded by telling him for the first time of his own frustration, that the Lord had kept him in India when he'd wanted to go overseas.

"But you know, John," said Benjamin in his silky voice, "I have learned that there is no wasted time with the Lord. There are no wrong turns. Time belongs to him, and he uses it to teach us and mold us."

There was a long silence, both of them thinking their own thoughts. Then John made the decision that he now knew the Lord had already blessed. He looked into Ben's eyes.

"Will you come work with me, Ben? I can only afford you part-time, but we can see where the Lord takes Big Life, and us." He smiled that shy smile. "Maybe we can get a church-planting movement started."

Benjamin smiled back, and his reply came with no hesitation.

"Of course I will work with you. And by the Lord's grace, we will plant many churches."

"I don't know how much to pay you, Ben. To be honest, I'm not even sure where it will come from; but as I told Kathy recently, the Lord will provide."

"Of course he will," replied Benjamin, still smiling. "We just have to trust him. Whatever God wants to pay me is fine by me."

Benjamin was going out in faith as much as John and Kathy had, and John knew it. He felt humbled.

"Thank you, Ben."

They stopped to pray. Then John opened his eyes and stood up. He had a plane to catch.

"Well, your first job will be to organize our first official Big Life trip in November. Kathy is coming over with some ladies, and I want you to show them India."

John visited with the missionary briefly to tell him as politely as possible that the Lord had told him that the Big Life ministry lay in a different direction. He thanked him for everything.

Big Life was official. Benjamin, Kathy, and John were taking on the world, committing everything, all their resources and their hearts, to success. By the world's standards, it made no sense; they were certain to fail. The world would chew them up and spit them out. But they knew that by faith, they had everything they needed to succeed. They had Jesus Christ.

KATHY

"Some trust in chariots and some in horses,
but we trust in the name of the Lord our God."

Psalm 20:7

Full-Time

She was trying to find the right moment to talk to him. Since he got back two days ago, Kristen and Jack had claimed all his time. They had missed him terribly. He was happy, happier than he had ever been after a trip, like something had been settled, progress had been made.

She had found them a smaller home. It was in poor condition but so cheap that it was a bargain even after remodeling. So they were able to add a little more to the Big Life budget. Even so, Kathy was alarmed at the outflow of funds. They had always had income, good income, even after she had stopped working, but now that had stopped. She had prayed constantly while John was away, and she filled her mind with the sure knowledge that God is in control; but they needed to be responsible and work to some sort of agreed budget. She had to talk to John.

A few days later, she thought the moment was right. She had cooked a great meal, the kids were in bed, and she and John were relaxing in the living room. He was so upbeat. He started describing the trip, that it was a complete disaster until the exchange with Jim on the Darjeeling road. He thanked God for sending Jim on this trip to confirm his purpose. Big Life absolutely needs to work with Benjamin.

Then he turned to her, smiling, and pulled the rug from right under her feet.

"So I offered Ben a job, just like that. And he accepted right away. How cool is that? Now we can make some progress."

Kathy blinked.

"That's great, John. You mean we're paying him?"

"Well, yeah. Part-time."

"And what is he going to do, part-time?"

"Right now he's organizing your women's trip. The first Big Life trip. We're not working with the missionary anymore."

She was searching for the right words.

"John, I'm a little surprised at the direction our bank balance has gone in a short time, and…"

"We can afford it, Kath. Having Benjamin part-time is perfect. He can start planting churches and still keep some of his other jobs."

Kathy frowned.

"But as it grows, Big Life will need more people, right? How are we going to pay them?"

John looked away, sighed deeply, then turned to her again.

"I don't know, Kath, but I know that God knows. We'll raise funds, get donations. God will work it out. We just have to trust him."

Late into the night, while John was sleeping, Kathy quietly rose and went to the study to read the Bible and to pray. At 5:00 a.m., she woke him. He lay staring up at her, not fully awake, as she leaned over him. She was breathless, crying softly, her voice faltering.

"John, I've been talking to the Lord, and he's spoken to me. He told me that Big Life can't take Benjamin on part-time." She wiped away a tear.

"It has to be full-time, John, full-time."

Later, he picked up the phone and dialed Ben's number. He was full of apprehension. Ben lived in a city where work was a precious commodity. John didn't even know if he had the right to ask him to give up what little he had. He would even have to give up his teaching. And if he said no, John was back to square one.

After some small talk, he just decided to say it.

"Ben, Kathy had an incredible touch from the Lord this morning, and we feel he is telling us…"

"Yes, John?"

"He is telling us that you should come into the ministry full time. Ben, I know this is short notice, and I understand the huge consequences of this decision for you, but I…"

But Ben interrupted him.

"It's okay John. The Lord has spoken to me too. I am with you, my brother. We will go forward in the darkness together, with the Lord as our light."

"Thank you Ben," said John. He didn't know what else to say.

"And John, we have had a touch from the Lord as well."

"What's that, Ben?"

"He gave us a beautiful daughter this morning. Her name is Abigail."

Crash Course

Kathy went on her first trip to India with Pat Stuart's wife, Jeanette, and three other ladies from First Baptist Church. The planning was more stressful for Benjamin than for the women. How was he supposed to keep five American women that he'd never met busy in Kolkata for nine days? It was a true test of his resourcefulness.

After that incredible touch from the Lord, there was no longer any doubt in Kathy's mind that God had his hand on Big Life. Their financial situation was a secondary issue. She was eager to see where the Lord would use her and to get a taste of what John had experienced. And she had to meet Benjamin. Even though he was from a culture she did not yet understand, from John's description, he was clearly a remarkable man of God.

It was a crash course in Kolkata. If the objective was to show Kathy and the ladies Indian life and religion then Benjamin had the contacts to do just that.

They spent three days working at an informal Christian school, teaching street children from five to fifteen about Jesus. These children were collected each day on the street corners by the 'Good News Bus' and taken to the school, a fairly primitive structure that could house a couple of hundred in crowded conditions. These children were the untouchables who had no prospects of education, simply because they were of the lowest Hindu caste, born into poverty. Their parents allowed them to go because even Christian education is better than none at all, and better than having their kids just roam the streets.

The bus brought them to the school, and the children were bathed and given a simple uniform to wear. Then they were taught basic reading, writing, and math, along with stories of Jesus in Bengali. The classroom was open, with no walls, just a cement floor, with the ceiling supported by wooden beams. But Kathy counted seventy, of all ages, squeezed into an area the size of a small garage. They were remarkably well-behaved, and Kathy wondered at this, until she realized that they knew that if they weren't, they may not be brought back, and the chance for a free meal, some fun, and freedom from the harsh streets would be lost.

Kathy taught through an interpreter, telling Bible stories by using puppets, which the children loved. She taught them lines from Christian songs and showed them how to pray to Jesus. The women were touched by the children's plight, and they tried hard to witness to them, but mostly, they felt that in the time available, they didn't get through to them.

Benjamin had the women address chapel at some Christian schools. They walked the streets, picking up the sights, sounds, and smells of Kolkata. Kathy soaked it all up, but she knew in the back of her mind that none of this was what had fanned the fire in John. Toward the end of the trip, however, she found it.

They went out to visit a Muslim village. It was just after noon, and the men of the village were away, working the fields, or in the markets earning their living. The women were gathered on front porches, chatting, caring for their little ones as they worked at crafting with their hands. As the American women arrived, Benjamin was careful to introduce them. The Indian women were friendly, smiling, intensely interested in the visitors. They happily showed off their babies. Soon, they were teaching their visitors how to weave. They were wonderfully dexterous with their hands, working the thick skin of the jute, a plant that thrives in the soil that is so well-watered by the late summer monsoon. They produced hot pads, chair coverings, curtains, rugs, baskets, and other household products that are sold at the market.

The Americans described their country and then began to talk about Jesus. The village women were attentive and even allowed their visitors to pray for them. They all joined in some praise songs, clapping hands and laughing together, encouraging the children to sing. Kathy was exhilarated, feeling that they were making real progress. When Benjamin interrupted, saying it's four o'clock, they have to go, she and the other women put him off, not wanting to leave. Fifteen minutes later, after being put off a third time, Benjamin put his foot down.

"Ladies, we have to go. *Now.*"

Kathy looked up, startled. Benjamin was staring straight at her, and for once, he was not smiling.

On the way back, he apologized.

"At four thirty, the men begin returning. I'm not sure they will be so friendly."

Kathy was silently praying, thanking the Lord, because she knew that at last she had seen John's vision. These women were housewives, mothers. They were social, friendly, skillful, and intelligent. Their culture was different; but were they, as women, so different from women everywhere?

But they didn't know Christ. She had seen in their faces this afternoon that many of them had never before heard his name. She felt an urgency, a desperate need for the women of this village to know him. And she knew that this was exactly how John felt. As they drove back, she was overjoyed, knowing that God had shown her something significant. It was his will. *Thank you, Lord, thank you.*

She glanced over at Benjamin, who was staring out the window, lost in thought. She smiled to herself. She liked him, but more importantly, she knew he was the right man, and she thanked God for him.

JOHN

"In this world you will have trouble. But take heart! I have overcome the world."

John 16:33

Beginnings

John was already back in India by early December. Sitting in his hotel room, Benjamin went over his rough strategy for the ministry, outlining the initial targeted villages and the resources and manpower needed. After prayer and discussion, they decided they would begin in the areas around Kolkata, North 24 Parganas and South 24 Parganas districts. They would prayer walk, then enter a village by asking permission to show *The Jesus Film*. A team of at least four per district would be necessary to handle equipment, talk to the villagers, and for security; there would be villages that would not welcome Christians.

The Jesus Film was the brainchild of Bill Bright, the founder of Campus Crusade, thought to be the largest evangelical organization in the United States. The film was based on the Gospel of Luke, and five hundred Christian and secular scholars were employed to research and ensure its Biblical accuracy. In 1981, *The Jesus Film* Project was formed to translate the film into alternative languages so it could be shown around the world. *The Jesus Film*, now translated into over three hundred languages, is the most watched motion picture of all time, with billions of viewings and hundreds of millions of decisions for Christ from those who have viewed it. It remains a powerful tool for bringing Jesus to the nations.

They saw that it was imperative that the Lord would bring the right men, and they committed much prayer to this. Many seeking work would claim to be Christian, so it made sense to begin the process of selection from Benjamin's many contacts. John was reliant on Benjamin here, and when they parted, he'd given him the task of screening prospects. But later that night, praying in his hotel room, John was given the first of these men. He was praying for guidance in how to maintain each new fellowship that was planted. It was vital to ensure that these new fellowships stayed healthy and alive while the teams went out to plant new churches. As he prayed, a name flashed into his head. It was Ani, the young interpreter that had impressed him so much. John knew that he had to contact him before he left for home. In the morning, he made some calls, and the next day, he and Benjamin met with Ani. After they outlined their vision, he had no hesitation in agreeing to work for Big Life. He was excited, and he told John and Benjamin that bringing the villages to Christ was the only thing he wanted to do with his life. The Lord demanded it of him.

Ani was from an area of West Bengal close to the Bangladesh border. As a young man, he achieved a BA with honors in history and was resourceful and streetwise. He struggled to find a career, but eventually found employment as a fundraiser, traveling the Hindu villages to raise money for the worship of idols at the Puja Festival. But he did this just to earn money, as he could not believe in the Hindu gods as his family did. Dissatisfied and without direction, he went to clubs, hung out on the streets, and spent his money on drinking and having a good time.

It was while he was drunk late one night in early 1993 that a Christian tried to witness to him. Through a haze of alcohol, he could recall only that this man had pushed a small book into his hand. Sitting alone on the sidewalk under a streetlamp two hours later, he opened it up and read.

"Jesus said, 'It is not the healthy who need a doctor, but the sick. But go and learn what this means: I desire mercy, not sacrifice. For I have not come to call the righteous, but sinners'."(Matthew 9:12-13)

Even in his drunkenness, Ani understood that this meant *his* sickness and *his* sin. He was deeply convicted that he needed to know Jesus. Over the next few months, he read that small New Testament, stopped drinking, and saw less and less of his old friends. When he finally gave his life to Christ, he was fearful, aware that the Hindu community would never understand or accept his salvation. But it was impossible to hide the changes that his new faith had wrought in him. Eventually, his uncle challenged him.

"Have you become a Muslim?"

"Who told you that?" Ani replied.

"You have Satan in you. Satan, Muslim, it's all the same."

Ani could not hold back.

"I have met Jesus Christ. I am a Christian. I will worship idols no more."

His family reacted violently. He was beaten, ostracized, and soon forced to leave the village. Baptized soon after, he was deeply convicted to preach Christ's salvation in the villages, and he soon connected with a ministry that was doing this, using *The Jesus Film*. He worked with that ministry for three years, all over South Parganas district. During that time, hungry for knowledge of Jesus and the Word, he also achieved a certificate in biblical studies.

Ani brought many to Christ but became troubled that the ministry did not always return to the villages they visited. When he returned to them, he found that the new believers were not regularly taught the Word, and other seekers were not brought into the fellowships that were started. Many fell away. In 2000, Ani decided to do it alone.

He often deliberately chose Muslim villages, knowing that their religion was less tolerant, because he saw them as trapped souls; it broke his heart. He was often beaten, rejected, and threatened, but he always went back, learning as he went. He studied their ways, how to approach them, and how to transition from their own Koran to the Bible.

He eventually returned to his own village in an emotional reunion and showed *The Jesus Film*. Twenty-five people responded, including many from his family, and he was able to begin a fellowship. Humbled, thankful, and tearful, Ani could hardly believe he was baptizing members of his own family.

John was so thankful for Ani. He called Kathy to share the good news, and she gave him some good news of her own. Friends at the church had organized a donation for Big Life. It was not a great amount, but it was a great encouragement. John knew exactly where it had come from, and he thanked the Lord for this financial blessing and for Ani.

By the end of December 2003, Benjamin and Ani had started four fellowships among the villages of North 24 Parganas.

Spiritual Warfare

In early January 2004, John sent daily emails to Benjamin and Ani, encouraging, sharing Scripture, and sharing ideas. Ani could not wait to get out into the villages with his team of church planters. Soon, he was suggesting that games (or sports, as he called them) should be introduced to the villages along with *The Jesus Film*. Benjamin was emailing church leaders, ministry leaders, old friends, and contacts all over India and Nepal, letting them know about Big Life, seeking the right men, the ones the Lord would bring. He began the search for equipment, supplies, and somewhere to set up an office.

They prayed constantly. They fasted.

Soon, Benjamin had found his man for South 24 Parganas. Atish Mondal, known as Mr. Mondal, came from a strong Christian background, his father having been a church secretary. As a teenager, his father sent him to military college in Lucknow, but he could not reconcile a military career with his faith. Later, he went into business as an electrical technician and was successful. This success led to financial freedom but little fulfillment, and it was only when he felt the Lord's call that he realized his true purpose, and he began to go to nearby Hindu villages to share about Christ. Soon, his wife joined him, and as their ministry grew, they walked away from their business and their relatively affluent lifestyle to commit full-time to the villages. A few months later, a friend introduced him to Benjamin.

Big Life was feeling its way, moving forward. Ani was everywhere, and he and Benjamin worked together as if they had known each other all their lives.

It seemed that the Lord was blessing the ministry. John was excited and flew out in January and February to assist Benjamin and support Ani and Mr. Mondal.

And then things started to go wrong. Mr. Mondal suddenly found resistance everywhere. He was denied access to village after village, as if someone were going ahead of him, poisoning his efforts. Ani suddenly found it harder to obtain permission to plant fellowships, even in villages where people had come forward to accept Christ. Both men moved to different regions in their districts, but this seemed to make things worse. They encountered not just resistance but aggression and occasional threats.

They discovered that a large church in Kolkata had put out the word that the Big Life people did not represent the Christian church. People seeking to know Christ should come to church. Benjamin was bewildered because this particular church was always empty! He rushed over to explain Big Life's vision and to ask if they could not somehow work together, but he was turned down flat. The church wanted nothing to do with him, or Big Life.

Mr. Mondal had seen no fruit for all his efforts, and Ani's progress had slowed. Their frustration was growing. John flew out again in April to regroup, and he and Benjamin went out to villages with Mr. Mondal to try to figure out the problem. They had some success, but they felt this was because of the interest in John. It was frustrating; they were trying to find a sustainable model on which to build Big Life, and it didn't involve John being on every visit. The day he flew home, all he could do was encourage and support the team and pray with them. As he flew back home, anxious and concerned, praying fervently, he remembered the words that had come to him on a previous flight, the words that now described Big Life's mission: "Empower and Equip." He now needed to add another *E*—Encourage.

John was desperate that momentum should not stutter so early in their ministry. For hours on the flight home, he prayed, asking the Lord for his protection against this spiritual attack in India. But he was soon to discover that the attack wasn't confined to India. It had followed him home.

KATHY

"But the Lord is faithful, and he will strengthen and protect you from the evil one."

2 Thessalonians 2:3

Disaster and Blessing

t was the first day of summer vacation. John was suddenly awake, senses on full alert. Something was wrong, and his heart was pounding like a drum. Glancing at the clock, 6:30 a.m. registered somewhere in his brain. He was in Kristen's bed. There was a loud noise, an unfamiliar noise, like someone was shaking a drawer full of cutlery. He headed for the kitchen, but as he reached the hallway, he heard it much louder now, coming from the garage. He turned to see smoke rising from under the laundry room door. He went through it, opened the door to the garage, and held his breath as the heat and the smoke hit him all at once. He saw fire, red and orange flames streaming out from under the hood of his truck.

Slamming the door, he raced down to the master bedroom. He had only got back from Tampa at 1:30 that morning, and he had climbed into Kristen's bed, as he knew that she and Jack would have crawled into bed with Kathy. He opened the door and shouted.

"Kathy, get up! Get the kids out the house—the truck's on fire! Hurry!"

Kathy reacted instantly, reaching for Jack. John shepherded them out the front door then hastily put on some jeans and a shirt, grabbed his cell phone and wallet, and followed them out. Kathy took the children to the next-door neighbor, while John ran around to the front of the house. Taking a deep breath, he opened the garage door. The flames were bigger, but the fire was still contained under the hood of the truck. He backed off and took out his cell phone to call 911. A neighbor across the street came running with a hose, and then another. But as John finished the call, he turned and was stunned to see that the entire truck was ablaze.

The flames were rising, and although the men persevered with the hoses, they were soon driven back by the intensity of the heat until the hoses were completely ineffective. Before long, there was a solid wall of heat driving the ever-growing crowd across the street. The truck was completely engulfed now, and Kathy's car had begun to burn. There was nothing more that John could do but watch. *Where was the fire department?*

Where was the fire department? Kathy had joined John across the street, and they just stood and stared at their burning garage. The house was old, and she knew it would burn quickly and easily. There was a *whoosh* and a surge of red and blue flame when the fuel tanks caught alight, and then the house itself began to burn fiercely. By the time the fire trucks arrived fifteen minutes later, it was out of control. The firemen hosed it but only to ensure it didn't spread to the other houses. The fire was too far gone to be stopped.

It felt surreal to Kathy, watching her house burn down. Even more surreal was watching it with the firemen standing next to her. On impulse, wanting just to do something, she grabbed John's phone to call the insurance company, and then she prayed to thank the Lord for waking them, sparing them. She was calm, and as she watched, she found herself thinking not of the house but of things she knew that were in it: photos, her flute from when she was small, yearbooks, and her drawings and poetry— her dark, angry drawings and poems. Memories, both good and bad, being swallowed up by the angry flames, rising to heaven like a sacrifice.

John's trip to India, scheduled in just two days, flashed through Kathy's mind, and then a stab of panic as she thought of Kristen's school recital that evening. Looking down, she saw Kristen and little Jack next to her in their pajamas. There was no way they were staying at the neighbor's house with all this going on.

Immediately, her maternal instincts kicked in. It broke her heart that her children were barefoot and poorly dressed like this with all these people here. Then she realized that she had no clothes to dress them, no money, and no wallet. She didn't even have somewhere to take them. She felt completely helpless. Bending to pick up little Jack, to love and protect him, she felt a hand on her shoulder. It was a distant neighbor she waved to occasionally.

"Can you use these?" She handed Kathy a bag and turned to go. Opening it, she found children's clothes and shoes. For a second, Kathy stood bewildered. *How could she know?* She dressed them right there in the street. The clothes fit both of them perfectly, and she prayed a silent, emotional prayer to thank the Lord for this small gift of grace in her time of need.

But she could not feel emotional about losing her home. Although her neighbors and friends offered words of support and sympathy, she was really okay with it. It really showed her that she had left material things behind. She smiled ironically as she recalled that she and John had recently decided to scale down, clean out the excess. Well, they sure had done that today.

By the time Kathy's parents arrived, half the house had been reduced to a smoking pile of ash. The rest was riddled with burn, smoke, and water damage, and the stench was appalling. Kathy's father looked around silently at all the devastation, and he turned to Kathy with a pained look of love, sadness, and compassion. His daughter was in trouble, and although he desperately wanted to help her, there was nothing he could do. As she looked into his face, she finally let go and broke down in tears.

The next day, they all went over to see if anything could be salvaged. It was hopeless. Kathy's father bent to pick up a toothbrush as Jack came running excitedly with a burned Lego table. He sat and cleaned it with Jack perched happily on his knee. The two of them were an oasis of calm and hope in a desert of devastation. It was a poignant picture that Kathy would always remember.

As the firemen left, Kathy suddenly remembered the recital again. It was tonight at a downtown middle school. With a stab of anxiety, she remembered the handmade dresses that Kristen was to wear. They must be in the trunk of her car. She grabbed John's phone again and called the dance teacher. "Mary, it's Kathy. Do you have any idea where Kristen's dresses are?"

"Why, they're here, Kathy, with me. No need to worry. I don't know why you left them here last night. I was going to call you, but I got busy and just put them away safely for tonight."

Kathy breathed a sigh of relief, closed her eyes in one more silent prayer, and then got down on one knee to talk to her six-year-old daughter.

"Are you okay, honey? Do you still want to dance tonight?" Kristen frowned.

"Sure I do. Why wouldn't I?"

And she sure did. She danced her heart out, and her proud mother gave thanks to the Lord for her daughter, her dresses, and for reminding her that day of his love, protection, and faithfulness.

And it didn't end there. They went to a hotel to find space to think and rest. Someone arrived with new swimsuits for the kids. It was just what they needed, and they swam for hours. Who would think of buying swimsuits?

The house sat for six weeks while Ford Motor Company investigated the fire. A faulty cruise control was the cause. Insurance would enable them to rebuild the home and maybe buy two used cars, and that was it. But their church responded and surrounded them. Over the next couple of months, John and Kathy experienced God through the generosity and love of friends and strangers alike. Cars, food, clothing, toys, bikes, and most everything else they needed was provided for them. Even before they had finished rebuilding the house, furniture started to come.

One man was closing a furniture store and had the inventory all stored in a warehouse.

"Take what you want," he said.

"I'm redecorating my daughter's room. Would your daughter like her bed?"

"My mom's in a nursing home. We're replacing the dressers. Can you use them?"

But the most remarkable blessing came the day after the fire. The Heeremas were in a restaurant having breakfast, trying to get back to some normality, when a smiling couple approached their table. Kathy recognized them; she thought the woman was a teacher at First Baptist Academy, the school affiliated with their church, but she didn't know them. Their two children were in the same classes as Kristen and Jack.

"Hi. I'm Kevin Carter, and this is my wife, Jennifer. We heard you guys had a fire at your home."

"Our ex-home," said John, smiling. He introduced Kathy and the kids.

"We're really sorry," Kevin went on. "We were just talking. We have a rental property, a condo, that maybe you could use until you get settled."

"Well, thank you for thinking of us. Where is it?"

"It's in Bay Colony."

Bay Colony! We can't afford Bay Colony. John could only smile.

"Thanks anyway, Kevin. I appreciate it." But Kevin persisted.

"Think about it, and we'll talk later, okay?"

They traded phone numbers, and the Carters left. Later that day, watching TV in the hotel room, John got a call from Kevin. He told him very directly that there was no way that they could afford Bay Colony, not even with the insurance payout, so there really was no point in pursuing it. A short while later, Kevin called back.

"John, Jennifer, and I will agree to take whatever the insurance pays out."

John shook his head in bewilderment at Kathy, sitting across the room.

"Kevin, that still won't work. We're not sure yet that we'll even get an insurance payout. Besides, we don't want you to lose rental on your condo with the season coming. So thank you, but no."

John was relating this strange conversation to Kathy when the phone rang again.

"John, Jennifer, and I want you to stay in the condo for as long as you need. This is not about money; it's about helping you guys."

"Kevin…"

"And we won't take no for an answer."

The Alley

At lunch the next day, Jennifer told Kathy the reason for the Carters' insistent generosity. They had recently experienced the Lord's protection and mercy in a life-changing way, and they wanted to pass on the blessing. Even as the fire raged, word had reached First Baptist Academy, and the teachers had hurriedly gotten together to pray for the Heeremas. As she prayed, Jennifer clearly heard the Lord telling her that she and Kevin should offer their condo to the Heerema family. That evening she told Kevin, and they resolved to call the Heeremas the next day. The very next morning, they were amazed to find the Heeremas breakfasting at the same restaurant. Kathy was intrigued. What was this experience that the Carter's had had? She was all ears as Jennifer explained.

Alligator Alley is the name given to the section of Interstate 75 that crosses Southern Florida from Naples to Fort Lauderdale. It cuts right through the Everglades swamps, and travelers can see swamp and alligators all along the route on either side, hence the name. The Carter family was driving east in their Mercedes SUV to spend the weekend in Miami. They had tickets to the Miami/Florida football game.

They had only recently moved to Naples from Memphis, Tennessee. After visiting Naples several times, they felt very drawn to it, and to First Baptist Church. Kevin ran a successful business from home, so they decided to make Naples their home. They had two children, Josh, seven, and Lindsay, five, a beautiful home, a great church, and a perfect life. In fact, that is what they were discussing as they drove along the Alley that Friday at noon. The Lord had blessed them so much, and they felt they needed to become more involved in ministry at their new church. Kevin's recent prayers had been requests for the Lord to place him in a ministry where he could serve.

It was a beautiful, sunny day. It seemed the whole world was going to the game because there had been heavy traffic all the way. Kevin glanced over to see mile marker 40 go by, and as he looked ahead again, he saw a dark, forbidding wall of rain coming toward them. It was enormous and angry.

"Wow, Jen, look at that!" he commented. Kevin had heard how the Florida rainstorms just creep up on you, but he had never experienced it. Before long, he drove into it. It felt like passing through an invisible curtain; this side dry, the other torrential rain. The noise was deafening, and he had the windshield wipers working overtime just to see.

Suddenly, Kevin felt the rear of the SUV slide left. He tried to correct it but couldn't. He braked but kept sliding, and he knew they were hydroplaning, heading toward the swamp on the right. With a sickening feeling, Kevin realized he'd lost control. All he could do was grip the steering wheel.

"Oh, no, Jen!" was all he said. His first fear was that he would hit another vehicle. There was a bump and then a crash, then silence and another crash, and silence again. Although they were moving fast, it was all in slow motion, like a dream.

Lindsay screamed, "What's happening?"

Jennifer held on to the handrail on the roof with one hand and the side of Kevin's seat with the other as she turned her head towards her children.

"It's a ride, honey, like Disney!"

They seemed to still be moving at high speed. There was a high-pitched screech from the roof, and the reeds and grass sounded like an old typewriter as they slapped the windshield. In some strange way, it was like a Disney ride. Jennifer prayed silently, "Please, Lord, don't let us hit anything, or be impaled."

And then they stopped. There was sudden, total silence. The ride had come to an end. For a couple of seconds, no one moved, and then Kevin and Jennifer both reached for their seatbelts, then Lindsay's and Josh's. They were disoriented, panicking, and as Lindsay fell hard onto her head, they stopped, realization coming that the vehicle was upside down. They were now all sitting on the inside roof of the car. It was eerily dark and gloomy, almost phosphorescent, and strangely silent. Jennifer looked around frantically, saw the horn, then put her foot on it, and pushed. It gave a tiny blast, and then trailed off to nothing.

Feeling around his door, Kevin grabbed the handle and pushed hard with his shoulder. It opened a couple of inches and then jammed. But as he opened it, a flood of water burst in. He slammed it shut as the reality of the situation hit him. They were completely under water. He had to get his family out of here. Holding back the rising panic, he tried again with his shoulder, giving it everything he had. He got two more inches, and a whole lot more water inside. He tried again, and this time the door would not budge. As he slammed the door shut once more, he knew he had to stop this. The water was already up to their waists.

He was breathing hard, trying to stay calm, to think it through; but then he saw through the gloom that water was trickling in through the air conditioning vents, and it filled him with dread. The water was now above their waists, and still rising. They were running out of time.

Kevin turned and found Jennifer's eyes in the dim light. He shook his head slightly.

"I don't know what to do." He said it calmly, but his eyes told Jennifer that her worst fear was real. He couldn't open the door wide enough for them to escape. If he tried, he would drown them all. He couldn't save them.

Jennifer, panicking, reached for the button of the sunroof, thinking they could escape that way. Kevin tried to stop her but was too late. It opened a tiny crack, water bubbled up, and then it stopped. That too was dead, and now more water was seeping in. She climbed in the back to see if they could get out that way, but the luggage was wedged somehow, and she couldn't move it.

Josh spoke, quietly and urgently.

"What are we going to do?"

They grabbed the kids, Lindsay with Jennifer, and Kevin with Josh, and they prayed. The water was now almost up to their chests. They prayed. They cried out to God to save them. "Lord," cried Jennifer, "please save my children. Please save my children." Through her tears, she heard Lindsay, quite calm. "Mommy, if we die, will we be with Jesus?"

Jennifer gripped her as tight as she could and bit her lip.

"Yes, honey, we'll all be with Jesus."

Suddenly, Kevin's door opened, and as the water poured in, a white-shirted arm came around, fingers probing, gripping, and pulling the door. Kevin reacted instantly. He turned to face the door, wedged himself as best he could, and then pushed with his legs.

The door gave a little. Kevin pushed again, both legs straining. He screamed out in despair and panic, and the door opened eight inches. It was enough. Kevin quickly squeezed Josh through, then took Lindsay from Jennifer and pushed her through the gap as Jennifer yelled.

"Swim, you two! Swim just like in the pool!"

Jennifer was next. Kevin had to hold his breath as he squeezed through, as the water was now over his head. He swam to the embankment and pulled himself up onto the grass. Jennifer was on her knees, holding Josh and Lindsay close to her. It was still raining. Kevin looked back, hardly believing what they had just been through, and all he could see were four tires poking up from the water. *Were we in there?* he thought. Jennifer was hugging the kids, talking to them, comforting them. Kevin closed his eyes and prayed, "Thank you, Lord, thank you, Lord," and then he turned to their rescuer.

"Thank you so much." His voice faltered with emotion.

"I was passing on the other side of the highway," the man said, "and I saw you slide and go through the fence and then roll over and over. Nobody seemed to be stopping, and I felt I just had to help you, so I turned around at the median and came back. I'm glad I found you alive."

Kevin stared at him. He wanted to say so much more to this kind stranger, but he just couldn't find the words. How do you thank someone for saving your family? The man was soaked to the skin and covered in mud, the suit and tie he wore now ruined. He nodded over Kevin's shoulder.

"You better check on your family."

Kevin turned and sat next to Jennifer. She was holding her children as if she was never letting them go. The four of them were shoeless and plastered with mud. Jennifer looked up at Kevin with wide, tear-filled eyes.

"Kevin, we are all okay."

He smiled and nodded, not understanding, still in shock.

"That's great, Jen."

"No, Kev, I mean we have just been in a major accident, and none of us has a scratch or a bump. This was a miracle, Kevin."

Then Kevin thought of a question he wanted to ask their rescuer. Is he a Christian? Does he know Jesus? Would he pray with them? He turned to ask him, but he wasn't there. He had gone.

They wept as they prayed because they knew the Lord had spared them this day.

The rain stopped, and the sun came out clear and bright to dry them and warm them. The man in the dive suit disappeared under the water, looking for a place to attach the winch. Kevin wondered vaguely what his SUV would look like when they towed it out. He looked at the two policemen stationed on either side of the car, shotguns at the ready, eyes scanning the water. Kevin hadn't even thought of alligators and snakes, but these guys took them very seriously. One policeman, eyeing Kevin carefully, asked him if he was sure they were all okay, because he reckoned they had rolled four times.

Later, at the hotel in Miami, they tried to remember the man who had saved them. Kevin thought he was young and blond, and Jennifer remembered him as middle-aged and dark. Why hadn't he stayed or even given his name?

The day after the phone calls between them, John and Kevin also met to see where this friendship might lead. John also had a surprise for him. Kevin's name had struck a chord with John when they first met in the restaurant, and later that day, he realized who Kevin was. Jim Powers had told John that there was a guy in his Bible Life Group that had been showing intense interest in Jim's India trips and in the Big Life ministry. He often came to Jim privately with questions about India, asking to see photos. Jim asked John to pray for this man because the Lord was clearly stirring his heart. His name was Kevin Carter.

"You know, Kevin, I've been praying for you," said John, smiling at him. Kevin looked puzzled.

"You've been praying for me? You don't even know me."

"I know that you are in Jim's BLG, and I know you are interested in Big Life."

"Wait a minute," Kevin said, pointing at him. "John, you're the John from Big Life! The other India guy!"

"That's right, and I'm going in two weeks if I can get Kathy and the kids settled. Come with me," said John, smiling.

Kevin thought for a second and smiled back at him.

"Sure, why not. It's time I went, I think," replied Kevin.

It was the start of his new spiritual journey and the Lord's answer to Kevin's recent prayers.

Jeff and David

Kevin Carter was not the only man to be fascinated by Jim Powers' stories of Big Life and his trips to India. Jeff Gibson also attended Jim's BLG. He didn't know Kevin, and he had no idea that someone else was being drawn in to Big Life just as he was. But Jeff cornered Jim often, asking endless questions.

Jeff had no idea why. Up until a short while ago, the thought of missions left him cold. When the pastor talked about missions, it irritated him. Mission work was for missionaries. But something about this Big Life thing made him think hard about people on the other side of the world that didn't know Jesus. Jim's stories were so graphic. They made these Indian people seem like, well, like real, ordinary folks who need Jesus. And there were millions of them. It was staggering. It seemed like Big Life was making a difference there, and Jim was on fire when he spoke of it. Jeff wondered why, and he began to have thoughts of maybe going to India to just check it out. But all he did for months was talk to Jim.

Then early one morning, as he was going to the dentist, he saw John Heerema sitting in the coffee shop next door. His next appointment was the following week, same day, same time. As he drove there, he thought about India and John again, and he said aloud, "Lord, if I see John Heerema at that coffee shop, I'll ask him if I can go to India."

Sure enough, there was John, sipping his coffee, working on his computer, but Jeff lost his courage and walked straight past. "Lord," he said, in the dentist waiting room, "if John is still there when I leave here, I'll ask him."

John was still there. Jeff took a deep breath, went in, said "hi," sat down next to him, and dived right in.

"John, I'm really intrigued with your Big Life ministry, and I know this sounds crazy, but I was thinking that maybe I should go on a trip to India."

"Sure, Jeff. Jim's leaving next week," replied John with no hesitation. He picked up his phone and started making calls, and seven days later, Jeff had a ten-year visa, all his injections, and he was on the plane to Kolkata.

It was not the first time that the Lord had spoken to Jeff. One Saturday night in the fall of 2001, two years earlier, Jeff and his wife Frances were attending church, and before the service began, Pastor Wicker addressed the congregation.

"I have a special appeal tonight," he announced, "for a boy named David Nicholas, who will die unless donors can be found."

Jeff couldn't believe it. David? Chuck and Debbie's son? He knew these people. He had rented their guest house when he first came to Naples.

The pastor went on to say that David had cystic fibrosis, a disease of the lungs. Two donors were desperately needed, as only a double-lung transplant could save David. It was the pastor's fervent prayer that at least one donor would come from David's own church. The pastor asked for prayer and for willing people to come forward to be tested, to see if they could be a match. The donor would have to be in good physical shape, O+ blood type, below forty years of age, over six feet tall, and a non-smoker.

But there were other conditions, apart from the medical requirements. If chosen, the donor would have to fly to Los Angeles for surgery, paying all their own travel, insurance, and expenses. They would be unable to work for several months. It was tough.

But as Jeff sat there, he felt the conviction of the Holy Spirit pouring all over him. The Spirit said, *That's you, Jeff. You're a match. You meet all the criteria.* He wondered what Frances was thinking. She had not turned her head to look at him even once since the appeal was made.

The service went by, and Jeff took in none of it. Not one word. He couldn't speak or turn to look at Frances. He was completely filled with the Holy Spirit telling him that he had to do this for David. Toward the end of the sermon, he found a prayer card and a pen and wrote, "Do you know I meet all the criteria the pastor talked about?"

He handed it to Frances. Still not looking at him, she read it, took the pen, and wrote back,

"I know. It's all I've been thinking about. You have to do it."

Later, at home, they talked and prayed until early morning. On the credit side, neither of them had a shadow of a doubt that Jeff was being called to offer his lung to help save David. On the debit side, they had two young children, the youngest not even a year old.

What if something went wrong with the surgery? Jeff had just taken sole ownership of his business. How could he leave it for months on end? Where was all this money going to come from? What about air flights, hotels, medical expenses—all kinds of other expenses. Lord, how can this be? It was completely illogical. Crazy. It was as much a risk for Frances as it was for Jeff, but she insisted that all she wanted was to follow the Lord's leading. Eventually, they were too tired to think, so they went to bed agreeing that they would decide for sure in the morning.

They both woke up feeling absolutely certain of the Lord's will, so they drove to the Nicholas home. When they arrived, they prayed in the car, and Jeff cautioned Frances that they must be tactful, carefully establish the facts, and not make rash promises until they and the Nicholas family were comfortable that they were all in agreement that it should be done. Frances nodded her assent. Nervous as a ninth grader on a first date, Jeff knocked on the Nicholas' front door. As Debbie opened it, he smiled and opened his mouth to speak.

But Frances spoke first.

"Jeff is going to be the lung donor," she said. Jeff just turned and stared at her, speechless.

Debbie invited them in. She was calmer than both of them. She hadn't been to the service the night before, as David was unwell, but she was pleased that the pastor had made the appeal. She listened to Jeff explain how they'd listened, and how they'd prayed.

"Well the bottom line, Debbie, is that Frances and I were both convicted to help David, so we would like to explore if I could be a donor. We have no idea how we will pay all the expenses, but…"

"What do you mean, Jeff?" Debbie interrupted.

"The air fares, the medical costs, the—"

"Oh, no," she interrupted again, "there must be some mistake. All costs are covered."

Jeff blinked at her for a few seconds, then looked up to the ceiling and breathed in deeply—really deeply. *Thank you Lord, thank you Lord. Now all I need is for the angel Gabriel to manage my business for a year, and everything's covered.*

Debbie spoke, very quietly and deliberately. Frances could see the exhaustion in her face.

"You mean, you two were prepared to do this for David, even if you had to pay everything?"

There was silence for a second, and then Debbie lowered her head and began to weep.

"Debbie," answered Jeff softly, "it's not about what we are prepared to do. It's not about us. We just have to do what the Lord wants, and we feel the Lord telling us to do this."

Jeff had the tests. They chose other donors. He thought the Lord was testing him, just as he had tested Abraham with Isaac. The ram in the bushes was, of course, the chosen donor. In some strange way, Jeff was disappointed. He prayed, "Lord, you know I would have done it, you know it."

But the Lord wasn't done. Jeff got a call a day before the surgery was scheduled. One of the donors had backed out, and they wanted Jeff for more tests and possible surgery. The next day, he and Frances flew to Los Angeles, and on that flight, he recognized a man from his church, a Bible Life Group leader. They chatted, and yes, this man had also put himself forward for David, and he was also going for tests.

Jeff was selected, but this man, a true brother in Christ, stayed at his side at the hospital to encourage and support him as he went through the surgery. By the time they were back in Naples, they were firm friends, and Jeff and Frances were soon attending his Bible study group. This man was Jim Powers.

Jeff gave one-third of his right lung to David. The young man lived another four years and six precious months. Jeff thought it was entirely worth it, not just for David, but for him. He felt that the Lord had blessed him in a very special way. He was amazed at how the Lord moved. In making this sacrifice for David, Jeff had met Jim Powers, who led him to John Heerema. Now he knew the Lord had a plan and a purpose for him, and it involved India, and Big Life.

JOHN

"Great is our Lord and mighty in power;
his understanding has no limit."

The Lord Moves

India was where the real focus had to be. After his return from the last trip, John had enlisted prayer partners at First Baptist, praying for protection against this spiritual attack and that the ministry would continue to receive the Lord's blessing. The success of the ministry was in God's hands and his hands only. John was now not prepared to make any decisions without him. He prayed and fasted, and the Lord began to move. Suddenly, Ani was on fire again, and Mr. Mondal began to see success. Benjamin was quick to note that certain evangelistic approaches were bringing early success, and from this, a strategy began to develop.

The Big Life church planting teams always prayer walked a village before approaching it for permission to show *The Jesus Film*. While setting it up, they played games with the villagers. As evening approached, they told the villagers about Jesus, showed the film, prayed, and then invited the villagers to come forward if they felt led to follow Jesus or know more about him. Their initial aim was to establish a weekly fellowship immediately. In the case of a Muslim village, the fellowship was known as a Jamat.

Medical camps were a special blessing. The Big Life teams liked nothing more than partnering with Christian doctors to bring medical help and drugs to villages that were suffering from disease, disaster or hardship. Many fellowships were begun as a result of reaching out in love in this way.

These fellowships would most often be accepted and allowed in the villages with the approval of an elder or influential figure within the community. Many times, this man didn't just allow the fellowship, but he offered his own house to conduct it. The regularity with which this happened was a great encouragement to Benjamin and John because they knew that this man was the 'man of peace,' taken right out of the Gospel of Luke.

> After this the Lord appointed seventy-two others, and sent them two by two ahead of him to every town and place where he was about to go. He told them, 'The harvest is plentiful, but the workers are few. Ask the Lord of the harvest, therefore, to send out workers into his harvest field. Go! I am sending you out like lambs among wolves. Do not take a purse or bag or sandals; and do not greet anyone on the road.
>
> 'When you enter a house, first say, 'Peace to this house.' If a man of peace is there, your peace will rest on him; if not, it will return to you.'
>
> Luke 10:1–6

Obedience to Jesus' teaching in these verses became standard practice for the Big Life church planting teams. They sought the man of peace with boldness, knowing that it was the Lord's will, His very own strategy.

Baptism of converts took place at the earliest opportunity. The Big Life church planter would attend each week, until God raised up the natural leader, or pastor, and the fellowship was functioning.

A pattern developed. Villages began to open up to the gospel message. Elders were allowing *The Jesus Film* to be shown, and people were coming out to see it. In one village, 500 people crowded around to watch. Fellowships were forming, Bibles were distributed. But other things began to happen, things that were amazing even Benjamin.

People told the Big Life teams to go to the village up on the hill, where their uncle lived, or over the river, to their cousin's village. They wanted to see *The Jesus Film* too. New believers were coming forward, offering to be the leader of the fellowship, wanting to be the one that reads from the Bible. And soon, as the fellowships matured, people were approaching the Big Life teams, usually young men full of the Holy Spirit, asking if they could join them in their work, wanting to travel to other villages to tell people about Jesus. Young men like Bablu.

When Ani's team first came to Bablu's village to show *The Jesus Film* he watched with his friends, expecting to have a good time. But as the movie progressed he found himself drawn in. A defining moment was when Jesus raised a young dead girl back to life. Bablu was amazed. He was a true Hindu, and believed in many gods, but none of them could do this. He did not sleep that night, nor the next, and he only found peace in his heart when he accepted that Jesus is the true living God. He bought a Bible, was baptized by Ani, and grew in his faith. He attended a fellowship and was soon boldly telling his family and his village to stop praying to idols made of wood that cannot answer prayer. After some months of evangelizing he asked Ani if he could join him in his work, and Ani let him operate the projector.

Ani sent Bablu to Christian Bible Club for a year, and then trained him to be a church planter. He soon planted five fellowships of his own, totaling about 280 people. Each week in these fellowships there were prayer requests for healing of sickness, addictions and relationships, provision of jobs, and other needs. Each week he heard how the Lord had miraculously answered these prayers, and he saw clearly how He was at work in people's lives.

John was soon amazed and humbled by the growth of the ministry. He continued to fast and pray constantly to stay close to the Lord and to discern his leading. He and Kathy now had Jim Powers, Jim Evans, Kevin Carter, and others working with them, volunteering their time, energy, and resources. Jim Evans, an MBA, was a numbers man, and he began the necessary but difficult task of tracking the numbers of fellowships, their locations and size, and how often the church planter visited. They built a website, moved into a larger donated office, and made plans to support their now completed ministry mission statement: "To Empower, Equip, and Encourage local believers to reach their own people with the gospel of Jesus Christ."

Big Life was exploding, but so were the costs. John and Kathy could not support this growth alone, and they needed to raise funds. Their church family had been more than generous in continuing to donate, but it wasn't going to be enough.

They staged Christian music concerts with First Baptist as the venue. The concerts raised awareness of the ministry, but as a source of revenue, they were not successful. John was challenged to think differently, raise funds more creatively, but in the end, he rested in the assurance that God would provide, just as he always had and always would.

By the end of 2004, Big Life fellowships were alive and flourishing in forty-five villages in West Bengal.

BENJAMIN

"…more and more men and women believed in the Lord and were added to their number."

Acts 5:14

"But the word of God increased and multiplied."

Acts 12:24

Acts in Action

I t was early February 2007. He had just put down the phone after talking to John for some time. He sat back in his chair to consider the news. So it seemed his old dream of going to the USA was finally going to come true. Not only going there, but preaching at a major church. There was to be a function at First Baptist Church of Naples in April to raise much needed funds and prayer partners for Big Life, and he, Benjamin, would preach to the people of Naples. John wanted him to touch their hearts.

How could anyone's heart not be touched by what God had done over the past three years? How could he even describe it?

India is a country of 1.25 billion people, and 75 percent of them live in villages, just like the ones Ben's church planters were visiting every day. Although Christianity had been introduced to India 250 years ago, the country remains 80 percent Hindu with Muslims accounting for a further 13 percent, and Christians numbering less than 3 percent. India produces sixteen million children every year. That is three-quarters the population of Australia—every year. India has the complexity of 6,400 castes, 1,618 languages, six ethnic groups, and twenty-nine major religious festivals. *Big Life has much work to do*, Ben reflected, and it was important that he impress these facts upon his audience in April, so that they understand the urgent needs of the ministry.

The book of Acts records the beginnings of Christ's church, how the disciples, empowered with the Holy Spirit, by faith in Jesus Christ, grew the body of believers through love, service, miracles, and discipleship. From a dozen disciples and one apostle, hundreds and then thousands came to salvation in a remarkably short span of time. In cities, towns, and villages, they had met to fellowship wherever they could, in any available house, often changing the venue as persecution followed them. But the venue was not important, as the church back then was not a building but the growing body of believers. The reason for their meeting, the spreading of the story of salvation through Jesus, was everything, and they were driven to tell the Good News throughout the known world.

Over the past three years, Benjamin had seen God's plan repeated, and he gave the title "Acts in Action" to the work that God was doing. The Big Life teams had prayed over hundreds of sick, addicted, and troubled village people, and this was a serious business because to most, prayer was their only recourse. The vast majority of them did not have ready access to a doctor, had never even seen one, and many could not afford to get help from the local witchdoctor, so they prayed sincere but futile prayers to their gods.

But God's response had been miraculous. Where prayers were offered in the name of Jesus Christ, villages reported healings of long-standing illnesses, diseases, addictions, provision of work, and reconciliation of families. The testimonies of these people went out not just to their own village but also to surrounding villages. Soon, many other people were seeking Jesus. Perhaps their own prayers would be answered?

Ben also saw God's hand in the people's obedience to baptism. In the western culture, baptism represents a commitment to Jesus as Lord and Savior and a passing from the old life to the new life in Christ. In India, Christian baptism represents all of this but is also a rejection of all other religions, gods, and practices that were formerly followed. As a consequence, families, communities, and tribes can be deeply offended when one of their numbers is baptized. There is often more persecution after an individual is baptized than when he initially declared his salvation because it is his declaration that there can be no going back.

God was working in other ways too. He had raised up many men and women who were now serving as church planters and as house church pastors. Benjamin was amazed at how many of these men and women had quickly shown themselves to be natural disciples and disciple makers. Many had felt the call to spread the gospel before being directed to Big Life and had begun one or two fellowships on their own, just as Ani and Mr. Mondal had done.

These men found that they had a gift for teaching and encouraging others and were eager to put it to use. The Lord had shown the Big Life leaders both in India and in the USA that discipleship was paramount in the plan he had orchestrated, and he was now showing them the strategy.

Benjamin saw this strategy illustrated clearly in the early church in Paul's words: "And the things you have heard me say in the presence of many witnesses entrust to reliable men who will also be qualified to teach others" (2 Timothy 2:2).

This incredible verse, just like the strategy, is simple, clear, and powerful. Men are to be taught the gospel and then taught to teach the gospel—Paul to Timothy to reliable men to others. That is four generations of discipleship.

Ben had quoted and taught this verse often to his leaders. It became the guiding principle on which the ministry grew, and they all knew the scripture as " 2-2-2." It was a reality in the ministry, and over the past six months, the multiplication of churches had threatened to outstrip the church planters' ability to disciple them all. God's answer to this was the second part of 2-2-2. The "reliable men" that had been raised up were now being trained to teach others, so that third and fourth generation churches were empowered and equipped to continue the process. With this discipling method, there was no barrier to explosive church growth. It was multiplication, and it truly was Acts in action.

The ministry was financially supporting church planters to free them to devote their time to the work they loved and were called to. Benjamin was extremely cautious in selecting them, mindful that 2-2-2 demanded "reliable men." Selection would come after much prayer, and the candidates were required to show complete commitment to Christ and the strategies of the ministry as a team member for a number of months, and demonstrate a hunger for the lost. Only then would a permanent position be considered. Benjamin always assigned experienced men to disciple and train them. They were expected to bear fruit in the ministry within this training time and to be undeterred by spiritual attack and the threat of persecution that would inevitably come. Provision came from the fellowships they began and mentored in line with Luke, chapter ten, once more: "Stay in that house, eating and drinking whatever they give you, for the worker deserves his wages…When you enter a town and are welcomed, eat what is set before you." (10:7-8)

Benjamin reflected that over the centuries different cultures in all parts of the world have worshiped many gods. Many fantastic temples, testaments to man's ingenuity, were built in their honor. But over time, these are all destined to end in ruins. There is only one God, and his everlasting temple is alive in the hearts of all believers through the Holy Spirit. The early church was successful in proclaiming the good news in pagan cultures against all odds, and Acts in action was again apparent in the developing of Christian community as the Big Life fellowships grew in numbers and attendance. Many were coming to Christ because they saw the love that these Christians have for each other and for everyone they come across, just as in the early church.

Ben knew that God was not just blessing Big Life but driving it. Ben was just a facilitator, a channel, as were John and the other leaders in the USA. At the end of 2005, there were 102 fellowships meeting weekly, and by the end of 2006, this had more than doubled to 215 with 2,795 villagers attending. What would 2007 bring? Benjamin was confident it would bring a harvest because the Lord continued to bring the right leaders to Big Life—men like Robert.

Born into a strict Buddhist family in Calcutta, Robert was a rebellious child. By thirteen, he was experimenting with drugs and drinking rice beer. His parents sent him away to school in Darjeeling to remove him from the bad influences in Kolkata, but he became aggressive and soon began drinking hard alcohol. He developed a love of music, and soon discovered that the only time he found relief from the anger he felt inside was when he played guitar and sang.

He rejected his parents' religion because he saw no reason to worship his ancestors as they did. But he knew he was seeking something because it constantly troubled him that he felt no peace in his heart.

"My aunt, a Christian, told me to pray to Jesus; he will help you," Robert said, "but I was with a bad crowd and would not listen."

Then disaster struck in 1987 when his father became mentally ill. He was unable to recognize anyone, to speak or hear, and appeared to be in a trance. The doctors could not help, and his mother tried everything, even witchcraft and mediums, but with no success. Eventually he was institutionalized. Without his father's income, Robert's family was threatened with ruin.

"My aunt took my father to a Christian fellowship, and they prayed over him many times. A month later, he was completely healed and back at work, and the doctors had no idea what had cured him. I will never forget how the Lord saved him. My parents and my brothers and sisters converted to Christianity immediately."

But Robert didn't. He thought Jesus was a powerful god, but just a god of healing. He went back to Kolkata where he became seriously ill himself. His drug and liquor abuse had accelerated, and although he knew he was killing himself, he could not stop. Through the pain, at last, he cried out to Jesus as he lay in a hospital bed.

"Lord, if you will forgive my sins and help me on the right path, I will give my life to you. Please help me." Robert was 22 years old.

He left the hospital a week later an energized, changed person, knowing that the Lord had healed him just as he had healed his father. He met a pastor from Sikkim who discipled him, and he became hungry for the Bible, reading it at every opportunity. Soon, he was evangelizing and preaching, and had planted three fellowships in Calcutta. He found he had a gift for teaching, and he became well-known among Christians all over the city. In 1998 he was offered a teaching position at the Shepherd's Discipleship school in Siliguri, and he worked there for eight years. By 2006, he had taught over 2,000 students.

But he felt the Lord calling him to something more, something bigger. Previously, in 1997, at age twenty-seven, he had met Benjamin in Calcutta when they preached together at a Christian gathering. They talked about God's calling, and Benjamin told of his dream to bring the gospel to the villages. Robert was enthralled and began thinking about the villages constantly. By 2006, he was convinced that God was calling him to plant churches, and he resigned from the school. He had no means to support himself, and for a while lived only on peanuts; but he rejected an offer to go back to teach, saying he only needed the support of his wife and of his Lord, and he had both.

After a joyous reunion with Benjamin in Calcutta, his journey with Big Life began. Robert went back to Siliguri, a perfect base to oversee work in Northeast India, Nepal, Bhutan and Sikkim. He currently oversees 128 fellowships in these regions, and is seeing constant growth.

"Before I joined Big Life, I had no strategy. Now the young men come out to join me. Benjamin has helped me so much, and John Heerema has been given a vision from God. I want to make disciples and pour my life into them. I know that the younger generation watch me, and they know my story, and they see how my life has changed, and they follow the path to Jesus.

"He is my master, and I am a worker in his field. He has shown me that if we take on greater responsibility, he will equip us because he is faithful."

The Lord had also shown Benjamin that the ministry was not to be confined to West Bengal, India, or to any human borders. God was weaving a global tapestry. Work in Nepal had taken shape and was growing through the leadership of Prem. Born in Nagaland, in the far northeast of India, Prem was brought up in a strong Hindu family that worshipped thirty-three gods. As a teenager, Prem excelled at school and was a gifted musician. He developed an inquiring and astute mind. Although his rational thinking told him there must be a God, he could find no peace with Hinduism, and he talked to religious leaders and read religious books copiously, searching for the one true God. He met with a church pastor who listened to him patiently then told him that one day the Lord would call him. There is only one way to eternal life, he said, and that is through Jesus Christ. He is the one you are seeking. Soon after, reading the Bible, Prem was riveted by Jesus' words.

"It is not the healthy who need a doctor, but the sick…for I have not come to call the righteous, but sinners" (Matthew 9:12).

Prem remembered that the Hindu god Krishna had said, "I have come to kill all sinners, and save the righteous one." He was riveted by the truth of Jesus, and he knew that at last, he had his answer. Falling to his knees in tears, he asked Jesus to come into his life. He was a sinner, and through pure love Jesus had come to earth to save sinners like him, not to destroy them.

Persecution from his family was immediate. His sisters and brothers called him a low caste because Christians eat cow. His father agreed and warned him that Christians and Muslims are not allowed in his house. Prem, seventeen years old, more knowledgeable than all his family, demanded to know where it was written that Christians are low caste, or Muslims, for that matter. His father physically threw him out of the house.

For three years, he lived on the charity of Christian brothers, doing whatever menial work he could find. Desperate to finish his education, he worked in the day and attended night school in the evenings, and he prayed each day for the Lord to soften his parents' hearts and to bring them to salvation.

Then, almost four years after his expulsion, his father unexpectedly sent word for him to come home. Prem was terrified, not knowing what to expect, but a Christian friend, a convert from a high Brahman caste, agreed to go with him. The reunion was tense at first, but then Prem's parents asked many questions about the Jesus he was worshiping. Prem answered them all, silently praying for the Holy Spirit to help him. Then, as Prem played guitar and sang Christian songs, his friend quietly brought both his parents to tearful salvation. Prem wept with joy, thanking God for answering his prayers.

He knew he had to grow in the Word, and a pastor gave him admission forms for Grace Bible College, three days' train journey across North India. His father gave him the money to travel there. He was so excited he didn't even fill out the forms, and when he arrived at the college, another prospective student tearfully told him she had been rejected because she had not sent her admission forms in before arriving for the interview. Trembling, Prem found an empty room, filled out the forms, and prayed for the Lord to help him. Later, waiting in line with many others, he saw a man watching him. Eventually, the man called him out and took him to an office where he questioned him. It took Prem some minutes to realize that this was an interview and that the principal was conducting it.

"I will accept you for six months, and if you work hard, I will make it the full three years," he concluded.

Prem earned a bachelor's degree in theology and went home to Nagaland to work in the Baptist church where he served as an evangelist, then as youth pastor. He spent four years in Hyderabad, South India, working at Discipleship Training School before going home again to be pastor of his home church.

Because of his fluency in Nepalese, Prem was asked to accompany a missions team from Santiago, Chile, to Nepal. This was to change the direction of his life. When they arrived in Katmandu, Prem felt the Lord calling him, and he knew he had to come back to this place to evangelize. Some months later, he resigned as pastor of his church and returned to Katmandu.

He found work teaching music at a school and started a small house church, which rapidly grew. It grew so rapidly in fact, that the local Baptist church forced Prem to stop it. "This is our area," they claimed. "We have rules and regulations here." The church took over the fellowship, but within two months, it had stopped meeting, so Prem started a new one, which quickly grew to over one hundred members. Eventually, the people raised funds, and a church was erected. This soon grew to be a congregation of almost two hundred from the surrounding villages, supporting Prem as its pastor. He was joyous, believing that God had revealed his plan for him. But God had other plans for Prem.

In 2001, Prem was asked to speak and sing at the Christian Youth Connection event in Katmandu. This national gathering, held annually, was attended by thousands of young people in the cities of Nepal. Prem met another speaker there, a small dynamic man from Kolkata by the name of Benjamin Francis. They were instant friends and stayed in touch regularly. Ben captivated Prem with his vision of bringing Christ to the villages, forming a house church in every single one. Prem was gripped by the stories of how God was working through Big Life.

Four years later, Ben came to visit Prem with Jim Powers, and Ben and Jim asked him to join Big Life. Prem was taken aback.

"But what about my church?' he asked.

"Prem," Benjamin replied softly, "It is a wonderful thing that you are called to be pastor of your church, and that you care so much. But what if the Lord is calling you to be pastor not of one church, but of a thousand churches?

It was a turning point. Of course, Ben was right. Prem prayed right there for a new vision, a God-sized vision. God answered that prayer too, and part of the answer was turning his church into a training facility, where today, Big Life church planters are discipled every week so that 1,000 churches can be planted for his glory.

Benjamin smiled as he thought of his brother Prem, and his smile widened as he suddenly thought of his precious four-year-old Abigail. What would she say about him going to America? Just the other day, she had sat him down for one of their talks. She looked up at him with her gorgeous brown eyes.

"Daddy, why do you have to go away so much? I miss you. Where do you go to, anyway?"

"Well, my darling," Ben replied, "I go to tell all the people about Jesus because they need to know him, just like we do. Everyone has to have the chance to go to heaven."

Abby frowned.

"Did Jesus tell you to talk to them, Daddy?" she asked.

"Yes, he did. He told me it is very important."

She made a decision.

"Then, Daddy, you must go. You have to do what Jesus says. I will tell everyone that Jesus said."

Benjamin bowed his head. He prayed that the trip to Naples would be successful, that the Holy Spirit would give him the words to touch the people's hearts, that prayer partners would be found, and that the fundraising efforts would bear fruit. He prayed that his words would honor God, give him all the credit, and glorify his wonderful name.

KATHY

"…do not worry about what you will say…for the Holy Spirit will teach at that time what you should say."

Luke 12:11–12

Kingdom Mathematics

They had moved into the new house in January 2005. It was smaller, simpler, and all that they really needed. It hadn't taken long for Kathy to turn the house into a home, even with all the donated furniture, and she was happy here.

It was a blessing having Benjamin stay at the house. She was nervous about cooking him curry, but he was a gentleman and a charming guest, and he ate hamburgers, pizza, and hot dogs as if he had done it all his life. She enjoyed having him around with his constant smile and easy manner, and she was looking forward to hearing him speak in a few days.

One evening, chatting in the living room with friends, Benjamin cornered her and surprised her.

"Kathy, you need to come back to India."

She considered him. *Was he serious?* She hadn't been to India since 2003, almost three and a half years ago.

"I don't think so, Ben. The ministry is doing fine…"

"But I have a great burden for you to come back, to lead a women's conference, to teach our women."

"Ben, we are empowering locals to reach locals. They don't need me in India. You guys can organize the conference. You have amazing people around you. My role is here, to support John and the team…"

"Will you pray about it, Kathy? I think you will find I'm right."

He smiled. She found his smile and his confidence a little disconcerting.

The sanctuary was full with 2,000 people, and he didn't disappoint. He was humble and humorous. He was soft and powerful. He was passionate and mesmerizing. He made light of the bullying he had suffered as a boy.

"They used to say, 'Hey, shorty, what's it like being so small? How's life down there?' And I would reply, 'You know what? I'm four feet eleven, but I know I'm going to heaven, and that makes me feel ten feet tall!'" There was applause as the audience warmed to him.

"People in my grandfather's village paid the old man to hit them on the head with a stick to cure them of headache," Ben declared. This was met with open laughter. "But this was no joke to the villagers; it was part of their belief system. How sad is that?" The laughter turned to silence.

He talked of his beginnings with Big Life.

"A friend said to me that he thought it was risky for me to leave my job to join a ministry without even being certain of pay. I told him there was absolutely no risk in giving up what I knew I would eventually lose for something I was certain to gain forever."

He talked of how Big Life was evolving.

"God constantly changes Big Life. I know I'm on the right road, but I never know what lane I'm in. The goal for 2007 is four hundred churches. It is only April, and we already have three hundred. The Lord is teaching us mathematics. He says you think one plus one is two, but in My kingdom, it's eleven! Kingdom mathematics is multiplication, not addition, and the Lord shows us how to achieve it.

"The harvest is plentiful, but the workers are few. So we pray to our Lord, asking him constantly for workers, and he sends them. Not a week goes by without someone asking to join us in our work. You see, the Lord goes before us, and he prepares their hearts. And yes, there is persecution, but the presence of God is the provision of God to go before, through, and over any danger that may come. So we persevere, like Paul. I discovered today that by this time tomorrow in West Bengal, there will have been eighty-seven baptisms, twenty-five of them Muslim."

He told of God's great works in the ministry. He told stories as he pointed to photographs on the giant screen.

"This woman was a powerful medium, worshiping the goddess, Kali. In this picture, you see her house full of hundreds of idols, and in the next one, you see them all going up in smoke as she burns them in a pile in the center of the village after giving her life to Christ. Can you imagine the power of her witness to the villagers there?

"This teenaged boy was full of anger and hatred. He was so violent they had to chain him to stop him from hurting people. After the villagers prayed to Jesus, he was healed, and here you see him smiling, arms around his family.

"This woman, Tapashi, was beaten and forced into prostitution by her husband. Here she is being baptized. Soon after this, she was able to forgive her husband, and she brought him to Christ. Today, they evangelize together.

"Here is the ice-cream seller who came to Jesus after reading a tract. He now travels village-to-village, selling ice cream and giving out tracts. He has three fellowships. This man is a snake catcher and has become a great preacher. When he preaches, you can be sure he has everyone's attention! This lady, Ethika, is a schoolteacher, and on weekends, she plants churches. This lady, Martha, was spending her life savings building a temple until Jesus stopped her in her tracks. There are so many more stories like these, stories of transformed lives."

His close was an impassioned plea that showed his heart.

"As a child, I loved to lie next to my father, and I would put my ear to his chest to hear his heartbeat. I was spellbound, listening to it beating so powerfully. It went *ba-boom, ba-boom*. Now I listen to my heavenly Father's heartbeat, and I hear it saying *ba-boom, none should perish; ba-boom, none should perish*. As long as I hear this, I must keep moving, because I cannot stand still. Please, won't you join us in our ministry?"

Before he left to return to Kolkata, he had one more plea to make. He asked Kathy one last time to come back to India. Since she and Ben had last spoken, she had prayed about it and talked it over with John, who supported the idea, and Ben was delighted that at last she agreed.

WOW

Kathy had no ideas, so she spent time in prayer asking the Lord what he wanted to achieve with this conference, how it was to be structured, and who would attend. Soon, two things happened that made the whole idea come alive for her, and they both involved Gillian, Benjamin's wife. It was Gillian that came up with the name Women of the Word, or WOW as it became known. The name gave the whole venture structure and purpose, and Kathy began to get excited. The second thing was that Gillian emerged as a gifted organizer. Communicating by phone and email, the two women hashed out all the details, problems, and strategy of the conference, which was set for three days in October. Kathy was responsible for the content of the conference, and Gillian was to communicate with the ladies, enroll them, arrange travel to Kolkata, and find lodging.

Putting together a teaching program was a real challenge for Kathy. It had to be relevant and practical, something the women could relate to and be inspired by. But there were multiple languages to deal with and a completely different culture. Some of the Big Life leaders' wives were actively involved in the ministry, such as Mrs. Mondal, but most just looked after their homes and the children while the men were away.

Kathy knew these women had no idea what to expect from such a conference. Their husbands met often for discipleship training as this was standard practice now in Big Life, but the women didn't. She had nagging doubts. *Would they have the motivation to even want to come? What would the women take back home with them from the conference?* She was acutely aware of her reliance on the Lord here, and she prayed earnestly.

For Gillian, the conference was a logistical nightmare. She was attempting to bring these women into Kolkata from all over West Bengal and as far away as Siliguri. Nothing like this had ever been attempted before. It was unheard of for village women to leave their village. None of them had attended anything like a conference, none of them had been on a train, none of them had been to Kolkata, and few of them knew each other. It was a terrifying prospect for each one of them. She was careful to enlist the agreement and help of the church planters, as they too would have concerns about their wives' safety. Gillian found and rented a facility with a huge meeting room and dormitory style bunks and prayed that the conference would fill the entire place. She dealt with endless questions from dozens of concerned church planters, leaders, and others with endless patience and love.

Kathy worked hard on a teaching schedule with three friends from her Bible study group, who had also agreed to go with her. One of these was Jody Carroll, a trusted and faithful friend. Jody had been an unwavering supporter of Big Life even from John's days in Iran. The women planned to talk about God's portrait of marriage, parenting, and spiritual gifts. There would be workshops, testimonies, and forums. It was a big undertaking. She was nervous, and when it was prepared, she gave it to the Lord, asking him to bless the event and everyone attending it.

Eventually all the plans were laid, and the two women could do no more. Kathy called Gillian, to encourage her, and to seek encouragement.

"So, Gillian, everything is in place. You've sent the invitations?"

Gillian's unusual Indian-English accent made her reply upbeat, as it always did. "I have. I also contacted every church planter and fellowship leader one last time, asking them to pray about allowing and encouraging their wives to come. But I stressed that it is voluntary, as we agreed."

There was a silence.

"They have to come, Gillian."

"They *will* come Kathy. The Lord will bring them, you'll see."

Three weeks later it was Gillian's turn to call Kathy. She was quiet, hesitant, and Kathy was immediately apprehensive.

"I think I have most of the replies from the ladies, Kathy."

Kathy's heart started beating faster. "You don't sound happy, Gillian. Is it bad?"

"I'm sorry, I'm just so emotional. Kathy, one hundred and fifteen are confirmed. It's incredible. I'm so humbled. The Lord is so good."

"Praise the Lord," was Kathy's breathless response. She was too stunned to say more.

They were uncertain and nervous. They came in like lost sheep, sat down, and didn't move. Nobody spoke; they just stared impassively at Kathy. She smiled and went along each line, welcoming them and shaking their hands, but they were clearly uncomfortable with this. Some of them even seemed to recoil from her. She sought Benjamin, desperate to find out what she was doing wrong. He calmed her and told her gently that shaking hands was not the way. He put his hands together in front of his face and gave a slight nod. "Like this, Kathy. Relax; it's okay."

It was okay. The Lord took control. Over the next three days, the women bonded beyond Kathy's wildest expectations. These women, pastors' wives, church planters' wives, were challenged to rise up as Christian women and get involved in their husbands' ministries and even begin their own ministries. They responded magnificently. Gillian was a revelation. She was energized, knowing that the Lord was showing her his plan for her, the plan she had waited for before she had even met Benjamin. A natural teacher, she confronted and stimulated the women. They responded, expressing their thoughts and their fears, and sharing ideas. They laughed and they cried together.

On the last morning, they began the day with praise and worship, and it went on for the entire morning, right through the teaching time. They sang and prayed in four different languages, raising their hands and their voices in praise of Jesus Christ. They were on fire for the Lord. It was glorious, and Kathy openly wept with joy. It was beautiful and God-honoring, and Kathy believed they all experienced a small glimpse of heaven.

At the end, Kathy addressed them all, expressing her deep appreciation to all of them. As she put her hands together, preparing to say good-bye the way Ben had shown her, a tiny woman sitting in the front row silently rose and approached her. Kathy stopped speaking, taken aback by this. Then the woman, suddenly full of smiles and tears, flung her arms around Kathy in complete abandon, and hugged her hard. Before she could react, there was another, and then another, all embracing her, all crying joyfully. Kathy burst into tears herself. There was no other possible reaction. She was so happy to experience this.

She had prayed for a mountaintop experience here, but God showed her she was aiming way too low. She knew the Lord was talking to her. *See, I am opening this door for you. Come join me in my work.*

Kathy thought back to her earlier years, before she knew the Lord. He had lifted her from years of pain and uncertainty to a life of purpose, peace, and blessing. She now lived with the sweet joy of Christ at the center of her life. *He is so good, so good*, she reflected. Her heart soared as she thought of Paul's beautiful words in 2 Corinthians 5:17: "…if anyone is in Christ, he is a new creation; the old has gone, the new has come!"

She would be back. He had more work for her to do.

JOHN

"My name will be great among the nations…says the Lord almighty."

Malachi 1:11

"Be still, and know that I am God;
I will be exalted among the nations,
I will be exalted in the earth."

Psalm 46:10

Awesome God

He finished praying, got up off his knees, and sat down at his desk. The peace and tranquility he had felt as he prayed stayed with him, and he began to reflect. It had all happened so quickly, but here he was at the end of 2009. The Lord's blessing of the ministry was an awesome, humbling thing. From the beginning, John had always tried to think God-big, but over the years, he was discovering that thinking God-big was something that everyone in Big Life could aspire to but never achieve. God's big was beyond imagining.

They had set an optimistic goal of 500 churches to be raised by 2010. At the time, mid-2006, there were just over two hundred. After consistent prayer and to remind themselves that they were aiming for world impact, in January 2007, they doubled that goal to one thousand. Then, to honor God, they doubled it again. They settled on 2,010 churches to be raised by 2010. That's a ten-fold increase in churches in two years. It seemed like they were reaching for the moon.

But 2,010 churches were raised before the middle of 2009. It was as if God was saying, *Why reach for the moon? Can't you see the stars?* By the end of 2009, just a few months later, the official number was 2,755 churches. Forty-four thousand four hundred ninety souls, previously Hindu, Buddhist, and Muslim, were now worshiping and praising Jesus Christ as their Lord and Savior and meeting weekly to study his Word and grow in their faith. It was astounding to John that at the end of 2009, the Lord had almost doubled the number of churches existing at the end of 2008, and the number of people attending had more than doubled—in one year. Since 2004, Big Life had shared the name of Jesus with over one million people.

The Good News was now flying ahead of the Big Life teams, carried on the wings of personal testimony and active discipleship. Prayer was being answered, and people were telling other people, teaching other people, and training other people. And God was being glorified. Wasn't this the purpose of the Great Commission? Big Life leaders were now also actively assisting in training, encouraging, and discipling other evangelical movements wherever there was a need.

The Big Life leadership team had a dream, of third and fourth generation churches multiplying and spreading the gospel everywhere. Could this dream come true? They had believed that with prayer it could, because nothing is impossible for God. And it was happening. There was still so much work to do, but God is faithful, and they would persevere.

God had shown them the 2-2-2 strategy directly from his Word. Following 'Acts in Action', the approach of disciple-making discipleship through indigenous Christians has led to multiplication of believers and churches. John prayed ceaselessly that Christians would get back to this realization, and that more ministries like Big Life would be raised.

John smiled to himself as he recalled some of the challenges Big Life had experienced, and how God had provided the solutions. The dramatic growth of the ministry inevitably had led to some questioning about the numbers of churches/fellowships and the number of believers attending them. *Christianity Today* expressed interest in publishing an article about Big Life in the fall of 2008, and they approached the South Asia director of the International Missions Board for verification of Big Life's reported numbers. He called for a report from two senior field operatives and eventually made a statement to *Christianity Today* that in their opinion, the Big Life numbers were too low.

John had immediately realized that the authenticity of these reported numbers is of prime importance, and he gave over the management of it to Jim Evans, who had joined the ministry immediately on his return from that first incredible Big Life trip. Distances, time delays, and cultural contrasts make accurate reporting challenging, but Jim insists on having complete records of each church planted, including the church planter, the church/fellowship pastor, and the number of attendees each week. If these details are not available, kept, and updated, the fellowship is not included in any report. This means that the numbers reported are always lower than they actually are and always some months behind, but it is a situation that John and Jim are comfortable with. If the numbers are beyond reproach, they can focus on the real task of winning souls.

Another area in which the ministry had to be beyond reproach was the integrity of the employment process. This was tested when a ministry that was vacating West Bengal offered eighty-four of their trained workers to Big Life. This ministry sent these men out in teams of two to show *The Jesus Film*. It was a great deal; if Big Life would take them on, the outgoing ministry would pay half their salaries for two years. John was excited at the prospect of instant church planters at half price. Benjamin personally screened them, but it was found that their primary motivation was the salary, not their faith. Big Life didn't take one of them.

Overall, John was pretty pleased with Big Life's employment record. Of all the hundreds of church planters, and in seven years, they had lost just over thirty. One made a morally poor decision, eight went over to other ministries, and twenty-five left because they found the work too demanding.

John was also humbled at how economically the Lord had structured the ministry. He had read that it takes most ministries worldwide an average of $200 to reach a lost soul for Jesus Christ. But Big Life employs local church planters to reach the lost in their own country. In India, the cost of living is very low, and a dollar goes very far. A church planter earns $100 per month. This seems an amazingly low figure, but it will support his family and his ministry needs—Bibles, tracts, traveling expenses, etc.

Because of this, and the fact that the overwhelming majority of funds received in Big Life go directly to the mission field, the average cost of reaching a new believer is currently $26. That's the cost of five fancy cups of coffee.

But funds were always an issue because even though the costs associated with the ministry had been remarkably low, Big Life was growing, and growth requires funding. There never seemed to be enough, but they always got by.

Fundraisers, particularly those held at First Baptist, were a real blessing and brought in not just regular donors but committed prayer partners, who John knew were more valuable than money.

There had been disappointments. There had seemed to be an opportunity to begin work in North Africa, and many meetings were held to explore this possibility. But in the end, after much discussion, fasting, and prayer, it was felt that the Lord was not leading Big Life in this direction yet.

There had been personal challenges too. John had lost his sweet mother, Jean, to stomach cancer in June 2006 after a six-month illness, and then the following year, little Jack had to spend two weeks in the hospital to overcome orbital cellulitis, an invasive infection that threatened his sight. For one terrible week, Jack had not responded at all to treatment, and John and Kathy were on their knees begging for the healing that eventually came.

In the middle of 2008, Kathy had been made a very attractive job offer back in the business arena. The salary was excellent. But after prayer and fasting, both Kathy and John felt the Lord telling them that she was to stay in the ministry. If it was another test, they'd had bigger ones.

John was so proud of Kathy. Women of the Word had exploded, and Kathy had gone back three more times after that first conference to lead others in Nepal, Siliguri, and back in Kolkata. She was energized, telling John that she had been inspired by how these ladies had grown spiritually in such a short time and how blessed she was to be part of their lives. The women reported that they were active, front porch evangelists at home, and they were now supporting their husbands in a more meaningful, vital way. They were leading Bible study groups in their homes, discipling other women, and many of them even began to travel with the men, being part of the Big Life teams at medical camps and at follow-up visits. Their numbers had also grown significantly.

Gillian was still teaching, organizing, and encouraging. Right now, she was leading a group of women to teach others how to disciple. Kathy was working on a new training method, a four- to six-week small group study based on women of the Bible that can be reproduced and passed on, some of it oral, as in the village tradition, and some of it written. She wanted to continue to challenge these ladies to be women of faith.

And John had stayed faithful to the men that the Lord had sent to him. Pat Stuart, living far from the Big Life home base but still with his heart in the ministry, was elected to the Big Life Board, as were John Van Proyen, John's friend in Christ since middle school, and Forrest Head. Jim Powers had eventually felt the call to ministry elsewhere, but John would never forget Jim's huge contribution to Big Life, the constant encouragement, the countless trips, the unfailing loyalty, the way the Lord had used him to bring Jeff, Kevin, and later, Jason Gerlach to Big Life through his passionate BLG leading. Jim would always remain John's brother in Christ.

The others were now fully engaged in the ministry— Jim Evans as director of statistics, and Jeff Gibson as director of development and the one responsible for fundraising. Kevin Carter, after his life-changing accident, committed to Big Life after that first India trip and is director of administration, while Jason Gerlach is director of prayer.

Jason came to the Lord in college through his sweetheart Jody, who was later to become his wife. They moved to Naples in 1999 when Jason took a position as a golf course superintendent, just as John had seventeen years earlier. Driving into the club for his first day of work, Jason saw a rare sight: a fox was eyeing him from the cover of the bushes. He stopped to look at it, as foxes are usually nocturnal and shy, but it was gone in an instant.

Jason and Jody were soon attending First Baptist Church and Jim Powers' Bible Study Group. As Big Life began to take shape in 2003 and Jim began to recount stories of the villages, Jason was deeply touched by the lost spiritual condition of the Hindu and Muslim people. Jim introduced Jason to John, and soon Jason and Jody went together to India. A second trip followed, with Jody leading a Women of the Word conference with Kathy and Jason visiting Muslim villages and a mosque. He was thrilled to witness to an Imam and have him accept a Bengali Bible.

Jason felt deeply committed to the Great Commission after reading Herb Hodges' superb work, *Tally Ho the Fox!* a brilliant manual for the Great Commission. The book describes through Scripture how Jesus' strategy for reproducing discipleship enabled the early church to see explosive growth. Hodges then shows the relevance and urgency of that same strategy today.

He makes the point that thousands of men and women have a vision for global impact and hundreds formulate a strategy, but only a few go out in faith and complete obedience to do it. Jason was taken by this, and he saw John Heerema as one of these men.

The book ends with the explanation of the title. Hunting dogs will sleep, accept other dogs, and live to secure their own survival until a fox goes by. Then their sole purpose is a single-minded chase to catch the fox. In the analogy, the fox is Jesus Christ, and the dogs are his church, following the scent of the Great Commission.

Jason took over the prayer duties from Jim Powers in 2006, and he came onto the staff of Big Life in 2009. On his last day of work at the golf club, Jason was stunned to spot another fox, the first he had seen since his first day of work ten years previously. It immediately brought *Tally Ho the Fox!* to mind, and he resolved there and then to follow Jesus and the Great Commission, come what may.

During his journey with the Lord, John had learned the importance of staying close to him in prayer. The Lord had always moved when Big Life was working in obedience. One of John's principles now was to seek him and listen for his voice in order to be in step with him and not ahead of him nor behind him as he had been so often in the past. John and Jason began to issue a weekly Prayer Wall email, and they called for prayer partners worldwide to give a commitment of thirty minutes each week to pray for both general and specific Big Life needs, from major ministry issues to requests for healing for individual villagers in the remotest areas. It is a striking fact that as prayer partner numbers increased, numbers of churches increased in parallel fashion—a humbling but compelling reminder of the power of prayer.

And of course, there was Aaron working in Pakistan.

He and John had become close friends since the baseball days, and Aaron had kept tabs on John's progress. He had traveled to India and seen the Big Life model achieving great things. Aaron was convinced that it would work in Pakistan, and he began working closely with John in 2008 to implement the Big Life strategy there.

From a base in another country, Aaron had spent time studying Christian efforts in Pakistan. The country has 2.8 million Christians, about 1.6 percent of the population, but these are largely "cultural Christians" that have Christian roots dating to British colonial times. They are treated as a low caste group by the Muslim population, and so persecution of Christians continues to be common and widespread today.

Officially, there is "freedom of religion," which means that other religions aside from Islam are allowed to exist; but there is also the blasphemy law, which forbids any overt or implied criticism of the Koran. Christians that evangelize run the significant risk of falling foul of it, and this is what happened to Peter, one of Aaron's Pakistani leaders.

Peter had put together a massive distribution in Karachi of thousands of New Testaments and DVDs of *The Jesus Film* around Christmas time. A colleague was arrested by the police but betrayed Peter in exchange for his own freedom. Peter was arrested on four different blasphemy charges, each of which was punishable by death or imprisonment. Christians managed to ship him out of the country just in time, and Peter was later granted refugee status by the United Nations.

Even as a refugee in a foreign country, Peter went out daily to evangelize and disciple and brought many to salvation. But he was broken for Pakistan and became depressed, thinking that his dream to bring his country to Christ was over. Soon though, he and Aaron put a plan together. Peter chose ten Pakistani men that he knew as obedient Christians and invited them to his new country for training to begin a new ministry. They came, and Aaron and Peter equipped, empowered, and encouraged them.

These men were the first Big Life leaders in Pakistan. Every week, Peter contacted each of them to follow up on their progress, and mentor them. Then he and Aaron would find ways to support them and supply their ministry needs. Two months after that first meeting, Aaron flew in to Pakistan to meet with them and set up formal discipleship training for men that these leaders had chosen to be church planters. Over the next three months, a total of 120 men were trained. Two months later, there were eighty house churches active and a total of 996 decisions for Christ. Aaron was astounded.

He knew that Muslim villages in Pakistan were not like Hindu villages in India. One didn't just go marching off to a friend in the next village to tell him that he's discovered that Jesus is the way, the truth, and the life. In Muslim villages, there is a stigma of fear about strangers. Anyone coming to call is regarded with suspicion, even other Muslims. For Christians to evangelize in a Muslim village, where a response could be a hand grenade thrown into your own fellowship, careful preparation is vital.

Aaron flew to Pakistan to check it out, to see these home churches in action, and to discover what they were doing to achieve such positive results. What he found was that the leaders were using the training they had been given to hone in on what they already knew about Muslim people. They knew that Muslims don't need more religion. They also knew that there are many who are desperate to find the living God who can save them and change their lives. And they knew that these people are not free to express their dissatisfaction or to ask questions about Jesus Christ.

So the church planters never mentioned the Bible. They shared their testimony, what had happened to them, and how their lives had changed. Five percent of people replied that they knew it's Jesus they were talking about and told them to stop. Seventy-five percent listened with little response. But twenty percent wanted to know more. This was where the Holy Spirit was working, and this was where the foundation was being laid.

Progress from there was rapid. One evening, Aaron called one of the leaders to get his report. The phone line was bad.

"Rafiq, I can't hear you. What did you say?"

"I said…sixty…"

"Sixty?…sixty decisions for Christ?" Aaron's heart soared. This was incredible.

"Sixty… to know…"

"To know what?"

"…about Jesus…"

The line went dead. Aaron's excitement turned to disappointment. He was pretty sure that Rafiq was telling him that the sixty were people that wanted to know more about Jesus—not saved. But the next week's call was a little different. This time the line was clear.

"You were telling me, Rafiq, about these sixty people. Were they saved?"

"No Aaron, they were not."

"So did you tell them more about Jesus?"

"Yes, I did."

"And how did that go?"

Rafiq laughed. "Well, this week's report is that all of them are saved, and fifty are baptized already. Praise the Lord!"

Baptism, a clear statement of Christian commitment and faith, is normally performed in secret. Reprisals can be swift and deadly, as many Muslims in Pakistan see baptism as a provocative Christian statement. It can take months of prayer and patient waiting before new believers can be safely baptized.

Aaron received word that one village in the southeast of the country was desperate. Crops had failed, there was sickness and disease, and many were fighting alcohol and drug addictions. People were at war with each other. One of the elders approached a Big Life church planter for help, and Aaron sent Ashraq, a master evangelist. An electrician by trade, Ashraq gave up his job to witness for Christ. He raised money by selling car parts that he collected on his evangelical travels. The Big Life churches he mentored called his car parts stash "the Jesus bank," and they called Ashraq "the truth warrior." The village was transformed. Ashraq brought the entire village to salvation in three days.

But along with success, there was the ever-present threat of danger. A regional leader, Timothy, was training two new believers to be church planters, and the three met in one of their homes to celebrate their first Easter. When Timothy left, neighbors kicked in the door and furiously demanded to know why they had allowed a Christian in their house. The two said nothing and were savagely beaten by the Muslim men before they left.

Two days later, they were dragged from their homes and interrogated. The same men demanded to know the name of the Christian and where he was from. The two believers stood firm, refusing to speak, and were taken away. Three hours later, the one believer's wife, at home with their four children, received a phone call telling her where her dead husband's body lay. Just down the road, the mother of the other believer received a similar call. A week after their first Easter, the two had gone to their eternal home with Jesus.

A few days later, Timothy sent a church planter to visit the wife and her children. It was a dangerous move, but Timothy was desperate for the welfare of that family. She told her visitor that she felt Jesus tugging on her heart. Islam made no sense to her any longer. The church planter brought the family to Christ. Less than a week after her husband's violent death, she and her children began to learn about the sweet love of Jesus.

Soon after this, the local Big Life leaders and church planters held an emergency meeting. John understood that they would be fearful, even reluctant to go out for a while. Perhaps some would lose heart and decide to give up. John, Kathy, and Aaron could only pray for them. But they were completely overwhelmed by the message that came from the meeting. It said they needed more church planters urgently because the gospel of Jesus' love needs to go out faster to prevent more people being killed.

John thought of Faizal, no longer a Taliban fighter but now a warrior for God, and of his incredible conversion. It's what happens when the truth of Christ meets evil.

God's Word, on a scrap of paper, the remains of a torn-up Bible, takes a man from the Taliban to God's army. Today, Faizal goes out to share the gospel every day regardless of the danger to himself and his family.

He and five others witness to the most extreme Islamic groups. They recently befriended six young men training for jihad who were attending a mosque known for its radical views. They showed them where the Koran points to Jesus, and the young men went home with Faizal, asking questions the entire night. By morning, all six were saved. When they told their families that they had accepted Jesus as their Lord and Savior, the families flew into a rage. It is a great privilege to have a son chosen for jihad, and to refuse is an insult to Islam. Their families would be disgraced, and the men would be branded as cowards and banished. But none of this prevented all six from being baptized soon after.

There was always persecution. John recalled the story of Samuel, a church planter in eastern Pakistan. Samuel was kidnapped by the Taliban in the spring of 2007. John and Kathy were heartbroken. At a church service one Saturday night, weeks after Samuel disappeared, Kathy broke down as the worship team sang, "My chains are gone, I've been set free." She thought of Samuel and how he was suffering in prison for his faith, just like Paul. She cried out to the Lord for Samuel's release and safety. At Bible study group class, she and John prayed with Forrest Head, and they all wept for Samuel.

They didn't know it then, but Samuel escaped the Taliban, and certain death, that very night. John and Kathy found out the following Tuesday that Samuel's chains were gone. He had been a captive for six weeks. But even though Samuel survived, John always struggled with how easy it was to be here, worshiping freely in America, and how hard it was for all these men to be there in Pakistan and all over South Asia, loving Christ in secret. And it was much, much harder when you knew most of them and loved them as brothers.

John's heart broke for these courageous Christians in Pakistan. On one trip, he met with all the leaders in a secret, remote place. They had a joyful time of praise and worship, and the reports from the regions were uplifting and positive. But John noticed something strange that the Pakistanis didn't notice at all. Although they were conducting the meeting miles from anywhere, whenever they spoke of the Taliban, the men spoke in a whisper. It was an automatic response to the fear that they lived with every day. But it didn't stop them from proclaiming the name of Jesus Christ every day. It touched John's heart and still affects him very deeply.

And the persecution wasn't just in Pakistan. In September 2008, John was devastated to receive the news that his beloved Ani, and two others, Waid and Rabiul, had been badly beaten by a mob of Muslim followers in West Bengal. The three had led many in the area to Christ and were meeting with a group of twenty-five Imams. The clerics had many questions and were showing peaceful interest as Ani used Koranic bridging to point to Jesus. But after some hours, a mob moved in, threatening and beating the three men. The Imams courageously stepped in to save them from probable death.

Particularly saddening was the sight of Rabiul's father screaming for his son's body to be cut to pieces and thrown into the river.

But John had also learned that where there was persecution, there was a powerful God ready to produce good from apparent hopelessness.

The situation in the Indian state of Orissa was at boiling point by mid-2009. The tribal peoples were alarmed at the anonymous threats to their religious leader, Swami Lakshmanananda Saraswapi. To them, he was more than a leader, he was a messiah. The people revered him like a god. From his base in Pulbarni in the Khandamal district he had devoted himself to the peaceful social upliftment of the tribal peoples for forty years. But as a Hindu he was vehemently opposed to their conversion to any other religion. There was tension between the tribal Hindus, the evangelical Christians, and the political Maoist extremists.

In August, the unthinkable happened, as Swami Lakshmanananda was assassinated. Anger erupted among the Swami's followers and mobs began to riot as the news leaked out. They wanted revenge, someone to blame. "It's the Christians!" someone cried out. "Kill the Christians."

Two hours after the assassination, in a village of 500 people not far from Kandhamal, a man came running out of the jungle. Although he turned many heads, he didn't stop running until he reached the house of Pastor Thomas, a Christian leader in this region. He opened the front door and slammed it behind him.

"You need to run," he said urgently, his breath coming in painful gasps. Thomas stared at him, confused.

"They have killed the Swami! They are looking for Christians, for Christian pastors. They are coming, you need to get away!"

Thomas looked at his wife. She immediately turned to gather the children. He turned back to the man. He was a Hindu from this village, and he had so far resisted Thomas's attempts to convert him, to enroll him in the 150-strong fellowship. But Thomas now knew he was a friend. "Thank you, Sunil," was all he said.

They barely had time to gather anything before they heard it. The sound of the mob came over, around and through the trees like thunder, angry and powerful. Thomas knew he had to get away before they surrounded the village. He also knew they would be looking for him. They would torture him and his family, and then slowly kill them. He moved his wife, his three daughters and his son to the edge of the jungle and he held them tight as he prayed.

"Father God, I thank you for alerting us, and now I beg you for protection for my family and for our village. Please, Lord, save us."

Panicked villagers were already fleeing, desperate to get away from the coming destruction. Turning to his family, he looked into their terrified faces. He pointed back, at the rising sound of fury and rage.

"You hear this?" They all nodded. "I want you to run from this. If we get separated, keep running, and always with this sound behind you." He looked into the eyes of his 17-year-old daughter. "Go with the little one, my darling. Look after her."

"Yes father," she replied. Then she took the hand of her 7-year old sister, who smiled bravely up at Thomas.

"And you two, stay together, okay?" The remaining two, his daughter, twelve, and his son, ten, also linked hands. "Let's go," said Thomas.

They joined the escaping throng melting into the jungle. They had no food, no water, no clothes. A small New Testament that he kept in his pocket was Thomas's only possession.

Staying together was impossible. Outside of their own village area it was easy to get lost in the dense jungle. They ran through it for three days before they realized that the two girls were no longer with them. Thomas and his wife were desolate, but there was nothing he could do except keep the four of them together, keep moving and pray that the Lord would protect his lost children. They had come across two villages where they knew Christians lived, and Thomas begged for food for his family. It was given to them, but they were told to leave immediately. The Christians were all gone, having either left or been ejected in an effort by the terrified Hindu villagers to prevent the coming violence.

They were told of a relief camp to the west that the police had set up to protect the fugitives, and Thomas led his desperate family that way. It took another nine days to reach it. They staggered into the camp exhausted, filthy and hungry. Driven by fear, they had stopped only to sleep, pray, drink water from the streams and eat fruit from the trees.

They were fed, assigned a sparse tent, and given clothes. As they recovered over the next few days in the relative comfort of the tent, Thomas could only think of his daughters lost out there, and weep, and pray. The stories began to filter through of the atrocities committed by the mobs. They had surrounded villages where known Christian fellowships existed, and tortured and beaten the pastors and the Christian followers until they denied Christ. Many did, to save themselves, but many did not. In all, fifty-five pastors were murdered in the villages around Kandhamal. Many homes were destroyed and burned, and many other people were killed. Horrific stories of children hacked to death and pregnant women cut up began to filter through, and confirmation of these stories added to the hopelessness in the camp. Thomas was on his knees, begging for his children, his people, his village, for the violence to stop.

He ministered to everyone he could, and began an informal fellowship. He encouraged the people to stay close to Jesus, and to keep their minds on their eternal home. His small New Testament brought hope to hundreds of people. Then on the fifteenth day, hope came to Thomas as his daughters arrived at the camp with a band of weary stragglers. He broke down in tears as he spotted them, frightened and exhausted. They were still holding hands.

After three weeks Thomas was summoned by the police officials and told he had to leave the camp. They told him that he could not take his family home. The district was in turmoil, and he, Thomas, was targeted for murder. He needed to be far away. They loaded his family onto a truck, took him to the nearest town, and gave Thomas a little money and train tickets to Mumbai. He was shocked; Mumbai was on the other side of India, and completely unknown to him.

The only work he could find there was manual labor. It was hard, and the family struggled. Thomas was heartbroken to receive the news from home that when the 200 rioters attacked that day they had killed two Christians in the village. One of these was his brother. In a neighboring village his aunt had been slaughtered. Most of the people who could not get away had suffered injury from machetes, swords, clubs, and homemade bombs, and many were seriously injured. Homes had been burned. It was a picture of devastation, of madness. And when they had finished their work, the mob went on to the next village, to do it all over again. His friends in Orissa told him he could not come home. They would kill him.

With his life in turmoil, Thomas was constantly in prayer, pleading for the Lord to show mercy to him, his family and his people. But when he received answers from the Lord, they were not what he expected. As he cried out for his people, for his own village, he began to feel a burden for the men responsible for these murderous acts. As Jesus was being nailed to the cross, he had cried out to the Father for forgiveness for those who were crucifying him. Thomas found himself weeping for these lost men in Kandhamal.

He was sent a DVD copy of a film taken secretly showing a scene in a market square in a town near his home village. It was taken from an upstairs room of a nearby building, and clearly showed the beating and torture of three Christian youths by a group of men, with dozens looking on, surrounding them. The film was dark and brutal, and shows the systematic killing of the three boys, one of whom was no older than twelve or thirteen. It broke Thomas's heart, but it also shocked him. This was no momentary outpouring of anger that could later be regretted. It was cold, calculated slaughter.

As the boys tried in vain to protect themselves, men much heavier than they stepped into the circle to mercilessly punch and kick them. As the boys doubled over in their attempts to evade the blows, the kicks were aimed at their heads and faces. As the men retreated, more stepped in to take their place. The boys were knocked down repeatedly, but desperately tried to stand, to cling to life. But after fifteen minutes they were just lying motionless on the floor, with men indiscriminately stepping in to kick them. Some stomped on their heads. But there was no crazed shouts or verbal abuse among the perpetrators, just cold, deliberate violence.

The film showed a growing pool of blood forming under the head of one of the boys. He was probably dead or dying at this stage, but still the blows rained down on him. The sickening ending showed a heavy-set man enter the ring weighing a large club in both hands. Standing over one boy, he raised it high and brought it down with great force onto his knee, crushing it. He then took time to position himself, and smashed the other knee. He carefully repeated this with the other two victims. Two of them hardly responded. Again, the mob was not shouting, screaming for blood. They just watched.

Thomas's heart broke as one of the boys, the smallest one, suddenly tried to get up. He struggled in agonizing slowness, and propped himself up on his arms, his back arched as he tried in vain to raise himself. The man with the club watched him for some seconds, then brought the club down viciously on the boy's exposed spine. His arms flew outward as the force of the blow somehow rolled him over. He lay motionless in the dirt on his back, his arms resting in the crucifix position, imitating the last moments of Jesus, his Lord and Savior.

One night, six months after his arrival in Mumbai, Jesus told Thomas in a dream to go home to Orissa. He wanted Thomas to continue his pastoral work, continue with his church. It made no sense, but the call was clear. He had to obey. Two weeks later he left Mumbai for Bhubaneswar, the capital city of Orissa, where he used his contacts, intending to start his life over. But the Lord spoke once more. He gave Thomas a clear message: not Bhubaneswar, but Khandamal. The Lord wanted him to go home. It was a terrifying prospect, but Thomas had no choice but to obey.

He wept as he stood inside what was left of his house. It had been demolished and then burned. He looked around the village, and there were many others just like it. The Hindu villagers were subdued, just staring at him, some of them clearly uncomfortable that he had come back. Most of the Christians had scattered, and nobody knew where they were. But as Thomas was driven away a little later, he had a peace, and he felt a purpose. After the violence, these people were without hope, and spiritually empty. They needed Jesus. Thomas had to continue his work. He rented a house fifteen kilometers from his village, and immediately began a fellowship. Six families, two from his village, attended twice weekly. Soon it was twenty families. In fellowship Thomas prayed for restoration and healing for the people, but he saved his most fervent public prayers for the men who perpetrated this violence in Orissa, that the Lord would forgive, and that He would do a mighty work in their hearts, to bring them to salvation through Jesus. There was much urgent work to do all over Khandhamal, and Thomas knew he could not do it alone.

One Sunday, after service, a man who had attended approached him, wanting to talk. His name was Raja, and he was with a ministry named Big Life. Raja had heard the story of Thomas's return to Orissa, and of the urgent need in Kandhamal. He offered Big Life's help. Thomas told Raja that the pressing need was to find and encourage the Christians, to find and help the remaining pastors and raise up new ones. It was imperative that Christian witnessing continue in Orissa. Raja assured him that this could be done. Thomas praised the Lord, knowing that Raja was an answer to prayer. Soon after, Benjamin Francis traveled to meet him, and Thomas began working with Big Life.

It took much effort to get the church in Kandhamal functioning again, but Thomas was on fire, completely obedient to the Lord's call. There were regular death threats, directed at all the pastors but mostly to him. But the Lord had told him to come home. He was where he needed to be. Soon, the Lord spoke again.

These men need to know me. They need my salvation. Thomas heard the Lord loud and clear. He had prayed continually for forgiveness for the men who had attacked the Christians, and now he stepped up the urgency of these prayers. He instituted a time of prayer at all services, for all Christians to cry out for the souls of these men.

It was during this prayer time at a service in his village that a man rose up and rushed forward, throwing himself at Thomas's feet. Thomas bent to help him rise. He was distraught, overcome with tears.

"Do you need prayer my brother?" Thomas asked. The man nodded. After some seconds, he lifted his head. The tears continued to flow, and his bottom lip quivered.

"Please forgive me, pastor."

"For what, my brother?"

"It was me, I was the one."

"What did you do?"

"I was the one who told them about you. I followed you, and I spied on you. I told them you were the leader, that the Christians would scatter if you were killed. The day they came, I was the one who led them to this village."

Thomas was shocked. He didn't reply. The man swallowed hard, then continued.

"More than that, I asked them if I could be the one to kill you. I was full of hate, and I was supposed to kill you that day. You and your family. Please forgive me." He wept bitterly once more, and fell to the floor again. As he looked down at him, a peace fell over Thomas, and he felt nothing but compassion toward this man. He bent down once more, to comfort him. The man turned his bloodshot eyes to Thomas.

"I want to know Jesus," he said. "I want forgiveness, and peace in my heart."

Thomas brought the man, Sirel, to Christ, and baptized him. Three weeks later, Sirel was working with a Big Life team in the tribal Hindu community, telling them of the peace and forgiveness of Jesus.

Over the next six months, over fifty fellowships were raised up in the district of Kandhamal.

A police presence has helped maintain the fragile peace after the riots, but the tension remains. Christians worship in the villages, but are still persecuted. They are often prevented from drawing water from village wells and from cutting wood in the jungle. There have been some attempts to disrupt Christian burial services. But the Christians in Kandhamal know that God is with them, that there is hope, and ultimately, there is victory.

The Big Life board had voted toward the end of 2009 that the ministry should begin to pay a salary to John and Kathy. John received his first paycheck in six years and his first ever from Big Life. He couldn't believe it was ten years—*had it really been that long? How had he and Kathy survived?* He had no idea, but the Lord had provided faithfully, just as he had promised. John had enjoyed this great adventure with the Lord, and he still believed in him, loved him, and trusted him with all his heart, all his mind, and all his soul. He would continue in obedience. *Where are we going now, Lord Jesus?*

The Lord has a plan and a purpose for each one of us, and he prepares us for it. John knew that his clubfeet and his near-death experience as a teenager had forced him to develop an unusual inner resolve to persevere. He needed to call on this determination years later as he struggled alone in India, sometimes overwhelmed with discouragement, making little progress while draining his resources.

In truth, John had felt sometimes as if he was on his own, but he later realized that he never, ever was. Step by step, lesson by lesson, the Lord had guided him and started this ministry. He had lost count of the number of overseas trips over the years, but it was close to fifty. *One every three months on average,* he thought.

And look at the people God had brought and was continuing to bring. Jim and Jeff had no interest in missions until God changed their hearts through Big Life. With the exception of Aaron, not one Big Life employee in the US or Asia has been formally trained for missions work. But God had raised up so many, at all levels, also wishing to serve him, trained only in obedience. They were his true brothers and sisters on this earth, people from vastly different cultures and backgrounds, but identical in their love for Jesus Christ—an army of faith. It was a comforting and satisfying thought that if John were no longer involved, Big Life would continue without him.

There was much work to do, and the task was daunting, but the people of God knew they had the promise of victory. All of India, Nepal, all of Pakistan, and all of South Asia would know Jesus. And so would Iran. He was still in contact with his brother, the Imam, whose faith remained strong in impossible circumstances. John treasured the prayer beads and often held them as he prayed for his brother and for Iran. Yes, John would get back to Iran. And then next—he didn't know what was next, but he knew that Jesus knows.

He was joyful, knowing that God was in control.

John smiled his shy smile. *What an awesome God we serve.*

PART TWO
June 2009

"From one man he made every nation of men, that they should inhabit the whole earth; and he determined the times set for them and the exact places where they should live. God did this so that men would seek him and perhaps reach out for him and find him, though he is not far from each one of us."

Acts 17:26–27

Aila

The van bumps along a poor, uneven road. It is a Tata, one of millions in India, somewhat hopefully described as an SUV. It is tinny, uncomfortable, and the air conditioning in this one is engaged by manually winding down the windows. Ten of us are squeezed inside, and it is 110 degrees, ferociously hot.

We are on our way south to the islands that have recently been ravaged by cyclone Aila. We are taking basic medical supplies to a village that Ani believes has been particularly badly hit not just by the disaster but also by post-cyclone flooding. Benjamin and his Big Life Indian team today, Ani, Patrick, Sam, John Thape, Tapan, Debu, and of course the doctor, Dr. Singh, have all commented that it will be pretty bad. We are praying that we will bring relief and the knowledge of Jesus to this village. We are only an hour out of Kolkata, and already there is water everywhere. It fills ditches on either side of the road, tumbles in fast-flowing rivers and streams and turns ponds into small lakes.

Kolkata—John and I arrived last night. After the long flight, via Dubai, there was the ninety-minute car ride to our hotel in the city. The traffic is heavy and noisy. The horn noise is an incessant blare in the dark. In New York, loud use of the horn is an aggressive statement, but here in Kolkata, it is just a polite "I am here." I find it amusing, but this morning, as we ride in the daylight, my emotions shift to apprehension and even fear as the reality check of Kolkata traffic hits home.

As the traffic lights change, I see that the road ahead narrows and five unmarked lanes turn to three. The blare from the horns rises like a battle cry as buses, vans, scooters, taxis, and motorized rickshaws rush headlong to get ahead. No one slows down. The vehicles miss each other by inches. I recall Forrest Head saying that Kolkata traffic is the world's biggest reality video game, and now I know what he means. Still staring out the window, I call out to Benjamin. "Hey Ben, how is it that these guys don't hit each other?"

"Count the side mirrors on the cars, my brother," he responds.

I look all over, and I can't find even one, so I turn to Ben. He's smiling and nodding back at me.

But I am excited to be here. John and Benjamin are leading the first national retreat in Darjeeling in a couple of days, and I will meet many Big Life leaders there. Some village visits are also planned, and having written already about the beginnings of Big Life in the United States, I am eager to discover more about the business end of this remarkable ministry, here in India. Who are these people that have brought salvation to almost 45,000 souls in just seven years?

This morning, rising early, we collected Dr. Singh, who will provide medical direction at the camp. He is wearing a white suit, which amazes me. While the doctor and Benjamin get into some healthy negotiations with a street pharmacy for medicine, I find some shade. Even out of the sun, it is oppressively hot. There are masses of people everywhere, and an endless procession of yellow taxis passes by.

Over the road stands a sidewalk teashop, some rough tables and benches positioned under the shade of a plastic sheet. I wonder at how uncomfortable it must be under that sheet, but the teashop is full of men, sipping tea from small plastic cups. Debu, a leader in the area we are to visit today, taps my shoulder and smilingly nods at the Tata. The medical supplies are loaded on top of the van next to the bags of food that were loaded earlier. We are on our way.

Sweat runs down my back as I introduce myself to Dr. Singh. He has taken off his jacket but still looks uncomfortable in his long-sleeved shirt, so I insist on him having the window seat while I sit in the middle. He speaks perfect English and is clearly an educated, cultured man. Below his striking jet black hair is a well-trimmed red beard with dramatic streaks of gray running through both. His gentle, friendly face is quick to smile. I ask him his story.

He was a Sikh from a high caste family. Ailing from a debilitating bronchial condition, he could find no cure until he found Jesus Christ, who miraculously healed him. He has dedicated his life to healing others with the gift the Lord has given him, while using his social position to share about Jesus.

Turning to my left, I nudge John. He has his head half out the window seeking air, but he turns to me with a smile.

"So what will we do when we get there, John?" I ask.

"We'll hand out the medicine, then we'll meet the man of peace."

"Man of peace?"

"Luke ten," he says. Knowing the importance of Luke chapter ten to the Big Life strategy, I reach down to the floor between my legs, recover my Bible, and read the passage over again. With today's village visit in mind, the Scripture tells me that we are to heal the sick and tell them the kingdom of God is near (verse nine). That we will do. And the man of peace will either accept us, or he will not (verse six). If he does, perhaps a church can be started. I turn to John again.

"So you expect to meet this man?"

"Absolutely," John replies. He leans his head out the window again.

The further we go, the more concerning it gets. The road is elevated, so our progress isn't slowed, but now there are only small islands of land on either side of us in areas where there used to be no water at all. Large trees have been flattened, some broken in pieces, like sticks. Soon, crude shelters line the road, dozens of them made of tree branches, reeds, and debris from the floods. We stop, and I get out to take photos. As the Big Life team hands out food packets and tell about Jesus, Benjamin explains that these people have had their entire village washed away, along with all their possessions, including their stores of food and grain. The side of the road is the only place they have while they wait and hope for the local government's assistance.

An hour later, we finally offload at a bustling market. I rush for the shade of a shop awning, but it is even hotter here than Kolkata, and the low bank of cloud above is adding humidity to the heat. It's going to be a long, uncomfortable day.

As always, there are people everywhere, and John and I attract a crowd, who stare at us quite openly. Patrick says we must take a boat, a *nowka*, across the river to reach the village, Chota Seari, some miles away, so we head off down a sloping lane to the waterside to board one. Fifty or so people climb aboard this strange vessel. It is shaped like a large Italian gondola and is difficult to stand in. The guys have a laugh at my expense as I dance awkwardly to the erratic pitch. The deck is filthy with what I take to be mud, but my nose soon tells me that cattle have left their mark. Patrick laughs.

"Can you imagine what Noah's ark must have been like?" he says.

"Yes, but I would rather have been on it than off it, Patrick," Benjamin replies with a grin.

John, Dr. Singh, Patrick, and I share the twenty-minute journey to the village on a motorized rickshaw. I ask the doctor what sickness he expects to find. He tells me he has bought extra drugs for stomach ailments, fever, and rashes because of the unsanitary water.

Again, the only dry area is the road, although much of it is under water and has to be negotiated. Patrick points out a flooded building.

"That's a school," he says, "and that was a soccer field."

I see the soccer goal about a foot above the water, which means the field is flooded by six or seven feet. There is water everywhere, and I can make out no huts at all, although people line the road on either side, and men wade waist deep in the water fishing for shrimp and crabs. Soon, the road becomes a path, and the path narrows and abruptly comes to an end.

Gathering our things, we see a woman working a water pump, filling aluminum containers. A pig roots around in the filthy mud at her feet, and goats stare defiantly up at us. We continue down another path, which is once again the only dry land in sight, and we all lapse into silence as the devastation of this place hits us.

The villagers have used the trees and bushes beside the road as a kind of retaining wall and have built makeshift huts using tree bark, palm branches, plastic sheeting, cardboard, and floating debris, loosely secured by homemade ropes. It is bleak, the crudest of dwellings, with no relief from the threat of rising waters and the constantly beating sun.

We are not welcomed, and the people are subdued. They glance at us then look away. I follow Benjamin on the narrow path for ten minutes, and we come to a large open area resembling a pond with several concrete buildings to one side. All but two of these structures have collapsed, and we climb over the rubble to get to the larger of the two. There is a shaded front porch that looks to be a good place to set up. Ani and Bablu are already attaching the yellow banner to the wall. It reads "Big Life Fellowship, Medical Camp," repeated in Bengali. Patrick and Tapan unpack the supplies, and blankets are laid down on the concrete floor for the Big Life team to sit on.

Sam points to the pond where a family of ducks paddles by.

"This was the village meeting area, the center of the village. Children would play here; the men would meet to talk."

I can't believe how high the water is and the extent of the damage.

"And they are expecting the waters to rise again tonight," he adds sadly.

A plastic chair is found for Dr. Singh, and six of us sit on the blankets in a line with our backs to the wall. Ani and Tapan will greet and organize the villagers, Mr. Singh will talk to them and write prescriptions, John Thape and myself will hand out the drugs, Patrick will explain the prescription to the people, showing them how and when to take the medicine, and Sam will hand out food packets.

They come slowly and hesitantly at first, but soon there is a large crowd—women with babies, old men, and children. They mill around and seem impatient, but I am surprised at how orderly and calm the villagers are. They talk to the doctor, pointing to their back, stomach, chest or head, then move along the line, collect their medicine and a small packet of food, and move off.

I try to make eye contact and smile at some of them, but they just stare with expressionless faces. They don't seem grateful at all that we are trying to help them. But as the villagers file past, I realize that these people are traumatized. They are in terrible pain. Aila has swept along and taken away everything they have, leaving them without hope. They are at a point where they accept everything that comes at them, good or bad. These people desperately need Jesus. My heart goes out to them, and I pray a silent prayer that the Lord will move today.

After some time, Debu begins to speak. Patrick translates for me. Holding up his Bible, he tells of the healing of the paralytic man in Capernaum. "The crowd that came to receive healing and hear Jesus preach was so great that this man's friends could not get close to him. But they had such faith that he would heal their friend that four of them carried him on his mat onto the roof and lowered the paralytic down through it, right in front of Jesus.

"The Bible says when Jesus saw the faith of his friends, he healed the man. He was healed by faith because they believed in Jesus. Jesus will heal you also and comfort you, if you believe in him. He is the true living God.

We would like to begin a fellowship here, to teach you more about Jesus and how you can know him. Let us pray together, and then you can talk to me or any one of us if you want to know Jesus now."

As Debu prays, I see that of the hundred or so here, thirty are praying with him, heads bowed, hands together in front of their faces. After the prayer, many of them come forward to talk to the Big Life people. Praise the Lord.

I am tired and stiff from the concrete floor, having handed out medicine for over two hours. About 150 have filed past, and the drugs and food packets are almost finished. There is a sudden sharp, harsh noise, a voice is raised, and all heads turn to the pond. Patrick goes to investigate. A large snake has apparently burst out of the water, seized one of the ducks, and disappeared back into the water with it. The remaining ducks noisily took flight.

There is another stir in the crowd, and two men push through supporting a sick man, his arms around their necks. They place him carefully on the floor, sitting in front of Dr. Singh, who immediately attends to him. This is very much like the story Debu just told about Jesus healing the paralytic, and as the two men watch and stare at the doctor, concern and hope etched on their faces. I drift off in thought, wondering what it must have been like on that day to be there in Capernaum when Jesus healed the people.

I take a break and find John and Benjamin, who are talking to the villagers. I see that Debu is surrounded by people wanting to know about Jesus. He and the other guys are taking down names.

Suddenly, a man comes forward from the crowd and stands purposefully in front of us. He clearly wants to talk. He stands out because although he is bare-chested, wearing a *dhoti*, or *sarong*, tied around his waist like most of the men, he is wearing a very thick gold necklace over his chest, which is incongruous in this setting. Benjamin smiles and approaches him, and they talk for some minutes. Eventually, Benjamin introduces the man to Ani and then turns back to John and me. I ask who the man is.

"He is a village elder, a businessman here," Ben explains. "His name is Ashosh Mondal. This building is his, and he has offered it up as a meeting place for the fellowship we wish to raise. He also wishes to attend."

I turn to John. He is already smiling his shy smile. I just met the man of peace.

Darjeeling

don't sing in Hindi, but the joy in this song is so palpable that I am laughing and clapping along with everyone else. I am discovering that praise and worship in Southeast Asia is a true celebration of the majesty of Jesus Christ. We are in a simple, large room on the ground floor of our simple hotel, which is serving as our meeting room. It is not air-conditioned, but up here in Darjeeling, close to the foothills of the Himalayas, we are twenty degrees below the incessant heat of Kolkata, so it is bearable.

As we joyfully give praise, I look around at the beaming faces. These men, regional coordinators and leaders, are all young, between twenty-one and forty, I would guess. They come from all over India, Nepal, and Bhutan, and are from vastly different backgrounds and circumstances, but they are bound in their common love for Jesus Christ, Lord and Savior of all. It is an honor to be here with them, and as I get to know them, I am excited not just to worship with them but to hear their stories and to trace their journey to Big Life.

The guitar is passed from Sam to Prem, from Nepal, and he leads worship, singing beautifully in Bengali. We stop to pray, and I feel the presence of the Holy Spirit in this place. Being here with these twenty-five Big Life leaders is a very precious, joyful time, and a moving experience.

The thirteen-hour train journey from Kolkata was an experience too. It was comfortable enough, although being woken by screaming vendors at each stop throughout the night was unexpected. They offered everything from chai tea to ice cream and vitamin pills as they marched through the train determined to make a sale. Then there was the hot journey by van from Siliguri up to Darjeeling, where our group met the others from various parts of India, Nepal, and Bhutan.

This, the following day, is the first morning of our three-day retreat together. John Heerema speaks about the need for focus.

"Remember the woman at the well? Look at what happens. The disciples go into town. These are the godliest men on earth; they've been following Jesus for three years. Nowhere does the Scripture talk about that town being impacted by the godliest men on earth. It says they went to buy food. They were focused on their own needs. They were brushing shoulders with the lost, but nowhere does it say that even one person was saved, because they were prejudiced against Samaritans. Then they are amazed that Jesus is talking to a woman, and a Samaritan. The woman was focused on Jesus, and after being touched by him, she goes back to the same people that the disciples ignored and tells them the Messiah is at the gate. The entire town comes to see Jesus, and many are saved.

"So we can be the godliest men in the world, but if we lose focus, if we think only of ourselves, we will have no impact. Keep your focus."

"We also need to be disciples, not just believers," says Ani. "Sometimes, the men who try to become church planters fail because they have not become disciples in their walk with the Lord. When Jesus was alive on the earth, his disciples were not real disciples; they were believers. They often faltered. When Jesus was arrested, they all ran away. After our Lord was resurrected and they received the power of the Holy Spirit, things changed. They were able to take all kinds of persecutions and beatings, and their work continues today. This is a crucial time for the Lord's work because he is coming back soon. It is time for men to finish the Great Commission. The great blessing of being a disciple is that we begin to see the character of our Lord in us."

Amit, the leader from Punjab, is nodding and smiling in agreement. He has been with Big Life less than a year, but the other leaders already call him "the healer." He is a jovial, energetic man, and he later tells me his testimony in English in his wonderfully melodic Punjabi accent.

"I was brought up in Jalandhar in a Christian family, but I did not believe in Christianity because my father drank and abused my mother. As a teenager, I discovered a talent for music, and I earned money from singing and playing guitar, piano, and harmonium, and I often used to sing and play Christian songs in our church.

"One morning, I finished playing and sat down to listen to the preacher, Sister Kathleen. There were 200 in the service, and in the middle of the sermon, she suddenly stopped and said, 'The Lord is going to call someone today.' I immediately became violently sick, and I was afraid because I suddenly felt the great weight of my sin upon me. I fell to the floor and shouted out, 'Lord, I am a sinner; save me!' Sister Kathleen rushed over and laid hands on me as I cried, and she told me God has chosen me. Later that day, as I was praying, the Lord gave me this scripture: 'Therefore, if anyone is in Christ, he is a new creation; the old has gone, the new has come!' (2 Corinthians 5:17).

"That night, I was awakened by a voice calling, 'Amit!' It was so real; I was afraid. When I went back to sleep, I heard it again: 'Amit!'

"I sat up and said, 'Who is this?' but there was no one there. It happened a third time, but this time, the voice said, 'Amit, I died for you; I gave my life for you. You will serve me, you will bring my name to many people.'

"I was terrified, and I sat up for the rest of the night. The next morning, I ran to the pastor, Pastor George, and he told me about Samuel. I read it in the Bible for the first time, and I could not believe the Lord had called me this way. I told my friends at school, but they laughed at me, saying Krishna is mightier than Jesus. Then the pastor came to my house and told my parents I must go to Bible school in Bangalore. I went for four months and learned to study the Word and how to fast and pray. I was so excited; I promised the Lord I would bring the lost to him.

"I was invited to work at a church in Delhi, where I led praise and worship, and then I was asked to pastor a sister church. I soon had many coming to my church because they said when I prayed for the sick, the people were getting healed. Soon, people were coming from far regions for healing, and many came back later to thank me. It was such a blessing. The other pastor said I was anointed and needed to grow more in Christ, and so I went to Grace Bible College for four years and earned a bachelor of theology degree. The principal of the college asked me to stay and teach, and I agreed, but I told him about my promise to the Lord to plant many churches.

"I spent some time in Thailand with Wycliffe, translating many Bible tracts from English into Punjabi and Hindi, and then I met a missionary from the US. We did medical camps and started home churches together, and then he introduced me to Benjamin. I saw straight away that his vision was the same as mine, so I left my job at Grace College, found a pastor for my church, and went back home to Jalandhar to work with Big Life. I left two very good salaries, but I knew the Lord had shown me my life's purpose. There are 700 Hindu and Sikh villages in Jalandhar alone, but we won't stop until we bring the whole of Punjab to Christ. In seven months, the Lord has used us to raise eleven fellowships with 600 people attending.

"I cry a lot for the thousands of villages. The Lord has given me a clear vision to plant churches, and raise up leaders and church planters to go into the harvest field. It hurts me to see the people worshiping stone and wooden idols. Big Life gives me wonderful support with Bibles, tracts, and everything we need."

> Let my teaching fall like rain,
> and my words descend like dew.
>
> Deuteronomy 32:2

"I praise the Lord that he connected me to Big Life."

Karma is from Bhutan. He worked as principal of a Bible college in India for many years and met Robert in 2007. He was fascinated to hear about the work Big Life was doing, and excited that Robert was searching for a ministry leader for his home country. He promised Robert that he would help him find the right person to begin work for Big Life in Bhutan.

Then the Lord began to work in Karma's heart. Over the years, he had taught many students how to evangelize and disciple, and the Great Commission had always been his passion. Students had contacted him years later to tell them of their success in church planting and missions and to thank him for his teaching. But over the years, Karma sometimes regretted that although he had filled thousands of young people with a fire to bring the lost to salvation, he had never gone out in faith to do it himself. His meeting with Robert had stirred these feelings once more.

About the same time, the Bible college approached him with a lucrative offer. They wanted him to move to Sri Lanka and to head up a larger Bible college there. It was the offer of a lifetime and recognition of his service and commitment. It put Karma in a quandary, and he spent hours on his knees, seeking the Lord's will. Eventually, he called Robert.

"I've found your man for Bhutan!" he announced.

"Wonderful," replied Robert, excited. "Who is it?"

"It's me, Robert. I'm your man."

Bhutan is a difficult, dark country. There is a ban on propagation of Christianity, and there is active persecution of Christians. But believers' testimonies passed on by word of mouth have been the Lord's witness. In the first seven months, Karma has begun six fellowships and now has three church planters working with him. They are excited about the future.

Lunch with Jonah is fun. He is short and thickset with glasses and a big black mustache covering his smiling face. When he speaks, everyone listens in anticipation because he is a natural comedian. He was brought up in a gypsy family and came to the Lord at age fourteen. He wasn't a good student.

"I failed class ten about eighteen times. Toward the end, when I went to take the exam, all the other kids thought I was the teacher!"

He felt a call to preach at fifteen but was never taken seriously.

"In one village, I was preaching about prayer. I was trying so hard, calling out the Scripture, but no one was listening. I noticed a very old lady was sitting with her head bowed very still and quiet, so I pointed to her and shouted, 'Look, that is how you should pray!' One of the men walked over to her then shouted back, 'This poor lady is dead!' They laughed me out of the village. I went to my pastor in dismay to ask what I'm doing wrong. He said, 'Jonah, I think your problems begin when you open your mouth!'"

But the Lord opened many doors for him, and Jonah has preached and evangelized all over India. He has a great burden for the eighty million gypsies in India to hear the gospel, and he feels the structure and strategy of Big Life will allow him to do this. He is researching and mapping gypsy areas and training his church planters how to witness specifically to them. They have already begun fellowships in thirty villages. Many people in the areas in which he works are illiterate, but Jonah grins as he holds up his hand to show me the 'hand gospel', each finger representing a truth of salvation.

"My vision is to make every home a worship center, and to make every believer a disciple," he says.

Jonah has known extreme poverty in his life. One time, he had not eaten for days, and he set out in the morning to preach and witness in the market to try to earn twenty rupees to feed himself. All day he preached, prayed with people, shared the gospel, but no one gave him a single rupee. As the great hot sun began to set hours later, he sat on the sidewalk and cried out in anguish, "Lord, you fed five thousand, why won't you feed me? Am I not worth twenty rupees?' He jumped up in anger and kicked over a trashcan, and as it rolled away, a brown paper bag fell out. Inside were fifty rupees.

As he counted it, with tears of joy and thankfulness, Jonah was deeply convicted.

"I had decided that day in my own pride that I would make twenty rupees my own way. I didn't ask Him or discuss it with him. The Word says that if I am in need, I should go to him, and he will provide. I have never made decisions without talking to the Lord since that day."

The next morning, Rajesh leads praise and worship. Once again, it is an emotional, spirit-filled experience. Rajesh is a talented singer and guitarist, having recorded two Christian CDs of his own music. He was born in Darjeeling, the eldest of five, and is now the Big Life coordinator in this area. His father abandoned the family when Rajesh was eleven, and his mother suffered a breakdown soon after. As the eldest boy, he had to take responsibility. He took menial work to feed the family but was often so hungry himself that he would pick up food that fell in the road. At fourteen, he was old enough to find manual labor work. It was cruel, backbreaking toil, but he was able to feed his family and buy medicine for his mother.

Rajesh harbored a deep hatred toward his father for leaving him and his family, and this hatred ran so deep that he avoided and mistrusted all father figures, even his friends' fathers. At fifteen, an aunt took him to church, and he heard the pastor say in his message that God is our Father and that he loves us with an unfathomable and endless love. Rajesh was deeply moved, and he fell to his knees and prayed that this could be true. He was overwhelmed with a feeling of such peace, love, and relief that he wept for hours. Jesus had begun the healing in his heart, and Rajesh surrendered his life to him.

In a terrible twist of irony, his Hindu mother and brothers that he had kept alive for years were enraged at his salvation and threw him out of their home. Discouraged and depressed, clinging to Jesus, he moved to Kolkata, where he found a church and was baptized. Eventually, he met Robert, who cared for him and discipled him. It was a time of great learning for Rajesh. He found himself drawn into Robert's dream to save the lost and returned home to Darjeeling to begin his work for the Lord. It began with his own family, and he brought his mother, brothers, and sisters to Christ, a blessing that he had prayed for ever since he had left.

But Darjeeling was a dark place of sinister beliefs, and he struggled to make headway for Christ. He became discouraged, and eventually, he gave up witnessing. But Jesus was to change that. He found work in a restaurant, and one day, a man came in to preach the Good News. He was deaf and dumb but wrote his sermon down, going from person to person until he had shown it to everyone in the place. Rajesh was immediately convicted. This man could not speak but was bold in his witness. Rajesh could not only speak but was blessed with the gift of song. The Lord had prepared him for ministry, so he must obey. He contacted Robert and asked for direction. Soon, he joined Big Life.

In 2008, The village of Bannockburn was a dangerous place, where murder was commonplace. It was the home base of a particularly violent criminal gang that was feared throughout the region. The village itself was full of Buddhist followers who were virulently anti-Christian. But he had one friend there who was Christian, and Rajesh felt the Lord calling him to witness in this village. He was nervous, but he decided to visit his friend.

Bannockburn is in hilly country, spread over the top of a sprawling plateau. Rajesh cycled for three hours, getting as far up the hill as he could, thanking the Lord for the old bicycle that he had bought recently for seven dollars, and then he walked up the steep road for the last half-mile, carrying his Bible. Coming round a bend, he saw four men lazing in the sun on the side of the road. As he approached, they rose to block his path. He recognized them as the gang members he had hoped he would avoid, and as fear gripped him, he silently prayed.

Rajesh glanced at all four of them. One was particularly fearsome. He had a hard, evil look in his eye. It was this man that spoke.

"Where are you going?"

"To visit a friend in the village," he answered. There was tension as the man eyed the Bible.

"You're not from here. Are you Buddhist?"

Rajesh was afraid but not prepared to deny the Lord.

"No, I am a Christian."

"You are not welcome here," the man snapped. He eyed Rajesh. "Do you know who we are?" he asked coolly.

Rajesh nodded. There was silence once more. The man considered him, his face like flint, and his eyes cold. Rajesh could see he was taking pleasure from this. He avoided his eyes, anxious at what he would say, what he would do. The others leered at him in the background, enjoying his fear. When the man spoke again, Rajesh was taken completely by surprise.

"Tell me about your religion, and I will tell you about mine," he sneered.

For the next hour, in this almost surreal setting, Rajesh witnessed and read Scripture to the cruelest, most feared men in the region. The man who had spoken asked many questions about Christ, without interrupting or making any comment. Then it was his turn.

He told Rajesh how many men they had killed and how they had killed them. They had recently cut one man up into a hundred pieces, like mincemeat. He showed him the knife and how they had cut him. They controlled all the drugs and criminal activity in the region, and the police were powerless because they fear them. Rajesh had no doubt that this was all true. He prayed as he wondered why the man was telling him all this, fearful of where it was leading. But then they let him go. He walked up the hill without turning, feeling their eyes on him.

When he reached the village, he was immediately approached by villagers demanding to know what he wanted. They saw the Bible, and soon, there was a crowd jostling him. One or two lashed out, and he took some blows, but others pulled him away to safety. His friend appeared, took him to his home, and cleaned him up. Later, when the coast was clear, he walked back down to his bicycle, thankful not to have met the gang once more. Rajesh was bruised and afraid but not daunted. He would be back.

A week later, coming around the same bend, Rajesh saw the gang at the same place. The same man stepped forward. He was obviously the leader.

"You again," he said evenly. "You are an annoyance."

"I am sorry. I have come only to see my friend," Rajesh replied, very conscious of the Bible in his hand.

The man stared at Rajesh for a long time and then motioned for him to sit on the grass. Without missing a beat, he began to question him some more about Jesus, his impassive face showing no emotion. Rajesh was once more nervous of his intent, but he answered all his questions with confidence, showing his deep love for the Lord. Soon, he realized by his questions that this man had given thought to their discussion last week. But he wasn't allowed to feel comfortable; one of the other men was cleaning a knife, polishing it while eyeing Rajesh. After an hour, they let him go; but this time, they followed him, Rajesh not knowing what to make of any of this.

When they got to the village, the gang leader suddenly marched forward and shouted to several of the villagers that Rajesh was to be free to wander the village and must not be harmed. The men nodded but said nothing, averting their eyes. They were clearly very afraid of him.

The next week, Rajesh found only the leader and one other on the road. In the middle of it sat a menacing pile of weapons: guns, shotguns, knives, axes, and machetes. The leader indicated that he should sit on the grass like before, and then he picked up the weapons one by one, demonstrating how they use them. He told Rajesh that if you put the bullets in the hot sand before you fire them, they explode with greater force and will blow a whole head or chest apart. He picked up a knife and showed how to turn the wrist to inflict the deepest wound. Rajesh was horrified. Then the leader smiled. It was the first time Rajesh had seen him do so.

"You know why we have made this pile?" he asked.

Rajesh shook his head. He wasn't able to speak. The leader looked away. When he turned back to Rajesh, he sighed.

"We are taking them to the police, turning them in. We are tired of killing. We no longer want to be criminals." Then he looked at Rajesh with a kinder face, one that Rajesh had not seen before.

"We want to know more about Jesus and the forgiveness you have talked about."

They went up to the village, met with Rajesh's friend, and the four of them prayed and read the Bible. The two men prayed to receive Christ, and Rajesh wept as he felt the awesome power of the Lord as the Word melted their hard hearts.

After this Rajesh began to go from house to house every week, witnessing to the villagers. He came upon terrible scenes and evidence of debased practices, but Rajesh found that as he prayed, God opened his mind and gave him the right words to say to the people.

Eighteen months later, fifty people from Bannockburn village were baptized in one month.

Prem shares about the work in Nepal. The Lord is blessing his team that has planted 150 fellowships in twelve districts. Prem is particularly excited to share about the six fellowships that have begun in the region of Dang, where there are no churches, and Jesus is unknown. There are problems in the country right now because of the unstable political situation, and militant Hindus are targeting Christians for persecution. Their newspaper quoted a report recently that there are one million Christians in Nepal. The militants said they have made one million bombs, and soon, there will be no Christians.

Prem says his team has encouraged the believers by reminding them that Saul was a great persecutor of Christians, but after meeting Jesus, he became Paul. Prem smiles. "All these devout Hindus can become Pauls, then they will move from being bomb planters to church planters."

The leaders cheer and applaud.

In another area, one church was bombed, and three people were killed. A woman confessed, and Prem's people are now praying for her salvation in prison so that all may see the power and compassion of the Lord.

There are often transport strikes in Nepal, and it is difficult to move on the roads, but Prem's people are targeting to plant 200 fellowships in the next six months.

Over dinner in Darjeeling, I get to speak to some of the leaders in a relaxed setting. All they seem to talk about is Big Life and bringing souls to Jesus, so I take the opportunity to ask some questions about the ministry.

"So, *The Jesus Film* is a good way to approach a village?"

"Definitely," says Robert. "Many villagers have never seen a movie, and do not know Jesus. So through the movie, Jesus can become real to them. Many Muslims and Hindus are led to believe incorrect things about Jesus. The movie helps us to make them understand that he is God. And there are other benefits, also. Although Jesus lived 2000 years ago, as portrayed in the movie, the style of dress in India today is not so different from that shown in the movie. The landscape is also not so different. So Indians can connect with the movie easier than westerners can in this way. Also, watching Jesus perform miracles in the movie has a powerful effect on the villagers, because they believe in miracles. Many have come to Jesus because he has performed a miracle in their lives, or the lives of those close to them. There have been many healings, overcoming of addictions, changed lives."

"Are the Hindus easier to witness to than the Muslim people?"

Amit speaks up this time. "They are not easier, they are just different. The hard thing with Muslims is that they become Muslims at birth, following only Allah as their parents do. This makes it a challenge for Christians to approach them. It's a cultural issue. Hindus, on the other hand, follow many gods, who they believe protect them and provide for them in different ways. This is a challenge too."

"In what way?"

"Well, when you have shown *The Jesus Film* to a Hindu audience, many can come forward at the invitation, wanting Jesus to be their God. But when you question them, some of them, maybe even most of them, want to accept Jesus as another god, an extra god, not as their one true God, their Lord and savior. The challenge is for us to show them who Jesus truly is. I had seventy come forward once, and after talking to them, only ten were truly saved. The rest would not give up their other gods. But we go back and witness to them, as fishers of men, and we catch them all," he says, smiling.

"Tell me about your training. How soon after accepting Christ do you start it?"

"Immediately," says Prem. "We teach T for T training, which began in China and has been wonderfully successful. It teaches new believers to tell their personal story in three minutes. They become Christian witnesses as soon as they are saved. Your own experience with Christ is the most powerful witness you can have. Part of our training is also to make our people understand that their goal is not just to become a disciple, but a teacher, able to disciple others to become teachers."

"And how do you manage the growth of the ministry, considering the dramatic increase in churches since Big Life began?"

Robert speaks again. "We have found that a church planter can raise, disciple and oversee five pastors and their five churches comfortably, so that those five churches are growing spiritually. As he or she plants more churches another church planter will have to be raised to oversee them, until they reach five once again. Similarly, regional leaders are responsible for five or so church planters, so there are twenty-five or so churches under them. Regional coordinators have five regional leaders, which is about one-hundred-twenty-five churches. It is a continual process of managing the growth. But five seems to be our number."

"Where are the church planters raised from?" I ask.

"The Holy Spirit raises them, mainly from the fellowships in the villages," Jonah replies. "We disciple them and include them in our teams that show *The Jesus Film*, or go on medical camps. The Spirit tells us when they are ready for more responsibility. Some of them fail, because the work is hard, and the enemy is always ready with discouragement and persecution. But we have never been short of church planters, because the Lord provides. We have also been blessed with many powerful men and women of God who came from other ministries."

Tapan Ghosh came from a strong Hindu family. He contracted tuberculosis in high school and spent seven months in hospital. The doctors told his family that he was critically ill and may not pull through.

"Every Friday, an old man, Pastor Das, came to visit me. He taught me about Jesus, who I had never heard of before. Pastor Das gave me a New Testament and always prayed for me. One day, he told me that Jesus had told him I would not die, as he had already healed me. I asked him why I was in such pain if Jesus had already healed me, and the pastor read this Bible verse from 1 Peter 2:21: 'To this you were called, because Christ suffered for you, leaving you an example, that you should follow in his steps.'"

"'What do I have to do?' I asked him, because I wanted to live. He replied that I only have to believe in Him. 'But when you are better,' he said, 'you must share with others how Jesus has healed you.'

"I read about Jesus in the New Testament every day, and I began to feel stronger. Pastor Das came to me a day before the doctors were to give me tests. I was nervous, but the pastor smiled and said there is no need to be troubled; they will find nothing. That night, I saw a white light in my room. I sat up and even stood on my bed, but no one was there. I felt a wonderful peace around me. It was beautiful.

"After my tests, the doctor told me I was completely healed. I went home, and I saw all the idols to Krishna and other gods as if for the first time. But my family would not listen about Jesus and threatened to expel me from my home if I did not stop being a Christian. I told Pastor Das, and he sent me away to Bible college for some months. I began work in a church, but I was also going to the villages with medicine to preach about Jesus. I knew Jesus was with me because I brought many back to the church for salvation and baptism. Eventually, I met Raja, who discipled me and introduced me to Benjamin. I baptized my mother with my own hands, and my sister also. I now have thirty-five fellowships and six disciples of my own."

While talking to these leaders, I am struck by how complete the conversion to Christianity can be. But it is not always this way. Ranjit Rai tells his story.

"I was brought up in a strict Hindu family. I had strong faith in many gods, because that was the way my father taught me from a very early age. As a teenager I heard about Jesus, but I thought he was a foreign, western god." At this Ranjit laughs out loud, and shakes his head. "This seems so ridiculous to me now." Then he becomes serious. "I remember my father telling me one day that the greatest sin a man can commit is to change his religion. I was deeply affected by this. I read about Jesus, and his life, and I saw that he was a holy man, a good man. I wondered about him a lot.

"Then one day we had a problem in our home. My mother became very ill. We tried everything to cure her, but no doctors, no medicine would work. We had given up in desperation. But some Christians came to pray for her, and we all joined hands to pray. I found myself praying to Jesus for the first time. The Christians prayed, 'Let these people taste and see Lord, that you are good.' And Jesus healed my mother. It was a miracle." Ranjit smiles, with tears in his eyes.

"My mother gave her heart to Jesus. But soon we went straight back to our normal life, and to our Hindu gods. We had forgotten Jesus. Then we had other family problems, and we prayed to Hindu gods. One evening, months later, we were all together in our house, all my brothers and sisters, and my parents, and I spoke up, even though I knew my father would be angry.

"We have been worshiping idols. We have been a family of great faith, but it was Jesus that healed you, mother. Jesus is the living God, not just a healer." I looked at my father, and he said nothing. My mother just cried. Then we felt the presence of the Holy Spirit so strongly, and we all broke down in submission. We all agreed to follow only Jesus. Today we are a strong Christian family.

We take a break, and Benjamin takes me to a café he knows in town that serves cappuccino. It is surprisingly good. As we sit, Benjamin talks about Raja. He speaks no English at all, but he clearly loves the Lord. He sings the name of Jesus. He has the reputation of being a powerful evangelist.

He and Ben were sitting in a café just like this one in Kolkata two years ago when they saw someone they recognized, sitting a little way away, alone and sipping tea. It was a notorious criminal, a terrorist, and a killer—a man to avoid. As they chatted, Raja seemed fascinated with this man, his eyes constantly drawn in his direction. Benjamin pointedly told Raja not to look at him, but he kept glancing his way.

Eventually, he turned to Ben.

"I think I should go and witness to him."

"What? Raja, that is a dangerous man. He will think nothing of killing you right here."

"But I think the Lord wants me to talk to him."

"Raja, listen to me…"

But he didn't listen, and suddenly, he was gone. Ben's heart raced as he watched Raja sit next to the man and begin talking earnestly to him. Ben was half out of his seat, ready to go, apologize, and get Raja out of there, but something in the man's expression stopped him. He was listening. He didn't react aggressively toward Raja at all; he just listened. Raja spoke for maybe a full minute, and then the man slowly nodded. Benjamin was stunned.

Raja met with that man several times over the next week, and he brought him to the Lord and discipled him. This man went on to witness to others like him, and he began a ministry, a fellowship of ex-criminals, witnessing to other criminals, having them turn to Jesus. Many with criminal backgrounds were being saved all over India through this man's testimony. And it all started in a café in Kolkata.

There is no doubt that Raja felt the Lord's call that day, but what would make him approach this man in such an impulsive and risky way? The answer may lie in an earlier testimony he gave me through Sam on the train journey to Siliguri.

"One day I was on a bus, and the Lord told me to witness to a woman in the front of the bus. I looked at her, but I could not do it because I was afraid I would embarrass myself with all the people. I made all sorts of excuses to myself. Then a coconut seller got on the bus and pushed his way to the front with his big sack of coconuts. He turned to everyone and started shouting how wonderful and juicy his coconuts were. He made a show of cutting one open with a big machete for people to taste. He was so proud of them he held them up high.

"But I could not hold my Lord Jesus up high because I was afraid. I was so ashamed I ran off the bus and cried out for forgiveness. I promised him I would never disobey or be ashamed of him again."

I ask Benjamin if opposition from other Christian ministries is still a problem, as it was in the early days of Big Life. He tells me that the church planters encounter it from time to time but learn to be adept at dealing with it. Then he tells a story with a different twist that illustrates his occasional frustration with the church in India.

"Some time ago, a young Hindu girl came to Christ at a church two miles from her village. She had been attending for some weeks, and in secret, so that her parents would not find out; but eventually, she had to tell them she had become a Christian. They were furious, and although they did not throw her out of the house, they would in no way support her until she stopped her childish nonsense and came back to her Hindu gods.

"But she grew in her faith and decided to be obedient in baptism. When she approached the pastor with her request, he explained that because she was just eighteen, her parents would have to sign a form of consent. She pleaded with him, saying that her Hindu parents would never agree, and she was a Christian now, not a Hindu. But the pastor said there was nothing he could do. He would not baptize her without their consent.

"She asked her father to sign the form anyway, but he laughed, telling her to stop her silly ideas and come back to her true faith. Then he would forgive her and forget her transgression. She had little choice but to give in to him.

"Some time later, she was shopping at the market, and she accidentally bumped into another woman. They both apologized then got into conversation and began to talk about Jesus Christ. The other woman was the wife of one of our Big Life church planters, and after listening to her story, she invited her new young friend to a fellowship service the next day. Today, the young lady is serving as a church planter.

"The point is," says Ben, "how many people fall away from their faith because of circumstances like that?"

As Benjamin and I finish our coffee, we see a young white girl sitting alone. She waves, and Ben invites her over. She is twenty, backpacking around the world, and will be in China next week. I tell her I think she is very courageous, and she smiles sweetly. We chat, and I ask her if she is a Christian.

"Of course," she replies. "I'm Canadian."

"I think what my friend means," says Benjamin, "is do you know Jesus?"

She frowns. "No, I don't think so. Do I need to? I'm a good person. I don't really think about stuff like that."

Ben smiles, and then speaks quietly in his silky voice.

"We are pleased when the door opens to let us in, and we switch on the light and marvel at the wonders of electricity. But we don't give a thought for the one who built the house. We will pray that you have safe and joyful travels."

She is looking hard at Ben, and I turn and see her eyes still on him as we slip out the door.

It's Sam's turn to take up the guitar. He leads worship at Grace Church in Kolkata, where Benjamin preaches, and he launches into several familiar songs and hymns. John and I are able to sing along this time in English.

Sam had a Christian mother and an abusive Muslim father. He suffered much as a child and became an angry teenager, dabbling in drugs and hanging out on the streets of the city. He was sitting under a tree with a friend late one night when Benjamin stopped to talk to him. He said he was a preacher. Sam had met preachers before, but Benjamin was different. He wasn't judgmental, and he had a way of getting through to him on a level he understood, so they became friends. Some months later, Ben came looking for Sam and asked him to go with him to Bangalore, where Ben was going to minister with his team. Sam thought it would be a month's free holiday, so he agreed.

Two weeks later, at 2:00 one morning, Benjamin was preaching on the streets of Bangalore surrounded by dozens of young people. Sam watched in awe as Benjamin poured out his heart for the love of Jesus and his fellow man. Sam had never heard such powerful preaching, and he came face-to-face with God that night. He broke down in his absolute need for Jesus and gave his heart to him.

Benjamin discipled Sam for a year, and by the time Sam joined Big Life, Ben had become his mentor and his father. Sam is now married to an American girl, Jennifer, and they were recently blessed with twins.

As I talk to these young men at breaks and in the evenings and listen to their testimonies, I am saddened by the persecution most have suffered, even from their own families. But some in this group have known the most heartbreaking kind of persecution.

Raju Chetri was born in Bhutan to Hindu parents. They lived in poverty, as his father wasted what little the family earned on his drug addiction. Soon, his father stopped working altogether, and Raju, fourteen years old, chopped and sold firewood to keep his family alive. Embittered, he prayed desperately to his Hindu gods, and even to Buddha, to find peace in his hard, empty life. Finally, he rejected God completely, declared himself an atheist, and followed his father into addiction. Depression followed, and he began to think about suicide.

One day, his little brother, unable to walk since birth, came stumbling toward him ecstatically declaring that Jesus had healed him. Raju's mother had been secretly taking him to church, and a man had prayed to Jesus for his healing. Raju was amazed at this. He sought out this man and told him of his hopeless life. The man read to him from the Bible and assured him there is always hope with Jesus. The word 'hope' touched and encouraged Raju. He began to seek out Christians, and outside a church, he was handed a pamphlet titled, "The Hope of Jesus." Raju was excited to come across the word 'hope' again, and he read it avidly, certain that the God he was seeking was talking to him. But some weeks later, he would find this new hope was all he had left in the world.

Raju and his family were deported to Nepal along with thousands of others and settled into a United Nations refugee camp. They were permitted to take nothing but the clothes on their back. But it was in a Christian fellowship, conducted in a plastic refugee hut, that Raju accepted Jesus as his Lord and Savior. He was fifteen.

He told his father of his salvation, hoping to influence him to accept Jesus, but he flew into a rage and beat Raju so savagely with a pipe that he was left paralyzed and bedridden for a month. Denied food by his father, he was fed secretly by his mother. But even as he slowly recovered, he found no relief, as the Hindu community in his new country persecuted him for his new faith. He refused to deny Jesus but was beaten and tortured until finally he ran away with a Christian friend to the town of Ilam, where they began a ministry to evangelize to the lost.

On 2nd September 1994, seventeen years old, Raju was arrested by the Nepalese authorities for illegally preaching the gospel in public. He was beaten, physically and mentally tortured, but refused to deny Jesus. Eventually he was thrown into prison, where he was kept in chains, just like Paul. And just like Paul, he brought many fellow prisoners to Christ. So many, in fact, that the authorities began to be concerned. They tried to stop him with threats, more torture, and beatings, but he would not be stopped; so after fifteen months, they released him. Today He still suffers from the physical and mental abuse of that time.

While in prison, he had prayed constantly for his parents' salvation, although they never once visited him. On his release, he went to visit them. They expected a contrite Hindu, and they discovered a triumphant Christian. When they saw the scars of his suffering on his body, they broke down and accepted Christ. It was the greatest day of Raju's life.

In 1999, he earned a bachelor of theology degree from Grace Bible College in Manipur, Northeast India. Today, he lives to please Jesus Christ and to bring his love to the unsaved Himalayan nations.

When asked if he feels anger or resentment about his past, his reply is simple: "For to me, to live is Christ, and to die is gain" (Philippians 1:21).

I finally get to speak to Tapan at 12:30 a.m. It is just the two of us, and Patrick, who is interpreting. We are in the large room where our meetings are taking place. It is quiet, apart from the *swish*, *swish* of the ceiling fan as it hurtles around its never-ending track. Tapan is a humble and gentle man, soft spoken. He says a few sentences then stops, waiting for Patrick to translate. There is a small smile on his lips.

In 2006, Bablu was praying and searching for a church planter to be raised up. Big Life was growing, and he needed this man to take over ten village fellowships in the eastern area of 24 Parganas. In one village, a woman was chronically ill with epilepsy, and her condition was deteriorating. Bablu brought believers each week to pray for her, and after some weeks, she began to recover. She was completely well in a matter of months. This woman was Tapan's wife.

Tapan was amazed. He and his family had paid for doctors, prayed to all their Hindu gods, and even tried witchcraft, all without success. Tapan knew that Jesus had healed her, and so did his family.

"I read that Jesus himself said 'It is not the healthy who need a doctor, but the sick.' He had come to call sinners to repent. These are the truly sick ones. I knew I was a sinner, and it completely overwhelmed me."

Tapan and his wife began to meet with Bablu to talk about Jesus, and they soon gave their lives to the Lord and were baptized together. They began a fellowship in their home, and Bablu met with Tapan each week to disciple and train him, as it was clear to him that the Lord had called Tapan to be the church planter he needed.

As he continues his testimony, Tapan becomes tense although he remains outwardly calm.

"In February the following year, 2007, I was part of a Big Life medical camp in a new village. Bablu was there too. I got a message that my wife was seriously ill, so I went home immediately."

He stops and frowns, as if searching for words.

"After I got off the train, I was walking down the road to my house. I saw people, but no one looked at me or greeted me. When I got close to my house, I saw something hanging by a rope from a tree. I looked up, and then I saw it was my wife."

He looks away as Patrick translates. For ten seconds or so, there is tense silence hanging in the air. The only sound is the *swish* of the fan. Then Tapan's soft voice again.

"My wife wrote tracts at night, and while I was away, she was going to the market and handing them out. She had led a few people to Christ, and she was excited. I was so proud of her."

Silence again. "Do you know who did this?" I ask.

"Yes, I know. It was my family, and my wife's family. But the people all said it was my fault for changing my religion. They said I killed her. They said if I remain Christian, they would kill me too, or have me arrested for killing my own wife. My wife's parents took my son away from me."

Silence. Patrick is blinking back tears. I don't know what to say. Tapan is now a picture of calm, his hands in his lap.

"I cried out to the Lord to help me out of this. I begged him to protect my son and to help me understand why my wife had to die. But I could not forsake my Lord, because he promised never to forsake me. So I carried on working, proclaiming Christ, even in my own village, and I waited for them to kill me too. Then some of the villagers came to me and told me they see that I have real faith in my God, and they would respect me. Some said my God had protected me and was powerful. Some wanted to know him. I praise the Lord for this. My in-laws were like this, and they allowed me to live with them. So I am now with my son, by the Lord's grace."

The last question is the hardest.

"How did you feel about the people who did this?"

"I read the Word over and over, where Jesus died on the cross. He felt the physical pain, but he felt the agony of our lost world. In spite of this unbearable pain, his prayer was for the Father to forgive them, all of them, all of us. So I have forgiven, just like Jesus. The Lord's love and his presence allow me to do this."

Tapan wears his slight smile again, and he looks blissful, as if he has crossed over to a higher place.

"With Christ, we have the victory. My mother used to worship many gods, especially the goddess Kali. We had a Hari temple right in front of our house, and my mother prayed to Hari on her knees every night. Today my mother worships Jesus Christ. My in-laws also came to Christ, and so did twenty others of my family, including the ones who killed my wife. I baptized them all with my own hands.

"I live for my son, he is seven now, and I live for my fellowships. I have seventy-two already, and soon, I will have one hundred fifty."

The retreat is winding down. John asks the leaders if they have final words of encouragement for their brothers as they all turn their minds to the journey home. He invites them to take the floor to address the group. The smiling Bakaj stands to speak.

"My region is in the middle of the cyclone area. There is heavy monsoon there in season. It is a frightening time. Now, at this time also is the ripening of the mangoes on the trees. The mango crop is important for food and for trade, and if they do not go to collect them, the monsoon will destroy the crop, so the men must go out for the mangos just as the monsoon sets in.

"This is not an easy decision. The rain is so heavy and swirls so wildly they cannot see. The wind is so strong it bends the branches high in the trees, and when they break off, there is a loud *crack*, and a heart-stopping moment as the men wait to see where the branch is falling. Lightning is everywhere, it crashes into the trees, and no one knows where it will strike next. But the men must focus only on the mangoes. They have to have courage.

"I believe when the Spirit of God takes over a man, this is a time of monsoon. In every country, in every person it is the same, if we are to be obedient. First you ask, then you see, and then you go. The mangoes are ripe. Some people have excuses—it's raining; there's lightning; it's dangerous. But if you have the Spirit of the Lord at the center your life, no harm can come to you. This is the time of monsoon, so let's go out and pick the mangoes! Take no rest and give the enemy no rest!"

Prem looks thoughtful. He stands, smiling broadly.

"Yes, nothing can harm us. Jesus told us this in Luke 10:19. He also told us in the same verse that he has given us authority to trample on snakes and scorpions and to overcome all the power of the enemy. I believe this authority has been given to every church planter and believer in Big Life. Wherever we go and do a new work, we are seeing healing. We see people released from demons, set free from the chains of addiction, and they are receiving Jesus with all their heart. The very next day they share what Jesus has done for them. All of this is from Jesus Christ. He is with us always. Let that be our encouragement."

Mr. Mondal is next.

"I praise God that by his grace I have many fellowships. In the beginning, it was not always that way for me, but if we are strong and faithful, he will use us, work through us. I see Moses standing at the Red Sea, and the Egyptian chariots are fast approaching. The Israelites were afraid, and the Lord said, 'Why are you afraid? Go forward.' Then he said to Moses, 'Raise your staff and stretch out your hand over the sea.' And suddenly, a new road came up on dry land. God said they must only trust, and he would deliver them, and that He would do the work. God has called all of us here to the Great Commission. We must obey and allow him to complete his work through us."

Raju speaks up. He works in Nepal. He was an alcoholic for many years and was completely dependent, but immediately after accepting Jesus, he stopped drinking. Everyone who knows him said it was a miracle.

"I joined Big Life to reach people who live without the knowledge of Jesus in this dark world. There are many Christian organizations in Nepal, but they are all in the cities. They rarely go to remote places. But Big Life makes a light in a village then goes back to put new oil, so the light shines always and can never be extinguished. We must not go to heaven empty-handed; we must work hard to gain the prize that the Lord has waiting for us.

"Jeremiah 33:3 says, 'Call to me and I will answer you and tell you great and unsearchable things you do not know.'

"The Lord's power and knowledge is so great. We must call to him all the time, and he will teach us."

Ani stands briefly, and points out that although the leaders are far apart physically, he is full of joy that they are all close in spirit. He laughs, saying he also has a teaching about trees.

"In the Sunderban forest, there is a big tree called *gorenkhat*. It has very deep, strong roots. In amongst them, entangled in them, grows the small sycamore. When cyclone Aila came along, many trees fell, but the sycamores were protected by the gorenkhat, which stood firm. This is how we must love and protect each other in Big Life. We are a family, in the family of God. Some of us have deep roots, and we protect, encourage, and instruct those whose roots are still growing. Big Life is our calling and our way of life."

Benjamin rises. He speaks on an old theme of his, one very dear to his heart. He is holding a sharp, rough stone.

"Some of you have come here to Darjeeling for the first time, and you may want to go to the shops and the market to buy gifts to take back for your family. How many of you will take back these stones?"

Everyone laughs. There are one or two comments. The smiling Benjamin persists.

"But why not, they are free! When I picked this up in the street, nobody stopped me! No, you don't want them. Nobody does. You see, these rough cut stones are the things in our lives that we are ashamed of, that we don't want to tell others about. They are also the places that we don't want to go in our mind, but where we do go in our spirit. And they are the things that Satan, the accuser of the brethren, always reminds us of to make us feel inferior and worthless. Yes, you are a sinner, you are weak, you cannot lead, and you will fail. He never stops. Rough-cut stones are your failures, reminders of the souls you didn't win for Christ. No, nobody wants these stones.

"But the Lord is interested in them. He wants these stones. You remember he told Moses that these stones were not to be dressed. No tool must be used on them, because the Lord wants them just the way they are.

"In the church, people do three things with these stones. Some people carry them everywhere as a burden. They can carry them for years, a whole lifetime even. They store them up to feed their negativity. 'This won't happen, that can't work. The Lord is good, but he can't help me with this.' They have many burdens, but it appears from their testimony that their biggest burden is their Christianity. Other people don't want to carry the burden of their stones, so they throw them at other people in the church. Many churches are divided because people spend their time throwing stones at each other.

"We in Big Life, we have the same stones. Where are you going? Bhutan is so difficult—let's just leave it! The villages have been Hindu, Muslim in that area for generations. No chance! You are wasting your time!

"But there is a third thing we can do. We can take these stones, and we can make an altar. These failures, these fears, can be put together and brought before the Lord. We can build an altar with them, an altar of sacrifice, of repentance, of praise, and of unity. Bring your stones to the altar and leave them there, and then you will find it becomes an altar of promise. You remember that the Lord told Abram to lift up his eyes on the land, and he promised that he would give him everything before him.

"David claimed that promise. Goliath was a champion. How does a man become a champion? By winning many times. The men of Israel did not want to fight Goliath because he was a champion. He had killed too many of them already. People have been preaching in India for 200 years, but the power of Satan has been ruling for many more years than that. He is a champion, and the people lose time after time. David saw things differently. There was no pressure on him to fight Goliath, because none of the men of Israel were willing to. Goliath had already won. But David stepped forward, and he lifted up his eyes, and he knew that the Lord would give him everything before him. He said, 'You come as a champion with the sword, but I come in the name of the Lord!'

"Let the enemy come with all he has because we in Big Life, we have the name of the Lord. We have the promise of the Lord. We must have courage and come out on the field to fight because the Lord has called us here. We only need one small stone from the altar of promise, and all the enemy's champion Goliaths will fall.

"Remember, it was at the altar where Jacob wrestled with the Lord all night. The place where we wrestle with the Lord is the place where we need to be defeated, where our sinful nature, our selfish wants, desires, and earthly ambitions are overcome for the glory of God.

"He gave Jacob another name. He told him he will no longer be a deceiver, he will be a prince, and his name will be Israel. Jacob clung to the Lord all night, and he said, 'I will not let you go until you bless me.'

"Before we leave this place, I want us to come to the altar and say, 'Lord, I will not let you go until you bless me with disciples, until you bless me with new villages and show me thousands and thousands more souls to save.

"These are the principles we live by. We do not work for Big Life; we are Big Life, as long as we live. Amen."

Nepal

The India-Nepal border is a busy place. It is mid-afternoon. With the retreat over, most of the leaders have gone home, but Prem, Amit, Jonah and I are joining Benjamin, Robert, and Raju, the leader in this area of Nepal, to visit one of his fellowships. John has traveled back to Kolkata. As I climb out of the van I am swamped by activity and noise. It is a spacious, busy area, full of shops, people and traffic. Raju and Prem begin quickly offloading our things from the van's roof rack, and Ben stands a little way off giving instructions to two other Nepali men in our group. I don't know what language he is speaking, but his message is urgent. They nod, smile, and move off to the shops. Ben then turns to Raju and shouts up at him, pointing to my backpack. As I collect it, I hear Ben behind me, speaking English this time. He is all business, wanting to get across the border.

"Okay, let's go." As I turn to see where we must go, Ben is already marching off across the road. I follow him towards the Indian border post, an old building that has the style of an English Colonial house. Inside I fill out forms, my passport is stamped and then Ben hurries me back outside. Back across the road, a rickshaw is waiting by the van. It is really nothing more than an ornate chair on wheels, pulled by an ancient bicycle. It is covered with fabric and ribbons that are so garish it seems all the colors are at war with each other.

The driver, or in this case, the cyclist, gives me an expectant toothless grin and presents his carriage with a wave of his arm. He is wearing a bright scarlet turban that sits slightly off center. I resist the urge to straighten it for him, and then I notice that all the activity has stopped, and everyone is silent, looking at me. I also notice the twenty DVD players that we brought with us, now stacked on the floor. Ben explained in the van on the way here that in some areas of Nepal there has been success showing *The Jesus Film* on DVD in home groups. These DVD players were to build on that success.

"Get in," says Ben, shortly. I climb up uncertainly as Ben continues shouting instructions, and as I sit, two DVD players are placed in my lap. Before I can react, there are two more, and one behind my back. Suddenly DVD players are being squeezed into every available space until I can't move. Then, between the pile on my lap, and the pile next to me, I see Ben's face.

"If they stop you, tell them you are a tourist," he says urgently.

"And what am I doing with twenty DVD players, as a tourist?" I ask. But he's already gone. I look up ahead and see the boom on the Indian side of the border being raised. The rickshaw takes off with agonizing slowness. Thirty yards on is another boom, with uniformed Nepali Border Guards manning it. My heart begins to beat fast, much faster than my grinning rickshaw driver is moving. As we approach them I see the guards are well armed, machine guns slung over their shoulders. As they turn to examine me, I pray for the miracle of invisibility, wondering what the inside of a Nepali prison looks like. I think about running far away. I could definitely run faster than this rickshaw, but I can't run anywhere, so I hide behind the DVD players instead. To my great relief, the guards don't shoot, or even show any interest in me. The boom begins to rise, and my driver passes it and slowly pulls off to the side of the road.

Before I can take a breath, Ben and the guys are there, and I am free of DVD players. It's all bustle and shouts once more as the van is reloaded, and we are off into Nepal. We will travel another hour and a half, then stay overnight at the home of a friend of Raju.

The service is conducted in a separate building constructed specifically for worship, located thirty yards behind the main house of the pastor, Kirrin Rai. It is not large, but large enough to accommodate the thirty-eight people attending today. Although it is hot this morning, there is a cool breeze, and the worship building is structured to take full advantage of it.

The whitewashed wooden walls have large square window frames, but they are open, without glass. The high roof is corrugated metal, lined with cardboard sheets to reduce heat, kept in place by bamboo poles. Eight strategically placed tree trunks support four crossbeams. A humming ceiling fan adds to the breeze. The floor is made of brown cow dung, polished to a high shine. This whole area has been carved out of the jungle, which surrounds it thickly on three sides about twenty yards away.

As we enter, we are greeted and asked to remove our shoes. There is an area set aside to store them. Then we are directed to the worship area, where a grass mat is set in place on the polished floor for each worshiper. I note that the men sit towards the front, and the women and children are at the rear. The men are dressed in open-necked shirts, but all are wearing long pants. They are friendly but reserved, nodding shortly at me as we make eye contact. There are some small smiles, but this is clearly going to be a formal gathering.

A wooden table serves as an altar, and is covered with a crisp white tablecloth with a large scarlet cross stitched onto it. A large homemade white board with a wooden frame stands a little way back, with scripture written on it in Nepali. A large picture of Jesus, hands raised in blessing, hangs from one of the beams in the front, and a huge old railway clock ticks off the last few minutes before 10:30. Scripture tracts, printed in black on plain white board, hang on the walls, their austerity in stark contrast with the many ornate and thoughtfully placed vases bursting with color from oversized exotic flowers. The worship building is carefully laid out and clinically clean.

Pastor Kirrin opens the service with a long prayer in Nepali, then introduces Benjamin, who steps forward to introduce the rest of the guests. When my name is called I stand and bow, as Amit, Prem, and Jonah did before me. Worship begins to guitar, hand drums and tambourine, and four songs are sung in Nepali. Kirrin prays once more, and after a short introduction invites Benjamin to speak.

The congregation all open their Bibles to the scripture Ben directs them to, and I note that they all have pen and paper ready to take notes. The response to Benjamin is instant. He speaks passionately for twenty minutes in Nepali, reading and quoting from the Word, and soon they are nodding, clapping and raising hands, calling out the name of Jesus. Towards the end, I hear 'Big Life' and 'baseball', then 'Coca Cola' and 'cricket', and there is an unexpected riot of laughter.

After Ben, Prem takes the guitar and sings a beautiful song in Nepali. I am asked to speak briefly, and after telling a little of where I am from, I take the people to Mark 11:24, stressing the need for us to pray with complete faith, expecting our heavenly father to answer us. Then Robert rises and speaks with great intensity. Everyone is nodding and clapping. Raju, sitting next to me, tells me that he is talking of the need for this entire church to be trained as disciples, and to teach others to disciple. Jonah is next, and it is not long before the laughter begins. His eyes twinkle above his great mustache as he tells his story as only Jonah can. Amit shares about the work that his Big Life team is doing in his area of Punjab, and this is greeted with applause. Pastor Kirrin closes the service in prayer, thanking Ben and the rest of us for visiting with them. As we close, many worshipers remain in the worship area to continue praying.

I am seated in an old but comfortable sofa with Kirrin as his smiling daughter serves us chicken for lunch. He tells me his testimony.

"I was brought up in a strict Hindu family. My father was a big influence on my religious life. We had many gods, and we followed witchcraft. But when I was nine years old, I had a vivid dream. There was a house, a beautiful house, and it shone so bright it was hard to look at it. There were no lights on and I wondered how could the house shine so? And in front of it stood a beautiful man, dressed in white. He shone even more than the house, and I could not take my eyes off him. I asked him, 'who are you, sir?' and he replied, 'I am the Lord your God.'

"When I awoke, the dream stayed with me, and I could not forget it. It worried me, and over the next three years I searched for this man. I met some Christians, and they told me it was Jesus, and they shared the gospel. One told me that in the Bible it says that when Jesus comes again, one will be left, and one will be chosen. So at twelve years of age, I asked Jesus into my heart. My parents were furious, saying Jesus is a low-caste god. My father said if you touch bad water you will become unclean. But Jesus' water is living water, and now my father has come to know the Lord, too. Jesus has cleansed and blessed me, and now I serve him in Nepal with gratitude for the joy he has given me.

"My life verse is Philippians chapter two verse two, 'Then make my joy complete by being like-minded, having the same love, being one in spirit and purpose.' This is Big Life, we are one in spirit and purpose."

I awake the next morning, and there is tension. Ben and the other leaders are in serious discussion with Raju at a cafe. I don't understand the language, but there is obviously a problem. As I sit down, Benjamin turns to me.

"I told you before about the political unrest in Nepal. We have just heard that a transport strike has been declared for today and tomorrow."

"And what does that mean?" I ask.

"Only emergency vehicles are allowed on the roads. If the political activists find vehicles on the roads, they will pull them off and burn them. Raju tells us that many vehicles have been burned and the travelers assaulted over the past months. We have to get back home today, and the border is an hour and a half away."

We all take a moment to pray for the Lord's leading in this situation, and then Benjamin spends the next thirty minutes animatedly talking on his cell phone. Raju is pacing up and down on the street doing the same. The rest of us chat and drink tea. Eventually the two of them get together to talk, and we all sit down to hear the news. Benjamin explains.

"We tried to find a Nepali ambulance to take us to the border, but they are all taken. We called friends in India to see if they would send an ambulance, but they are not prepared to take the chance."

"Is there nothing we can do?" Amit asks.

"A man in one of Raju's fellowships is a funeral director. When they have a funeral, the vehicles display a sign to indicate that they are part of the funeral procession. This man is willing to take us to the border with the sign displayed."

I ask the obvious question: "What do we do if we are stopped?"

Ben looks at me. "I have no idea. But the Lord will protect us."

We pray again, and we all agree that we should go. Ten minutes later, we are in a van headed for the border. There is no traffic at all on the road, and we are driving way over the speed limit. Ben, Robert, and Amit are in continuous prayer, and Raju, Jonah, Prem, and I are silent, anxiously scanning the jungle on each side of the road. After half an hour we see a ribbon of black smoke just off the road ahead to the left. As we pass it a minute later we see a van lying on its side, burning. There are no people around and we do not stop.

Forty minutes later we reach the border. The relief is immense. We get out and form a prayer circle, to thank the Lord for his protection, and to claim further protection for our driver and Raju, who now have to make the return trip.

This was an anxious time. I think back to the retreat, and Prem describing how difficult it is to work in Nepal with the political situation, and these constant transport strikes, and I remember they are targeting two hundred churches. I have a new understanding of this, and a new respect for the Big Life workers in Nepal.

Blessings of the Villages

U p at six and out to meet John Thape at seven. It is already hot, around eighty degrees, but John is on time, smiling and ready with a yellow taxi. We ride to the train station to meet Patrick at the ticket office. John Heerema and Ben have work in Kolkata, and I am looking forward to my day with Ani and his team.

The station is huge and alive with multitudes of people. I see policemen everywhere carrying long canes, and Patrick tells me with a grin that they use them to keep order when the people fight to get on the trains. We run to catch the train east into North 24 Parganas, and I grab a window seat, knowing it's not going to get cooler. Patrick tells me we have a three-hour journey east, and then Ani and Debu will collect us in a van for a two-hour ride to visit a new fellowship in a village called Shyastanagar, where Ani is baptizing thirteen people today.

The train carriage is soon packed with people but empties as we progress east. The journey is leisurely, and I am struck by the signs of continuous habitation with clusters of huts, brick dwellings, and cultivation in evidence the entire way. I glimpse an ornately arched three-story Hindu temple in a shady glade in the middle of nowhere.

As the train sways east, my thoughts turn back to Darjeeling and the retreat. As I recall the testimonies of the Big Life leaders, their hardships, and trials, I am reminded of the passage in Matthew 16. Peter declares that Jesus is the Messiah. In verse 18, Jesus replies, "And I tell you that you are Peter, and on this rock I will build my church, and the gates of Hades will not overcome it."

The gates of Hades—the entrenched, fortified gates of the bastion of hell. Jesus gives a vivid picture of his church successfully attacking this fortress. It is another command to go. And this is exactly what the Big Life teams are doing: they are entering enemy territory and attacking the very gates of hell, using the Word as their battering ram.

I coax the humble and self-effacing John Thape into telling his story.

"I was born in Kolkata and raised by my grandparents, who are Buddhist. I was shown little love growing up, and as a teenager, I became a drug addict; and more than that, I bought and sold drugs. One day, a Christian tried to tell me about the gospel. I told him I wanted nothing to do with foreign gods, but he smiled and said one day the Lord will take me for his work.

"I began to get sick from all the drugs, and I was coughing up blood, but still I could not stop. The doctor examined me and said I would die if I did not stop. My skin had turned very dark because of the poison in my blood.

"I met another believer who prayed to Jesus for my healing, but I didn't believe; I just said if I'm healed, why am I still coughing? Then he told me about Jonah, how he came out of the fish, repented, and had new life. He said he was sure the Lord wanted to use me, and I remembered the first man had said that. He said that if you do not accept Jesus, he cannot work in your life and heal you. So I prayed to Jesus with him. He took me to his church, and when he introduced me to the people of Jesus, they welcomed me with open arms in spite of my addiction. I had never known such love. I broke down, and I knew it was all Jesus, so I gave my heart to him.

"My grandparents said following Jesus was selling my religion, and they persecuted me. I had to hide my Bible and I read it in secret in the toilet. But the Lord has given me new life and helped me through this. Soon, the Lord was putting it on my heart to teach others about him. I said, 'Lord, I have a bad reputation, how can I do this?' Then I read that God told Moses, 'I will help you speak and will teach you what to say.'

"I had a dream that a letter had come from Pastor Robert in Siliguri inviting me to go there for Bible training. I thought, *Lord, I have no money, so how can I go?* Then in my dream, a lady gave me two hundred rupees for Bible study. I woke up suddenly and looked at my hand because it was so real! But there was no money. I prayed, 'Lord, please let me go to Bible school today. Let my dream be true.'

"So I told my granny I was going to Siliguri. I walked to the station to find out when the train was leaving and on the way I met a man who asked me where I was going. Remembering my dream, I told him I was going to Bible school, to Pastor Robert. I said I didn't know Pastor Robert, but the man said he did, and he gave me two hundred rupees for my journey. I knew this was my dream coming true and that it was from God. Then I met a Christian woman, and we had the same conversation. She also said Pastor Robert was expecting me, and she gave me one hundred fifty rupees.

"I rushed home to pack. I had one hour before the train left. My granny was sad, and she said, 'So, are you really going?'

"I said 'Yes,' and she took me to the market, where she bought me shoes. Before I left, she cried and said she had been told in a dream to buy me shoes for a journey I was taking.

"When I got to Siliguri, I searched for Pastor Robert, and told him my story. He put me in his Bible class, where he taught me and discipled me. A year later, I went back to Kolkata and started a fellowship. I called Robert to tell him this is what the Lord is calling me to do, and he told me to go to see Benjamin. That is how I joined Big Life in 2008."

Ani and Debu welcome us from the train, and soon, we are bumping along in the van on our way to the village. We pass through a town with a busy market with a host of shops selling all manner of things; clothing, food, chickens, pots and pans, Coca-Cola, soap, cell phones, and furniture. The whitewashed walls of the buildings are faded and drab and in stark contrast to the color and variety of goods on sale. The clamor is incredible, with vendors screaming out their wares, vying for attention. One shop sells radios, but the broken speaker outside blaring out Indian music is more an irritation than an advertisement. A sea of people moves this way and that, going about their business, the bright saris of the women offering a colorful contrast to the whites and grays favored by most of the men.

Ani says this market serves many villages, and as many as twenty thousand people. Our progress is slow, and the incessant harsh blaring of horns is everywhere as the buses, cars, vans, rickshaws, scooters, bicycles, and pedestrians jostle for the limited space, but eventually, we are through the town.

I am able to spend some time with Debu, who has worked with Ani now for almost five years. He came to Christ when Ani brought *The Jesus Film* to his village. He becomes emotional as he describes seeing Jesus on the cross. He could not believe that even in such pain he was praying for his enemies. Debu wondered how could there be such love? He couldn't sleep that night, and early the next morning, he set off on his bicycle to find Ani, who shared more about Jesus and brought him to salvation. Ani sent Debu to Bible school for a year and he continues to disciple him, just as Debu now disciples others the Lord has brought to him.

The fellowship at Shyastanagar village meets on the porch of Ram, the wealthiest man in the vicinity. It is shaded but uncomfortably hot, over one hundred degrees again. There are about thirty attending, mainly shy young women, all carrying Bibles. Ani leads us in prayer. Songs are sung in Hindi and Bengali to the accompaniment of guitar and hand drums. The people's early shyness of me passes as they sing out, clap hands, and praise Jesus, and many of them smile as I join in the clapping.

Debu preaches for thirty minutes, reading from the Scripture, using his hands and fingers to emphasize his points. The people are animated, smiling and nodding, enjoying themselves. There are many happy "hallelujahs." Debu leads prayer, and then announces that nine women and four men are receiving baptism today. There is more clapping and calls of "praise Jesus." Among the congregation are Ram and his wife, who have accepted Jesus and forsaken Krishna.

I am struck by the difference between this fellowship and the first one I experienced, in Nepal. The outward show of joy and praise here is in contrast to the more formal, reserved approach in Nepal. Both fellowships are full of people who love the Lord, but are expressing their adoration through their own natural character and style. Perhaps this is an Indian and Nepali cultural difference, or perhaps not. But I am impressed that these house churches have the flexibility to accommodate different styles of worship in a structured format.

Ani discreetly points out another lady to me, sitting quietly just outside the circle. She has been attending and watching for some weeks, and Ani has watched her.

"It won't be long before the angels in heaven are singing," he says, smiling. "I have seen this so many times before. Soon, she will belong to Jesus."

Those being baptized rise to go and prepare, and a woman on my right tells Patrick she wants to tell me her testimony. Her husband was a practicing Hindu and is an elder of the village. He discovered that some of the women were following Jesus, and he found a New Testament, so he called a meeting to tell them that if they did not stop, there would be trouble for them.

The next week, his mother became very ill. He prayed to all of his gods, but as the days passed, she became worse. Eventually, the village was preparing for her death when Big Life men came to the village asking to show a film about Jesus. Her husband refused and told them to go away. Before leaving, they asked if they could pray for anyone, and he stopped to think then said they could pray for his mother. The men surrounded her bed then held hands and prayed aloud to Jesus.

A few days later, his mother was up and cleaning her house, completely healed. He was astonished and sent for the Big Life team, wanting to know more about Jesus. Big Life began a fellowship in the village, and he was one of the first to give his heart to the Lord.

While she is telling me this, I become aware of a man sitting on my far right staring at me. I glance at him once or twice and smile, but he doesn't return the smile; he just stares. He has protruding front teeth, and I find his expressionless gaze a little intimidating. When the story ends, Patrick tells me this man wants to say something. He speaks briefly then continues staring. I turn to Patrick with a frown.

"He says he is nothing without Jesus Christ."

"And who is this man?" I ask.

"He is the husband of the woman that just gave her testimony," he replies.

Everyone walks down to the pond for the baptisms. The fellowship is four months old, Patrick says, and nineteen were baptized last month. There are many young women here, and children everywhere. I am given a cute baby to hold, seven or eight months old, I guess. Naked except for a thinly weaved rope around his waist, he looks at me with open curiosity, but is quite happy in my arms. Patrick takes my camera, and everyone squeezes up to be in the picture with me. Patrick and I switch places, and I laugh at him holding the baby so awkwardly.

Patrick smiles constantly, and I remember when I first met him, how he laughed out loud when I told him he looks like Elvis Presley. Nine years ago, at sixteen, he contracted a life-threatening illness. He lay in a hospital bed burning with fever. As he became weaker, he felt his own heartbeat slowing and his pulse decreasing until he stopped breathing. Suddenly, he saw a bright light, and a voice from the light called to him. "Patrick, do you really want to die?"

He called out, "No, I don't want to die!"

The voice spoke again. "Then in whose hands shall I leave you?"

Patrick answered immediately, "In Jesus' hands!"

He felt his heartbeat returning, and as he came back to consciousness, he opened his eyes to see his distraught mother, crying over her son whom she and the doctors believed had just died. Patrick was paralyzed on the left side of his face and body for some months, but he eventually recovered.

Although he was brought up in a Catholic home, Patrick had never believed in Jesus. But he knew now with certainty that Jesus had saved his life, so he set out to follow him. A year later, he discovered that the friendly economics teacher at school was also a preacher. He went to hear him the next Sunday, and he knew after that sermon that this was the man who was to teach him about the Lord. The close bond between Patrick and Benjamin continues to this day.

The people clap and sing as Ani conducts the baptism ceremony. It is clearly a joyous and meaningful occasion for them, and those being baptized are congratulated with hugs and smiles. I spend ten minutes with the children, who are excited to show me six tiny baby ducks swimming in a plastic washbasin.

One of the young women baptized today says she was controlled by evil spirits and prayed to Krishna for their removal. A friend in the fellowship told her that the Bible says Jesus casts out demons. She prayed to Jesus, and her healing was so dramatic that several other people, including her husband, were saved. As she learns about Jesus, he has taught her many things, even how to pray to him.

I am completely uplifted by this whole experience because Jesus is at the center of the work here. The fellowship is growing and will continue to grow and reproduce more churches. We serve an awesome, unchanging God, and I praise and thank him for his work in this peaceful village.

The day is not over. The team is showing *The Jesus Film* to a new village tonight. But first, we will have lunch.

Back to the town and down a narrow side street. The entrance to the restaurant is tiny, just a door with a small sign above it. It is clean, although modest, with formica tables and plastic chairs, and the air conditioning is a blessing. I read the menu while gulping down a second bottle of water. It says I am about to embark on a unique culinary experience. "The journey beings," it proclaims. It is "A test of the Orient." I pray that the message is not prophetic as the guys place the order because Indian food can be notoriously unforgiving on Western stomachs. But it turns out to be a simple, delightful meal.

We are on the road to a new Hindu village, Fatulapur Uttar Para, only it's not a road; it's a grass path with two dirt tracks, and we have been traveling on it for over an hour. The van carefully crosses over a rocky stream, turns a bend in the path, and stops. Looking around, I see a wide, natural grassy clearing surrounded by tall trees through which brick huts can be made out. We are parked next to another van, and soon, I meet Bipro, the church planter who is responsible for this village. He is a good-looking young man with a striking grin, and he joins the other Big Life guys unloading equipment and setting up for the sports and the movie that will be shown later. Villagers stand a little way off, taking it all in. Small children stare at me warily but soon edge closer, their curiosity overcoming their fear. They clearly have never seen a white face before. They have never heard of Jesus either, and I pray that very soon neither Jesus nor myself will continue to be a mystery to them.

While the guys work, I pull out my camera and take shots of the children. They see their smiling faces on the screen, and they screech in delight and line up for more. Their parents seem happy with all this, and as I smile and wave, several of them wave back. As the only white person, I am the center of attention, and even the cow standing a few yards away stops licking its calf's ear to gaze at me.

Thirty minutes later, the grinning Bipro takes the children over to the far side of the clearing to play games. I get some water and sit on the grass with my back against a rock. I drift off in thought, but I am brought out of my daydream by the awareness of someone next to me. It is a tiny child, a boy, and I turn to him and smile. Our faces are at the same level, and he is no more than a foot away. His beautiful deep-brown eyes are a perfect almond shape, and they roam all over my face. He reaches out his hand and touches my cheek, my nose, my glasses. I reach out and touch his tiny nose, and he suddenly comes alive, turns, and sprints back to his friends, his bare feet skimming the grass as he goes.

I pray that this precious child will come to know Jesus as he grows up in this village, along with all the others, now pointing and laughing at me; and I praise the Lord for directing the men of Big Life to this remote place, bringing with them His saving grace.

I wander over to Bipro just as he, Debu, and Patrick finish securing the canvas sheet to the branches of two trees. It's a little skew, but it will work fine. John Thape is balanced precariously, setting up lights in the one tree in the middle of the clearing. A microphone and a speaker are also set up. Being surrounded by trees like this, I recall Benjamin saying that if a house could not be found for a fellowship, then gathering under a tree will do just as well; and if something plops on your head, well, that's just one more blessing.

There is a lot of excited noise coming from farther away, where Ani now has the children running races. For the first time since I arrived in India, it seems, the heat and humidity are bearable. It will be dark in a couple of hours. Bipro speaks excellent English, and we sit while he tells me his testimony.

Coming from a devoutly Hindu family, Bipro was brought up worshiping idols. He started smuggling when he was a teenager, bringing gold and alcohol from Bangladesh. The police caught him crossing the river with a boatload of alcohol, and he jumped in to escape. Carried by the current, unable to stop, he gave in to exhaustion but had a vague memory of being dragged out and cared for by a stranger. He woke up alone on the riverbank the next morning.

He was convinced that he had been spared by God, and he set out to find him. Later, a Christian friend, a former Muslim, brought him to Christ with the tract that became his life verse: "So do not fear, for I am with you; Do not be dismayed, for I am your God. I will strengthen you and help you; I will uphold you with my righteous right hand" (Isaiah 41:10).

He soon found he had a burden for the Hindu lost and was introduced to Ani, who mentored and discipled him before asking him to join Big Life. Two years later, he now oversees fifteen fellowships. He grins as he tells me that this village will be number sixteen, even though it has taken him two months to obtain permission to show *The Jesus Film* today.

About 150 villagers watch the film, sitting in groups in the dark under the stars. Many adults are here, most of them women. As it ends, the projector is silenced, and the light in the tree clicks on. Ani takes the microphone and speaks powerfully to the people. I only find out later what he is saying, but his strong voice conveys his passion and conviction. He says that Jesus loves them, wants to know them, and have a relationship with them. As they just saw in the movie, Jesus died on the cross as a sacrifice for mankind's sin. But he rose again and lives and reigns in heaven, where he welcomes those who follow him. He ends with a question: "Who among you would like to follow Jesus? Come."

I am astonished to see several people come forward without hesitation. I can see that many of them are profoundly moved. Many are crying. Ani gives the invitation once more, holding up his Bible. More come forward. Ani now leads everyone in prayer, and many who have not come forward are praying, hands together and heads bowed.

One or two more come forward. Ani is furiously taking down their names. A man taps me on the shoulder and talks excitedly to me in Bengali. Patrick translates—he wants to know where can he get a Bible. "I will give you one," Patrick replies. Another smiling, chattering man waves a battered Bible at me. "He says he doesn't have to hide this anymore," Patrick laughs.

A little later, Ani takes the microphone and calls everyone together for the prize giving from the afternoon sports. The children are given medals with bright ribbons and candy, and the adult prizes are everyday household articles. The villagers are delighted, and I laugh with one man who holds up a plastic pail as if it were a football trophy.

An hour later, we are ready to go. Last to be loaded is the light that was in the tree, now burning brightly in Ani's hand, and the humming generator. As it is switched off, there is silence and darkness. As I climb into the van, I am hit all at once by hunger and fatigue. We have not eaten since the restaurant at lunchtime, which seems like yesterday, and I complain to Ani.

"There will be food back at the hotel," he smiles, "and cricket on the TV!"

It's already 9:30 p.m. I am exhausted but completely uplifted and full of joy. What a blessing and a privilege to see the Holy Spirit at work so powerfully tonight. So many came forward, and then the "man of peace" had appeared and granted permission for a fellowship to begin. Ani and Bipro will be back in a couple of days to oversee the first service.

The long, bumpy journey back doesn't seem so bad, and maybe I can catch some sleep. The guys are talking excitedly in Bengali, and I am full of respect for the passion and sheer hard work with which they serve their God. Suddenly, they are singing and clapping, praising the Lord. They are celebrating the twenty-one salvations tonight and the thirty other people who want to know more about Jesus. Okay, no sleep for me. Who wants to sleep in the company of men like these, anyway?

I keep thinking of the ones that responded that night, the ones who came forward at the invitation. Their immediate response was an indication of their hunger to meet their creator. How many more are searching right now in the depths of their soul for truth? How many in India, Asia, and the world, would recognize the one true God as soon as they see him in a movie, read his name on a scrap of paper, or hear his name called by a brother? Hundreds of thousands? Millions? Billions? It is a staggering thought. Each of these souls was fearfully and wonderfully made. The very hairs on their head are all numbered. We have to reach these people with the love Jesus showed us, to tell them at least one time that the one they are searching for is real, and very close.

So many of the men and women of Big Life found God in just this way, and now they are driven by obedience to proclaim the name of Jesus and to live a life worthy of the calling they have received, just as he has commanded in the Great Commission. The Lord has shown them multiplication, the very strategy that is illustrated in the book of Acts. They have been faithful in obedience to this strategy and faithful to the call of 2-2-2 discipleship, outlined so graphically by Paul to his own disciple, Timothy. They are the Lord of the harvest's laborers, obedient men and women prepared to dream God-sized dreams, regardless of the sacrifice, the cost, or the danger.

I read recently that many people in the West believe that faith is so important to the peoples of third-world countries because they have nothing and are constantly in need. Following a deity or deities (as in the Hindu religion) helps these people deal with their hopelessness. They have a God to lean on, who they believe will provide a better situation for them and their families somewhere in the future. But this is not what I have seen here these past nine days.

The people I have met say that they have sought the one true living God. I have heard that phrase repeatedly. These people have an innate need to connect with the God who created them, to find their purpose, and they earnestly seek him because they know he is truth. This is exactly as Paul described it in Acts 17.

The western world has largely ignored this need to connect, to search for God the way these people do, because they prefer to create their own god. Why embark on a difficult and painful search for truth when you can easily create your own? Absolute truth has been rejected in favor of a tolerance and relative truth that flaunts God's moral laws. I accept your beliefs as long as you accept mine.

Is it any wonder that God moves so strongly now in third-world countries while the West excludes him in so many areas of life? We claim we have freedom of religion, but every day, we are fighting movements that want to control where and how we worship, and even what we say in our churches. This is an insidious form of persecution in itself.

The homing beam from God is fuzzy at best because the gods of money, power, status, and pleasure are easier to attain, more immediate, and more appealing. We think we are spiritual but want nothing to do with religion, which is archaic and obsolete. We want control of our lives and refuse to accept the idea of being answerable to a higher authority.

The story of Big Life is an object lesson in what God will do through obedient people. Just as in so many Old Testament stories, the Lord has called ordinary people to trust and obey him. In simple faith, they have stepped out to obey. He has responded to their obedience, and he has used them for his work.

And the Lord has blessed this ministry.

The leaders I spent time with in Darjeeling are intelligent, driven, and devout men. Many of them left lucrative or comfortable positions within the church structure or in the secular world to join this ministry in obedience to the Great Commission. This was their decision, their calling, and their choice. Others come from abject poverty or broken homes and have had to struggle to maintain their faith against serious persecution. They have all suffered and made sacrifices in one way or another. But they all have one thing in common—obedience to Jesus Christ, their true Lord and Savior. They have an eternal mindset, and their hearts break for those lost ones who do not know Jesus and will not reach heaven.

Jesus Christ is doing a mighty work in Asia in a very direct and simple way. He is saying, "Come to me," and they are coming. He is the miracle worker, the teacher, the healer, the provider, and the comforter. Through simple house churches, the Word is being read and spoken, believers are being discipled to become disciplers, and God is being praised and glorified in remote places. It truly is Acts in action. The people are finding their one true living God, and they are discovering that his name is Jesus Christ

"All the ends of the earth
will remember and turn to the Lord,
and all the families of the nations
will bow down before him,
for dominion belongs to the Lord
and he rules over the nations."

Psalm 22:27–28

Afterword
by Mike Huckabee

Former Governor of Arkansas and
2008 Republican Presidential Candidate

When I was on the campaign trail in the last Presidential election, nobody knew who I was. It was tough running for President when nobody cared. My press secretary and I had just gotten off a plane in Denver to attend a fund raising event. We went to the car rental counter to pick up a car, and the press secretary handed our campaign credit card to the smiling young lady working there. The card said "Huckabee for President." The young lady read it, then said, "Hmmm, 'Huckabee for President.'" Then she looked innocently at me and said, "President of what?"

People ask me how in the world I got so far in the election with so few funds. I find myself asking the same question of the ministry of Big Life. I am astonished at what they are achieving with the resources they have. And they are actually winning.

It was only after the campaign that people began to act as if they knew who I was. I'd get stopped in airports and people would say, "I just wanted you to know I voted for you." It made me feel good, but I realized after a while that more people claimed to have voted for me than actually did during the entire process. It was TV that did this; hosting a show on Fox News Channel made me known.

So what exactly is being known, and what makes us believe we are living an important, big life?

I became a Christian on my tenth birthday at a vacation Bible school in a small church in Hope, Arkansas. I didn't want to go, but my big sister said they'd play baseball, and I could eat all the cookies and drink all the Kool-Aid I could handle, so I went. The pastor talked about what it meant to trust Jesus, and I found myself silently following him in a prayer of acceptance. I would never have imagined in my wildest dreams what God has allowed me to experience in my life since then.

It's like this for many Christians, and they feel they are living a big life for God. But I have come to learn that a big life is not how much money we have, or what car we drive, or even how many people know who we are. A big life is simpler than that. Jesus talked about it in the tenth chapter of John. He said, "I have come that they may have life and have it abundantly." Jesus was talking about a big life. It includes people who have nothing and yet have everything, people who happily walk miles to fetch water while we in America complain about the price of gas. We grumble about our electricity bills while whole villages have no electricity, windows or beds, or even blankets. Yet they seem more content with their lives than we do.

A big life is one lived according to higher principles than what one owns, or (as is often the case) what owns us. In times of economic crisis, as we are experiencing now, we might just be reminded of how little we are, and how big God really is. What keeps many people from the joy of living the big life is the big lie, the one that tells us that life consists mostly of our possessions, prestige, and power. But these are things we will lose, not things we can keep.

The reason we are having a tough time getting the Gospel to so many people across the planet is not because the task is too big, but because our priorities are too small. We have changed the big life into the big lie. We've acted like it's all about us, when in fact it should be all about Jesus, and the fact that he loves people on the other side of the world just the same as he loves us. If we in the West lost everything, all our assets, we would still be infinitely better off than seventy-five percent of the world's population. Many countries live in darkness and lostness and separation from even hearing the Word of God. We can turn the dial on a radio or flip through TV channels and accidentally hear or see more of the Gospel in twenty seconds than many people in most parts of the world can get in twenty months, even if they search hard for it.

As a teenager I worked for JC Penney, and I heard the story of this remarkable man, James Cash Penney, who built the retail empire and at one

A Big Life

time lost it all. He was a Christian, and he was generous, using his money to build churches, hospitals, schools, colleges, and libraries. When the economic crash came he was asked in an interview if he regretted giving away so many millions.

"Oh no, not at all," he replied. "You see, everything I gave away I still have. All those institutions are still serving the people. My only regret is that I didn't give more. It's only what I personally kept that I ended up losing."

You see, that is the big life. It's how big our view of God is in our lives. Big Life exists because some people had a big dream. God took a couple of lay people who decided to live this big life. As is clear in Peter's telling of the story, they had no idea what God would do with them. But what an incredible journey it has been. Big Life is a ministry that doesn't build buildings, it builds people. It is true kingdom work. And it's not only indigenous local churches that they are raising, but churches that have a perpetuating power to exist and multiply and grow. This past year has seen God not only raise church numbers and attendance just as dramatically as in previous years, with 70,000 decisions for Christ recorded, but Big Life has moved into Turkey, Cambodia, and other countries. In changing lives one at a time, it is changing the world, bringing hope to the hopeless.

When Jesus said, "I have come that they may have life and have it abundantly," he meant all of us. It's the young man, the teenage girl, the married couple who have never once heard the name that we Christians take for granted. They need to hear His name, and know him, so they too can live a big life.

—Mike Huckabee, February 2011

If this book has touched you, or if you have comments,
I would love to hear from you.

—Peter Hone

www.facebook.com/abiglifebook

www.twitter.com/abiglifebook

www.abiglifebook.com

Big Life Ministries can be
contacted at the following address

www.biglifeonline.org